Change on the Run

*Competing through
e-Leadership*

Change on the Run

Competing through
e-Leadership

Michael Kay

JOHN WILEY & SONS CANADA, LTD

Toronto • New York • Chichester • Weinheim • Brisbane • Singapore

John Wiley & Sons Canada Limited
22 Worcester Road
Etobicoke, Ontario
M9W 1L1

Canadian Cataloguing in Publication Data

Kay, Michael
  Change on the run : competing through e-leadership

Includes index.
ISBN 0-471-64519-2

1. Organizational change — Management. I. Title

HD58.8.K39 2000   658.4'06   C00-930762-1

Production Credits
Cover & text design: Interrobang Graphic Design Inc.
Printer: Tri-graphic Printing Ltd.

Printed in Canada
10 9 8 7 6 5 4 3 2 1

To Isabel, Kimberley, and Julia
and
Tyler who slept through it

Contents

Acknowledgements

In 1969, coming out of university, I joined Shell International's global staff as a management trainee. At that time, Shell was one of the few truly global companies and a leader in management thinking and practice. How was I to know that the methods I would learn would be instantly outdated? Over the span of my career, the industrial age has given way to the information age and I cannot remember a time when the specter of change was not present. So what is different now?

E-business is different, the Internet is different, and the degree of global integration is different. However, the key difference as we move into the new millennium, is that everyone in North America (at least) has adjusted to the idea of continuous change. We no longer have to convince people about change—the obsession of the 1970s and 1980s—or help them shift to continuous learning as in the 1990s, they are already there. The friction of resistance is much lower and shifts can happen much faster. Because we can change faster we will, and the ability to change at high speed will become a central part of competition. Indeed, in a turbulent world, adding more turbulence to drown your competitors may be a viable strategy when you know *you* can change on the run.

The central idea behind this book is that in a world where proactive change can be a competitive weapon, having a sophisticated capability in transformation is no longer an option, either for a firm or a leader's career. The six imperatives identified here (one per chapter) are the minimum skills needed.

Many of the ideas mentioned in this book have been part of the common intellectual property of informed business leaders for many years—at least since they were crystallized by such writers as Peter Drucker, John Kotter, Warren Bennis, Richard Pascale, and host of others. One absorbs them with the oxygen you breathe, and pinning individual ideas to specific sources becomes difficult. As a doer, I absorb ideas best by working with my clients in the rough and tumble of trying to resolve a particular problem. Yet, I have been deeply influenced by many ideas and freely acknowledge my debt to others even where I have not referenced it. My purpose in this book has not been to break new theoretical ground, but to try to put some shape around a phenomenon that is engaging everyone's attention—the capabilities needed to lead in an environment of perpetual turbulence.

That said, there are people to whom I owe considerable debts of gratitude and without whom this book would never have been written. John Jenner for his unswerving belief and design help in the accompanying games; Scott McRae, Jim Dustin and Darvi Jiang for their work on the Web site and the games; and Peter Jackson for his assistance and advice on Chapter 4. I have to thank my colleagues at PricewaterhouseCoopers: Rudy Bayoumi, for his help with Chapter 2 and Stacey Hodorek for Chapter 3, Howard Fromkin for his help with the Leadership Chapter, and Grady Means, Richard Hossack, Jay Hamilton, Doug Pirie, Gordon Fife, Edward Berryman, Ian Wells, Jim Niemes, Chris Rolyson, Michael Gourley, Tim Springham, Peter Harper, Mark Camstra, Peter Lawton, Peter Sedgewick, Jos DeSmedt, Daune Orsulak, and the many other colleagues and clients who helped form my thinking over 30 years. If I missed you I apologize. Also Bill Johnston and Iain Scott for support in the rough spots. I owe a considerable debt of gratitude to Karen Milner of John Wiley & Sons who sensed a book in my early incoherence and Ron Edwards for his insightful editing.

Finally, the birth of this book required enormous patience from my wife, Isabel, and my children Kimberley and Julia, as I locked myself away yet again for which I thank them.

Michael Kay
Toronto, Ontario

Introduction

Leading a transformation can make or break your career. But business in the e-world is in constant, rapid flux powered by technology and globalizing markets, and every leader—without exception—will be faced with managing a major change at some time. Everyone is at risk. E-world leadership *is* transformational leadership and this book is about the six keys to winning in this turbulent world. *Change on the Run: Competing through E-Leadership* provides hands-on guidance you will need when you face those make-or-break opportunities.

The business challenge to e-world leaders (e-leaders) is simple: build shareholder wealth through a period of intense turmoil. How turbulent will the next decade be? Without exception all firms and all industries will have to embrace the challenge of e-business as the Internet dominates communication; face ever more intense merger activity as global consolidation and industry convergence accelerate; and reshape their businesses more frequently to meet innovations and new competitors with lower costs. Even successful businesses will have to run harder to stay in place as they try to increase their returns. Those in protected niches will find their remaining protection stripped away as privatization, re-regulation, and outsourcing continue. There will be no hiding places from continuous transformational change for any leaders, whether they aspire to hero status or a quieter life.

This book is about winning in this business war zone. It is about wielding the weapons of successful transformational CEOs, weapons that can be fashioned to anyone's hand if you are willing to try. The six keys to success are discussed, one per chapter. You can learn to:

1. Change your business on the run by leading total transformational change without stopping the existing business.

2. Drive extraordinary financial results by achieving the cost sophistication that allows profit resilience in a turbulent word.

3. Unify thousands of people behind your vision and win their total commitment by aligning them intellectually, emotionally, and even spiritually.

4. Harness people's experience and get them involved in applying their real-world insights to improving the business and their own skills.

5. Galvanize change agents throughout the organization to implement critical initiatives that will transform the business.

6. Build a leadership army that will plant your transformational flag in every corner of the organization, inspiring people with their own commitment and dedication.

These are the weapons wielded by the top guns of business transformation. Some of these leaders are: Colin Marshall, the visionary who transformed British Airways from a joke into the "World's Favorite Airline" by attaining unattainable goals through a total makeover. Lou Gerstner of IBM used the hammer of financial efficiency to drive entrepreneurial spirit back into the world's biggest technology bureaucracy. Arthur Martinez enrolled over 300,000, mostly part-time, employees to revitalize a moribund Sears. John Browne led a stodgy, deeply indebted British Petroleum (BP) into becoming a dramatically more nimble organization by harnessing the experience and energy of people throughout the whole business. Jack Welch, the most famous transformational leader of all, seeded change agents throughout General Electric (GE), by teaching his values of winning the right way. Jacques Nasser is busy creating leaders throughout Ford who are carrying the torch of his vision at all levels in the organization. But it is not just the famous; those unknown to all but a few have contributed their experience to this book. Here you will learn what the weapons are and how to make them fit your hand. Here you will learn how to win.

Navigating White Water

The early 2000s will be a period of staggering change as the world's business and financial systems continue to integrate into a single global economy. Incredible wealth will be created as costs are squeezed out, vigorous new players emerge, capital is more efficiently allocated, and demand soars. Barring global warfare, *nothing is more certain*. Even if there are periodic slowdowns, as there were in the 50-year expansion in the mid-nineteenth century, driven by the Industrial Revolution, the fundamental drivers are already in place.

The breakpoint occurred at the start of the 1990s. In the four years from 1990 to 1994, national economies and politics throughout the world went through an enormous transformation, possibly the greatest ever in its impact on business.[1] Around 1990, countries all around the world started to pursue or accelerate the same basic set of ideas, four of which are key and probably irreversible[2]:

- The Shift to Liberal Democracy
- The Drive to Privatization and Deregulation
- Lowering Capital Barriers
- Mass Adoption of Low Cost Computing

The Shift to Liberal Democracy

Whether one believes that with the collapse of communism and the triumph of liberal democracy we came to the end of political history or not[3], the shift in political philosophy to more flexible forms of government, able to support rapid economic expansion in an increasingly competitive world was astonishing. This trend, in turn, stimulated others and even the most powerful liberal democracy felt the effects of this move. For those selling transformation services to clients, the Clinton election of 1992 was a watershed. In this election, every politician of note was calling for change—the only difference was in degrees of radical thinking. Swept up in its self-image as the leader of the liberal-democratic world, and coming out of the

---

[1] For further insight into these changes see William Wolman and Anne Colamosca, *The Judas Economy: The Triumph of Capital and the Betrayal of Work*, Reading MA: Addison-Wesley, 1997.

[2] Grady Means, unpublished PricewaterhouseCoopers thought paper, New York: 1999.

[3] Francis Fukuyama. *The End of History and the Last Man*, New York: Free Press, 1992.

depths of the 1990 recession with its heavy downsizing, America was ready for a new message, and the new vision was the idea of change. The impact on management was profound. Until that time selling change had been difficult. After the election, everyone believed that change had happened!

The Drive to Privatization and Deregulation

The early 1990s saw a global tidal wave of privatization sweep across nearly every public sector institution, extending the trend seen in the 1980s. Simultaneously, a shift from economic nationalism and state-controlled enterprise to public capital markets and private ownership formed the core of reform agendas. Hundreds of billions of dollars of state-owned enterprises were privatized in this period. Many countries swung from dominantly public to dominantly private sector in a period of four years. This represented a global capital market transformation and a massive shift in attitude to a shareholder perspective in business. Privatization requires a firm to deal with the mechanics of becoming a private entity, plus demanding a massive mind-set change to commercial thinking in its staff. It also has to face competitive markets for the first time, which inevitably leads to a drive for efficiency and a reshaping of operations and structure.

Lowering Capital Barriers

Today the flow of capital internationally is huge, many times greater than the flows of trade goods, and it is almost impossible for a country to insulate itself or move far out of line from the reasoning of market analysts. This is a world where capital dominates and the needs of shareholders must be met. It is no surprise that the concept of shareholder value is the dominant philosophy in strategic thinking today and the driver of continuous change.

Mass Adoption of Low Cost Computing

Computing power continued to follow Dr. Gordon Moore's Law driving a corresponding decline in prices. In 1975, Dr. Moore, co-founder of Intel, stated that a doubling of computing power from chip technology could be expected every 18 months. Time has proven him right and this pace is expected to continue until 2017 when the practical limits of transistor packing on integrated circuits will be reached. Incidentally, the doubling of capability on other aspects of computing technology such as hard drives is running at the same rate or faster. The potential for gathering and manipulating vast amounts of information at a reasonable price dramatically changed the perspectives of governments and businesses toward the control of sprawling, global business enterprises, making the execution of complex transactions quick, effortless, and encouraging globalization.

* * * * * *

The four themes just discussed are still working their way out and will continue to do so well into the millennium. They intertwine to create a business world of dramatically greater potential where the political, economic, and legal environments in countries around the world became more alike. Large corporations could now execute fully global strategies, acquire subsidiaries and set up in many countries, move goods and services more easily across borders, and finance businesses locally or on global capital markets. Companies could now see the world as a single market and act accordingly, and they did. The result was a race to buy up local firms and seek global presence by merger and acquisition. One specific example is Nestlé, the Swiss food giant best known as a confectionery and coffee company. It decided to take a major role in the world's ice-cream business, commissioned a senior executive to buy positions in all the world's key markets, and inside two years was a major player with about 10 percent of the market. But more interesting, is the fact that they looked at their investment from a global perspective and though the markets are local they operate globally.

This global consolidation was entirely predictable. In the fragmented world economy of the 1980s, the first round of internationalization had created many small, protected, and inefficient players. It was time to clean up. We can see the trend in the automotive industry with the steady decline in name plates, and such huge transactions as Daimler effectively buying Chrysler. In telecommunications the process is proceeding apace as the mega-companies like MCI-Worldcom, AT&T, British Telecom, Deutsche Telekom, and others, materialize as global giants. In consumer and retail the drive to globalize brands is on as everyone tries to emulate Coca Cola and McDonald's. Formidable domestic competitors like WalMart are taking their US formula global. Everywhere we look firms are consolidating into larger and larger global entities. Their strategic logic is that they need mass to compete at the global level as well as to prevent them from being swallowed by larger competitors. The implications for leaders in all firms, both those that merge and those that don't, are profound as they seek to either manage the behemoths they have created or compete in multibillion dollar niches. As if this were not enough, enter the Internet.

It is hard to believe that the Internet has only been around since 1994 in commercial form. Combine the public Internet with corporate Intranets and in the blinking of an eye a global communications network of staggering proportions has sprung up and is rewriting the rules of business. The Internet is transforming the value chains of nearly every industry and creating shareholder value at unprecedented levels. Companies have had to rapidly adapt to and adopt this technology to drive their business processes. Today, the principal advantage of being already in business has moved from being an incumbent with market share to providing a platform to create an entirely new business model before some techno-entrepreneur gets there first. Of course, many, perhaps most, don't move onto that new model and find they have to play catch-up on a global scale.

Future External Drivers of Change

It looks like the world of high volatility will continue. A cocktail of drivers will guarantee that. We have already met some of these.

Continuing Globalization

The trend to globalization is going to continue to expand despite the protests of labor and protectionists. In the period from 1970 to the end of the century, global export volumes grew over 20 times, but foreign direct investment grew by a massive 35 times. It is showing no signs of slowing down.[4] There is a rule in general systems theory that indicates that when the magnitude of a phenomenon increases by an order of magnitude (10x), it must reintegrate. We have seen this with global firms as they expand the boundaries of organizations, stretch their

---

[4] Export Development Corporation (EDC), *Creating Capacity: An Evaluation of EDC's Role in Canada's Export Credit System*, Ottawa: EDC, March 1999.

organizational structures, demand new formats—like global shared services—and change their leadership approaches. Globalization will demand continuous change as market strategies shift, and cultural and business boundaries are reshaped.

Rising Convergence

Convergence between industries will continue.[5] In the pharmaceutical industry, the emergence of gene therapy, previously the preserve of the small, entrepreneurial biotech firms, is restructuring pharmaceutical thinking. The alliances and acquisitions say it all: Corange/GeneMedicene, Genentech/Genvac, Bristol-Myers Squibb/Somatix, Rhone-Poulenc Rorer/Applied Immune Sciences, and so on. In the energy business the convergence of gas and electricity supply helped by privatization and re-regulation has stimulated the idea of an integrated energy company. The crystallizing strategy has been the potential of these ubiquitous utilities (particularly electricity) to own a close relationship with the customer, and provide them with a multi-fuel energy package. In finance, the four pillars have been converging for some time—retail banking, brokerage, insurance, and investment banking—Citibank and Travellers being a classic example. This convergence is being pushed again by access to the customer and the emerging technologies. In telecommunications, the convergence of voice and data is at the root of the merger spree, pushing such firms as Sprint, and MCI WorldCom together. From the convergence of the entertainment industry, the Internet, and digital television, to the linking of agriculture and biotech, pharmaceuticals and genetics, everywhere we look firms and industries are being reshaped by convergence. This is not going to slow down, indeed, it will spread.

Continuous Innovation

New product development sometimes creates the apparently bizarre, for example the microwave,[6] called the Microwave Bank, created by

---

[5] See various publications: Dr, Alan Walton, The Annual State of the Biotech Industry; "Gene Therapy and Big Pharma," *Biotechnology Business News*; "Energy, The New Convergence," *The Economist*, May 1999; "Telecoms Equipment: We Have the Technology," *The Economist*, October 1998; see the Dow Jones Interactive Publications Library.
[6] Geoff Martin, "A Catalogue of Convergence," *Ottawa Computes!* July 1999, ottawa-computes.com.

NCR, which hooks to the Internet to pay your bills, or the Screenfridge by Electrolux that does much the same, and the sometimes brilliant (to the housework-averse) robotic vacuum cleaner which searches out dust-bunnies automatically while you do something more useful. We live in a technology-driven world where invention is at its heart, and innovation—taking an idea to market—is a core skill. High-speed product development was a core competence we developed in the late-1980s and 1990s stimulated by the staggeringly fast pace set by the Japanese. The next few years are going to see those base skills deepen as new technologies open up for exploitation. Additionally, innovation has been happening for years in business processes, the most famous example being the Toyota System of lean production[7] with its emphasis on low inventories, just-in-time delivery, and intense supplier relationships. Every time a new product or process innovation appears it forces others to rethink, reshape or move aside. There is no reason to expect that innovation will slow down, indeed, with e-business roaring ahead, we can expect that there will be a whole new wave of innovative thinking. Innovation will be a significant factor in driving competition and continuous change.

Disruptive Technology

Truly revolutionary technology is highly destructive to established players.[8] The examples are legion—hydraulics taking over the earth-moving business from mechanical systems, the PC almost prostrating IBM, the micro-chip, the vacuum tube, and the small Canon copier taking a bite out of Xerox today, and of course we have the Internet. Disruptive technologies start out less sophisticated. Often starting with low efficiency they are typically cheaper alternatives. They are generally ignored by the established players who have heavy business and emotional investments in the old world. Moreover, the customers the established players talk to tend to decry the new approach as not

---

[7] For a full description of lean technology, see James P. Womack, Daniel T. Jones, Daniel Roos, *The Machine that Changed the World: Based on Massachusetts Institute of Technology 5-Million Dollar 5-Year Study on the Future of the Automobile*, New York: Macmillan, 1990; James P. Womack and Daniel T. Jones, *Lean Thinking: Banish Waste and Create Wealth in Your Corporation*, New York: Simon & Schuster, 1996.
[8] For a rapid overview of disruptive technology see Joseph L. Bower and Clayton M. Christensen, *Harvard Business Review*, January-February 1995; also see Clayton M. Christensen, *The Innovator's Dilemma: When New Technologies Cause Great Firms to Fail*, Boston: Harvard Business School Press, 1999.

meeting their needs, largely because it does not meet some quality standard. Then the new technology hits some threshold in functionality and becomes acceptable to the customer base.

The classic example is the Canon copier. This small machine came into the market at low cost, low quality, slow copy rates and questionable reliability compared with the huge Xerox machines. Canon slowly improved the technology and to Xerox's surprise it took off. The machine was suddenly good enough for a wide range of applications and cheap enough for small businesses and departments to have their own. It's improved operations combined with the desire to have control of one's own work drove sales ahead. The big Xerox machines were still needed, but the emergence of this new market gave Canon the boost it needed to become a formidable competitor in all segments. We live in a world of technology. We can safely predict the emergence of more disruptive technologies—the only question is when.

Ubiquitous E-business

E-commerce is only beginning to appear, but we can already see the trend and the adoption curve is vertical. We are in the middle of an e-enabled business explosion, with e-businesses set to grow by 2,000 percent between 1999 and 2002 according to DataMonitor. It also estimates electronic business at more than three trillion dollars by the same year, fueled by a 660 percent increase in e-business investment. The only thing we know for sure is that the actuals have always outperformed the forecasts. According to the US Department of Commerce,[9] the Internet's pace of adoption exceeds all technologies before it. It took radio 50 years to get 50 million users, TV 13 years, the PC 16, and the Internet four. E-business is driving new business models and reworking old ones, and it has just begun. This technology alone will keep organizations spinning for years.

* * * * *

Big concepts such as globalization, convergence, innovation, disruptive technology, and e-business seem remote, but the dynamics they unleash have dramatic effects on all our lives. Eventually, they translate

---

[9] For a major study of the emerging e-business world see "The Emerging Digital Economy," US Department of Commerce, www.ecommerce.gov.

into mergers, acquisitions, new operating systems, downsizings, new jobs, the creation and destruction of wealth, different roles, new competitors, the collapse and renewal of business models, and the relentless demand for ever increasing shareholder value which will put enormous pressure on your business to transform continuously.

No one is safe. Look back on our list of transformational leaders, none of their organizations has been able to stand still. British Airways is busy reinventing itself again in the face of intensifying competition. Sears is faced with the emergence of e-commerce. IBM is still trying to kick-start mega growth, BP faces tough markets and a race by competitors to also revitalize. GE is about to go through a leadership change attempting to replace a mythical figure. Ford, facing endemic Japanese competition and global industry consolidation has just entered the e-business world with a major procurement initiative. Even the most successful of the information age companies are under intense threat—Microsoft faces possible break-up and the dissipation of its desktop monopoly into many appliances. AOL acquired TimeWarner in a massive attempt at convergence in the entertainment markets. It remains to be seen if Disney, one of the world's truly excellent companies, is safe. After three transformations Intel is now faced with more intense price competition. Is IBM immune from take-over and break-up? Analysts have long said it would be worth more in bits. In the consulting industry the pressure of the Securities Exchange Commission (SEC) to ensure auditing independence is driving major restructuring. The Japanese colossus has been heavily affected by persistent recession forcing change in employment practices that will reverberate for years in that traditional culture. Like Japan, German industry is facing a major culture shock as it adjusts to a less respectful world. France is in danger of losing out as its labor protection weakens its global competitiveness. The pace of change everywhere will not slow and will probably accelerate. The white water looks permanent.

E-Leadership: The Competitive Difference

It was Harvard professor Rosabeth Moss-Kanter[10] who lectured that when the market is changing faster than the organization then you are in deep trouble, and she said this in quieter times. Modern markets

---

[10] Kanter is the author of the groundbreaking, *The Change Masters: Innovation and Entrepreneurship in the American Corporation*, New York: Simon and Schuster, 1983.

with their hyper-competitiveness are shifting at a tremendous rate, making leadership with the skill and insight to move the organization quickly, the critical competitive difference. As an e-leader you will be measured by your ability to drive shareholder value, and in a period of turbulence, this depends on the firm's capacity to change. How fast can it get an initiative in place? How fast can it drive through a learning curve to retrieve the most value out of a change? How well are costs understood so that accurate change is made? Preparing your organization to win in this world is what this book and the associated game and Web Site are about.

Becoming a great e-leader will mean building personal skills in transformation, modeling winning leadership behaviors, and building the organizational capability to transform continuously. In the six chapters of this book we address the six imperatives that will mark out successful transformational leaders, equipping you to be a winning e-leader. They are:

1. Change on the Run
2. Drive Extraordinary Financial Results
3. Unite People Behind Your Vision
4. Harness People's Experience
5. Galvanize Change Agents
6. Build a Leadership Army

1. Change on the Run

You cannot stop the world while you change your business. Successful transformational leaders have the capability to manage all-compassing change while keeping the business running at full tilt. How do they do it? In Chapter 1, "Change on the Run," we look at the differences between types of transformation—e-business, merger integration, installing major information systems, and profit collapses—and summarize the transformation implications facing e-leaders.

2. Drive Extraordinary Financial Results

The financial markets measure top leaders by their ability to build shareholder value in good times and bad. In the e-world, leaders need to make profits in the face of turbulence. In Chapter 2, "Drive

Extraordinary Financial Results," we look at profit resilience and how it is rooted in the sophistication of cost management. We look at the changes in approaches, tools, and perspectives needed to build profit resilience.

3. Unite People Behind Your Vision

In turbulent times strategy implementation often depends on the individual initiative of thousands of people. Get an organization aligned behind you and implementation of your strategic vision is a snap, saving up to 50 percent in total elapsed time. Chapter 3, "Unite People Behind Your Vision," discusses three of the key types of alignment open to e-leaders:

- Strategic alignment, getting an entire business lined up to implement a strategic vision, often during a crisis.

- Continuous alignment, involving everyone in the business in the restless search for value.

- Transcendence, a spiritual and emotional alignment which can take people to a higher plane of personal connection with their peers.

4. Harness People's Experience

The e-world is a knowledge world, yet after a decade of talk, the learning organization is still seen by many as an option. Chapter 4, "Harness People's Experience," redefines the problem of learning to make it a core leadership challenge. E-leaders will focus on creating the organizational conditions for tapping the knowledge of every individual. The chapter extends this theme into the area of personal learning and focuses on the frontier of "e-games," the use of the computer to provide experiences for business people so that they can learn about complex, holistic issues in very short time slots.

5. Galvanize Change Agents

The e-world will see firms continue to implement individual initiatives in large numbers. Getting initiatives in place quickly requires change agents with the requisite skills. E-Leaders will build a cadre of such individuals. Chapter 5, "Galvanize Change Agents," focuses on the issues of implementing single initiative changes and provides real-life examples of those middle-level leaders who won and lost.

6. Build a Leadership Army

The research says it all. Successful organizations have more leaders at all levels than less successful ones. As the traditional management structures continue to be eroded, the spreading of leadership skill to nontraditional places will accelerate. If you want to win in the tumultuous e-world you will have to create and enroll lots of leaders to join the journey. Chapter 6, "Build a Leadership Army," talks about the three keys to this problem: building the underlying leadership skill base, inculcating the skills of a modern leader, and lighting a leadership fire which will blaze throughout the business.

* * * * *

Each of the next six chapters stands alone. You can read them as a whole or just the chapters that interest you. Each focuses exclusively on a key aspect of winning at transformation. However, *Change on the Run* is more than a book, it is also an electronic experience. Whatever you do, don't forget to go to **www.changeontherun.com** and look at *Change on the Run: The Game*. It was built to display the potential of games to teach such holistic concepts as business strategy. As a player, you must transform your business as you compete in the marketplace. Also at the site you will find other ideas that will help you think about transformational issues. Whether you choose to start with the book or the game, have fun!

Change on the Run

The world is not going to stop while you transform your organization. E-world CEOs must drive the complex, multi-initiative programs that will determine the future of their business while keeping the present going. Leading complex change on the run is an imperative that could not be ignored at any time, but in the fast-changing e-world it will be a distinguishing skill of winning leaders. The ability to juggle the demands of the present and find the resources to address an ever-changing future will be obsessively important.

In 1999, Eleanor Clitheroe's world was getting more hectic by the minute. As the CEO of Ontario Hydro, she had been a prime mover in the recent privatization of the Ontario electrical supply industry. Now she had to deal with the aftermath. Ontario Hydro—the old utility—had been broken up, splitting the market operations of transmission, local electricity distribution, and sale of the actual electrons from the generation activities. Eleanor now ran Ontario Hydro Services Company (OHSC), a complex business operating regulated distribution and transmission, unregulated electricity commodity supply, plus interests in telecommunications, home service, and other potential businesses. The list of the issues she and her top team had to deal with would be daunting to anyone:

- De-merging the business from the old utility.
- Creating an entirely new organization.

- Developing a new strategic direction and getting everyone aligned behind it.

- Preparing in case the Ontario government decided to offer public shares in OHSC.

- Raising major debt financing for the first time as an independent entity with no track record as a private business.

- Dealing with an evolving regulatory environment.

- Working on reshaping the culture of OHSC from the old inward-looking monopolist to a flexible market oriented business.

And so it went on, down to such nitty-gritty issues as moving her whole staff to new premises. At one count, she and her management team had over 300 significant items to deal with. As one person put it, "We have lists of lists." Oh, and by the way, they still had to keep the business going, taking everyday operating decisions.

Eleanor and her team discovered at a deep personal level the blunt reality of major transformational change. No matter how much you reach down into the business for good people to help, no matter how many talented consultants you hire, no matter how many strategic retreats you use, in complex, holistic change the buck stops at the top. If decisions are to be made and the change program run effectively, the top team must act as a team, understand the issues, and put in 24 hours a day for weeks or months. This is the reality, and the first and overwhelmingly important leadership lesson for transformational CEOs is, *get the right people on your team*.

The primary reason for poor execution in transformation is "failure to put the right people in the right jobs...and the related failure to fix people problems in time." CEOs who fail are unable to deal with a "few key subordinates whose sustained poor performance deeply harms the company."[1] In the e-world, the ability to make these kinds of decisions will be even more crucial as time frames for action shrink. Assessing competence takes time and transformation demands that you seize the moment. You hire someone with the wrong credentials, carry someone incompetent over from the prior organization, or even worse give someone a change task because it will keep them busy even though they are not the best, and it can take you months to discover the disaster you have created. Time has been lost, the people throughout the organization discouraged, and money wasted.

---

[1] R. Charan and G. Colvin, "Why CEO's Fail," *Fortune*, June 21, 1999, 69-82.

Nothing—repeat nothing—is more important than this first lesson and the financial markets recognize it. A major PricewaterhouseCoopers survey of European businesses showed that organizations with leadership skilled in transformations that require changes to every part of the business at the same time yielded a 60 percent premium over firms that were not as skilled. No leader in the intensely competitive e-world can afford to give up that kind of premium to the competition.

The *mechanics* of change on the run are not complicated on the surface and have been the subject of endless numbers of change books and consulting proposals. The keys are:

- Have a clear business case rooted in external reality that you can express to the organization on why the change is necessary, then go out and sell it—relentlessly.

- Set up a governance structure for the change that ensures key decisions are made at the right times, then keep top management focused.

- Ensure that the program is owned either by you directly, the top team as a whole, or someone in the top team with the power to clear the way for those working on the details.

- Select a high quality change leader to manage a tightly controlled program office where all the many subprojects are coordinated, then support him or her effectively.

- If possible, keep the project separated from the main business while you parcel tasks out among teams so that those involved will put enough time in to make it all happen.

- Get the right people released to work on the program, square away their bosses so they are not in conflict, and give them incentive to get the projects finished quickly.

- Finally, from the very start, supplement the technical experts with people skilled in the techniques of change management so that resistance is minimized, then insist that they are used.

* * * * *

Thus far, thus simple. Obey the list, and you will have the shell of a major program. But, like all lists, it is just a series of items. It only comes alive in the cauldron of experience. Different types of transformation demand that leadership focuses on different issues, the generic has to be supplemented by insight into key strategic and operational concerns so that the change program gets the focused support it needs and the right questions are asked. The reality is that the circumstances surrounding a shift to e-business, where the elements of strategy are still evolving and are weakly understood by most leaders, are very different from those around a major merger integration. There, the issue is how to hold onto the combined value of the predecessor firms. Both of these are different again from a huge information systems installation where you are ripping up work processes, human relationships, and forcing major reskilling. In turn, all of these differ from a major profit collapse where you need to persuade people to come on a multiyear journey of refocusing, realigning, and reinventing the business. Finally, even a fundamentally sound business can no longer stand still for long. The restless pressure from the financial markets will ensure that they too must change on the run. In the next decade, a top leader of a multidivisional company will probably find him- or herself overseeing any or all of these types of transformation. Even in a smaller company, e-business is a certainty and any of the others could happen at the same time. E-leaders need to know what drives each type of transformation and why so that they know how to support the program. This chapter looks at four of these complex change environments to provide a feel for the leadership issues surrounding changing on the run and then lists the critical success factors for making the transformation work. The four transformations are:

- Transforming to E-Business
- Installing New Plumbing
- Making Mergers Happen
- When Profit Collapses

Transforming to E-Business

E-business will be the most consuming transformational issue of the next 10 years. If you have not started in this direction, you are already in deep trouble. The pioneers of e-business started their journeys up to a decade ago; they grew up with the Internet and had the luxury of time and few or no serious Internet competitors to make their changes. To them went the first round of Wall Street rewards. If you are just getting into e-business, you are now a follower, and in some industries, such as computers, a late-adopter. Unfortunately for those coming to the party late, e-business differs from all previous transformations. They were driven by the competitive economics of "things" where the primary concern was scale of operation. The more scale and capital you had, the better your chances. Moreover, many businesses were protected by the realities of geography with local knowledge or transportation costs keeping others out. In the e-business world, the competitive economics of information and knowledge apply and all firms can be global.

The economics of information are different from those of things. The reason Internet businesses give services away is that they are competing for mindspace and customers (globally) and in this way for customer knowledge. Get enough customers, the logic says, and you can learn more about them than your competitors. Use that knowledge to satisfy their needs and more customers come, eventually passing some point when you have the bulk of the market. At some point, your site becomes the premier place to go to because the customer can achieve the most there. You have effectively built a monopoly, for it is very difficult for others to dislodge you. The game is yours to lose. For example, if you want to buy a second-hand car would you go to a site with only a few sellers or one with 75 percent of the supply? If you need an entry point to the Web, would you go to an aggregator with a few services or one with hundreds of relationships? Capture the herd and you have won the game; competitors can never get enough traction to pass, as they do not have the customer knowledge or offering. This is the brass ring; things are different in cyberspace. This is the logic of Amazon.com, which grabbed customer loyalty before anyone was looking. Once you have the customer base you can migrate across categories, as Amazon.com has into videos, CDs, and so on.[2]

This doesn't just apply to business-to-consumer transactions, but also in the business-to-business world. Dell, a pioneer in the direct selling of computers, has integrated itself into the purchasing processes of major companies around the world, making buying from Dell simple.[3] Those companies are not going to create such relationships three or four

---

[2] For a detailed exposition of the economics of information businesses see Philip Evans and Thomas S. Wurster, *Blown to Bits: How the New Economics of Information Transforms Strategy*. Boston: Harvard Business School Press, 1999, and for further insight into the economics of e-business see W. Brian Arthur, "Increasing Returns and the New World of E-Business," *Harvard Business Review*, July-August 1996.

[3] "The Power of Virtual Integration: An Interview with Dell Computer's Michael Dell," *Harvard Business Review*, March-April 1998.

times. As long as Dell uses its commanding position to learn more and serve better it holds the winning cards. Look around your industry: which firm is doing this now? If it is not you, then you are in trouble. If you are too late to do it yourself then you had better join someone who has, as a supplier—quickly, before all those slots are gone too.

* * * * *

As the above illustrates, e-business is different. Leading a firm in its transformation to e-business requires that you understand something about this new world. The rest of this section addresses three key pieces of knowledge:

- What Does an E-Business Look Like?
- How Is the Industry Around Us Changing?
- What Is Different Strategically?

All these come with a caveat. E-business is new, business models are appearing daily, and most of them come to nothing. What is set out here is just the beginning of a long learning curve, so get on it soon and don't depend on the traditional sources of knowledge.[4]

What Does an E-Business Look Like?

There are two starting points in e-business: the pure Internet babies, like Amazon.com, and those that are or were classic businesses. For the vast bulk of firms the shift from classic is the issue and the starting point in e-business transformation is to have a picture in mind of what a mature (ex-classic) e-business looks like. Cisco is such a pioneer, having started down the road in 1992.[5]

In 1992, Cisco Systems was faced with the challenge of finding cost-effective ways to provide outstanding service for new products and customers. Revenue was nearly doubling each year with customer growth from internal product development as well as from

---

[4] E-business is beginning to evolve its own business press, for example, Business 2.0, Fast Company, Red Herring, and so on. As yet immature, these publications look set to give the traditional press, such as the *Harvard Business Review*, serious competition for insights into this emerging environment with its new business readership.

[5] This description of Cisco's journey to the e-business frontier was constructed from various public presentations and speeches by Cisco personnel and briefings by the Gartner Group *Cisco Reaps Huge Benefits*, March 1998, and Cisco and Internet Procurement, Sept. 1998. Numbers are indicative only.

acquisitions. The cost of maintaining this growth using traditional technical support approaches was becoming astronomical. Plus, at the expected growth rates, finding qualified technical people at all would become a problem. Cisco made its first move to a proto-Web environment, powered by this business question. Now, a decade later, Cisco's Web site, Cisco Connection On line or CCO (www.cisco.com), handles around a million log-ons a month. Its sales across the Internet amount to many billions of dollars and are Cisco's predominant way of doing business.

Today, 80 percent of the inquiries previously handled by Cisco's call center are answered electronically via CCO with growth in Internet log-ons handily outstripping phone calls. Cisco estimated that without CCO its support staff would have to be at least three times larger to handle the workload. For example, when Cisco added the functionality to CCO of allowing customers to print copies of their invoices, its call volume dropped by several thousand calls a month. In addition, while Cisco's inquiry workload doubled in five years, customer satisfaction ratings improved significantly. Depending on a problem's complexity, Cisco estimated that it saved up to $150 for every inquiry handled by its Web site, resulting in savings in the millions in support costs every month. When software distribution, paperless documentation, and reduced recruiting costs are added, the total savings attributable to CCO were calculated to be several hundred million dollars per year.

The technical-support information, which was developed initially for customers, and then for delivery to their Web sites, is now available to any entitled CCO user, including Cisco's call center staff. As Cisco customers use CCO, all of these troubleshooting data are captured for future reference. Cisco believes that the information available in this ever-evolving database allows its customer service agents to resolve customer problems more quickly, increasing overall productivity. As Cisco moves to an even more integrated customer care center this effectiveness can only improve.

In the high-tech industry, enterprises are looking to acquire solutions from partners, not products from vendors. The level of service is often more critical than the features or functionality of the products. CCO, with its round-the-clock global customer service and technical support resource, is an extension of Cisco's business partner network strategy and is characteristic of the principle that drives the company: profits and customer satisfaction have a strong one-to-one relationship. Besides providing more accessible service and support, and reducing related costs internally, CCO is intended to foster and build relationships with customers and promote additional sales.

A decade on, e-business thinking permeates the entire firm. Besides handling service and support calls, CCO is an important and lucrative sales channel. Recent press articles have touted how companies such as Dell Computer are achieving more than a million a day in sales through their Web sites. In comparison, by January 1998 Cisco had already achieved 10 times that in daily revenue from its Web site, and Cisco's sales and customer gain are even greater than the revenue numbers imply. Under the old system a customer communicated his or her idea of the type of product needed and how it should be configured to a procurement department, which then created the purchase order and sent it to Cisco by fax or e-mail. A Cisco customer service administrator keyed the order into Cisco's system. If it were correctly configured, with components that worked together, it would be booked and production would be scheduled for the next 24 hours. However, since up to 75 percent of orders were not configured correctly, the order would be rejected, and the customer had to be contacted, restarting the procurement cycle.

Today, the engineer configures his or her order on line and knows immediately if there are any errors. Procurement in the customer's firm would be notified but the order would go through immediately assuming the purchaser was authorized. With on-line pricing and configuration tools, 98 percent of orders are accurate, and lead time has dropped to two or three days. CCO allows only authorized customers to purchase through the Web site, but they can check the status of an order, get pricing and product data, review information on their contracts, register for seminars, and download software upgrades from an on-line library. Other features include an e-mail alert that sends information about software bugs to customers within 24 hours of their discovery.

Cisco has installed CCO remote distribution servers in countries throughout the world, including dedicated links in Australia, China, France, Hong Kong, Japan, the Netherlands, and South Korea. Users can access an integrated selection in the local language with content for that local country. Translated versions of the award-winning CCO home page, and many other key CCO pages, are available in 14 or more languages.

Cisco's supply chain is now entirely integrated with its customer ordering approach. Cisco has outsourced production to a group of different suppliers who act like a single enterprise. Everyone is involved in product introductions and there is one central forecast for the whole system instead of everyone trying to second-guess the next player in the chain. Data gathering on production needs is totally automated and by having the same demand forecast for everyone, the whole chain minimizes its inventory needs, so reducing total system costs. Shippers dispatch directly to the customer, eliminating the Cisco interface. Indeed over 50 percent of unit volume is shipped without Cisco involvement. Some statistics: lead time of product introductions to volume production has been reduced by a quarter, engineering change times have been cut by up to 70 percent, and annual operating costs cut by over $70 million.

Cisco's program manager of Internet procurement recognized that, just like the earlier customer inquiries problem, manual processing of purchases had no scale economies. Grow and you need to hire more people; in fact, the ratio of purchase orders to employees is roughly what you had before. Cisco had had success in streamlining procurement of direct goods by integrating electronic data interchange (EDI) with its Oracle manufacturing software. However, the requisitioning of support goods and services that did not go into the products directly had little automated support. As a result, Cisco estimated this labor-intensive process resulted in each purchase order (PO) costing $130. (Cross-industry processing costs are as high as $250 per PO.) At Cisco, the high unit cost was due to purchasing employees struggling with an inefficient manual process. The procurement manager's objective was to increase the proportion of direct-order items from 50 to 80 percent, so reducing the overall cost of POs from $130 to a target of $25. Cisco invited suppliers to a supplier day, where they were told how Cisco's internal catalog would be stocked. None of Cisco's major suppliers declined the offer.

Cisco has adopted most of the e-business themes known so far—Web commerce, customer support, international support, supply chain management, product customization and configuration, e-procurement, e-strategy, a full panoply of financial systems, and it now sits at the center of a customer/supplier/partner ecosystem. The effect is staggering. Cisco has revenue of about $600,000 per employee, compared with 3 Com at two-thirds of that, and Lucent at a third.[6] Clearly this is not comparing apples with apples as a firm like Lucent does much in-house production, but it does give an idea of the efficiency of the original equipment manufacturer (OEM) in a system such as Cisco's. Cisco, with Dell and a handful of others, is on its way to mythological status as the first of the great e-business success stories. Unlike Amazon, eBay, and the pure Internet models, Cisco built its success by moving from existing bricks and mortar operations to a true e-business, leveraging the advantages of the Web to access the best of everything, and focusing their own efforts on what they do best. With minor variants the Cisco story will be repeated over the next decade and the transformation will follow the two-step pattern of all information technology driven changes.

- E-business, like ERP before it, is a "package" driven change. To get into it you have to have an electronic platform. Just as ERP drove five years of staggering workload for the IT industry (accelerated by Y2K), so the next five years will see the mass installation of Web sites, customer management systems, e-procurement programs, e-logistics, financial cost management, and so on. Meanwhile, the established ERP programs—SAP, PeopleSoft, Baan, and so on—will be refined to adjust to the e-business world.

- Once the programs are in place and the trauma of installation over, benefits realization programs will follow as the firm seeks to get the operating and financial benefits that were advertised.

However, there is no guarantee that all this effort will make followers into winners. If someone gets there first and cuts you off from the customer then you may be headed for the scrap heap. E-business is not about technology, though technology is a prerequisite. It is about customer knowledge and how you use it.

How Is the Industry Around Us Changing?

It is very difficult for a firm to get too far ahead of its industry. Even pioneers need followers to join their Web enterprises or supply chains. Looking across a range of industries, they seem to fall into four states[7] of development:

---

[6] Cisco presentation, Q3 Revenues x 4 /employees as of Q3, 1999.
[7] This four-state framework was derived from various PricewaterhouseCoopers LLP internal thought papers.

- Isolated E-Commerce
- Locking in Extended Enterprises
- Creating Value Networks
- Evolving a Business Ecology

Isolated E-Commerce

Industries in this first stage are characterized by the launching of e-commerce sites by individual firms. These sites are usually able to conduct business with secure software for information sharing, order taking, payment, and catalogs. Such sites are often a reworking of more primitive corporate Web sites that had been set up purely for advertising purposes. For some, this event is the extent of their ambition, but for others it is a deliberate learning experience on the way to a wider e-business involvement. For business-to-business firms, the site is often an extranet, accessible via the Internet but only to the company's most valuable customers and suppliers.

At the time of writing, a commercial Web site can still provide a firm with an advantage over competitors who have not yet taken the plunge. E-commerce sites are still rare in many industries. Rarer still are Web sites that are effectively integrated into a firm's underlying, internal systems and business processes. To date, most sites have been launched as an experiment or for PR reasons, and simply laid on top of the existing business. This is true even of some highly sophisticated firms.

The result has been a rush of customer interest and an inability of the company to service its customers properly. A major Canadian bank discovered this when it had to back off its e-bank strategy because of back office problems. *The Economist*[8] traced this problem in the 1999 Christmas period when sales on the Internet were in the $6 billion range, with quotes from equipment suppliers scoffing at the poor quality back office operations of even sophisticated clients. However, the article also noted the basic belief of dotcom firms that they are in a race for market share—and mindshare—and it is better to be there and incompetent but learning than not be there at all.

---

[8] "Wish Fulfillment," *The Economist*, December 18, 1999.

Locking in Extended Enterprises

In this state, e-commerce has ceased to be a novelty in the industry. Customers are used to the new levels of immediacy in response and new service levels. E-commerce is beginning to make firms rethink their market strategies around new levels of service, lower prices, product customization, delivery and purchase convenience, and so on. Senior management is starting to realize that this way of doing business is more dynamic and surprising than anything previously known. The dynamism comes from the direct link with the customer and the increasing flow of information on customer preferences. This demands reactions in new products and services and levels of support.

Also, the volatility of the customer base is much higher than in traditional businesses where distributors may have relationships and customers have costs in shopping around. In the e-world, a new shop is just a click away and unless it is created no one has a compelling need to shop at the site. Any extranets with business-to-business customers and suppliers help create a relationship or deepen an existing one, as customers and suppliers start to modify the ways they do business. The traditional supply chain will be most affected. Old intermediaries may disappear and new ones emerge—the previous intermediaries will either find new ways of adding value or perish and be replaced by new players. This stage may also see firms start to outsource capabilities to others and focus on the areas where they can add value.

Creating Value Networks

Enterprises in this industry state extend themselves beyond their immediate group of suppliers and customers to embrace the whole networked community in their traditional industry. This opens up a wider array of suppliers and customers. The industry may seek to set standards in a collective effort to realize cost and potential revenue gains for all. This is happening in North America in the car industry, the grocery trade, and others. A profound change in the way the industry operates occurs as businesses focus on their core source of value and have others provide the other capabilities. Here we may also see the emergence of transient, virtual organizations that come together to create a product or service and then disband after it has run its course.

Evolving a Business Ecology

This world is characterized by the remaking of industry boundaries. In traditional business, products define industries. For example, we talk about the real estate industry, the house insurance industry, the property maintenance industry, and the home security industry. In the e-world the industry is defined not by products, but by customers. So the industry list above becomes the homeowner industry. In this model, the customers with their needs are at the heart, and products and services are clustered around it.

This is absolutely revolutionary. Not that it had not been envisioned before, but the Internet has made need-based, one-stop-shopping a reality—overnight and with no bricks and mortar costs.

Imagine the personal transportation management industry linking rental cars, car purchases, insurance, maintenance, vehicle interest groups (specialty sports car owners or racing freaks), public transport providers, taxi companies, and so on into a single package. This is a business ecology and to be successful the members of the ecological system have to develop cooperative and collaborative relationships for delivery of products and services in disparate categories. That adds value to the customer because of the coordination and integration. Such ecologies are beginning to emerge around home ownership, cars, and even such broad customer categories as gender. In the case of women.com, the ecology focuses on the specific needs of women, women's issues, and the products and services desired by women as women.[9]

In the business ecology world, competition is no longer between individual firms but between communities of suppliers, and your problem is to become a part of a community before it's membership settles and before the community gets a dominant position making it difficult for others to move in.

* * * * *

Different industries are in different states of development and different firms have started from different places. Most firms are in the simple e-commerce state, while others with EDI capability have

---

[9] Services, to date, include free e-mail, advice of fashion, home decorating, sex and romance, pregnancy, childbirth, and weddings, as well as shopping and advertising aimed at women.

already moved to the extended enterprise. The relationships inside a Dell, a Cisco, or a GE are a value network, an idea that will be extended dramatically when Ford and GM set up their procurement companies reshaping the whole car industry. In the value network and ecology worlds we have already seen the emergence of new specialist intermediaries—the infomediaries and aggregators—who provide advice and access to multiple products to multiple customers. The pace of adoption is rising as firms embed the basic technology in their systems architectures and major firms insist on working with suppliers that are e-business enabled: being part of the new e-world is now a prerequisite to survival.

What Is Different Strategically?

Industries are moving quickly through the four states described in the previous section and PricewaterhouseCoopers expects most industries in North America to have made significant progress to value networks and business ecologies by 2003. From a non-North American point of view, these firms will be projecting that market proposition worldwide. If you are not part of this integration in your industry, you will be left out of value creating opportunities. To get a grip on the size of this problem, it helps to understand what is new strategically about the e-world. Actually, much of it is familiar: firms formed strategy in the pre-Internet world; they reacted to aggressive competition; they tried to understand the customer, installed computer packages, and got people to use them. They also interlinked supply chains, created virtual relationships, had major channel conflicts (just as is happening with the Internet in, for example, the insurance industry where direct insurance sales compete with the traditional channels that the insurance companies still depend on). With the exception of specific things such as opening e-commerce Web sites, much of the e-world has reflections in the world we knew. This is true of every significant transformation. So what is different about e-business? Five things stand out:

- E-Speed
- Hyper-Intensity of Competition
- Transparent Prices
- Paramount Role of Knowledge
- Ubiquity of Communication

E-Speed

The opening up of cyberspace has some similarities to the land rushes of the American West, with firms in a headlong race to mark out territory through the setting up of Web sites whether they intend to "settle" on them immediately or not. Cyberspace seems infinite, and it is to the extent that new entrants will be able to get a foothold at low cost, and those who wish to sell their own products will always be able to use it as a channel. But, like all else in business, it will obey the laws of competition. First movers who use their sites to create a strong value proposition will claim mindspace with busy users of the Web and thereby a competitive advantage which will be rewarded in the financial markets. Amazon.com proved this conclusively when its ownership of the e-book business forced leading retailer Barnes & Noble to establish Web presence. Other leaders, such as Dell and Cisco, have built deep integration with their customers. Getting in yesterday and establishing a presence is absolutely crucial. Recently, American Express imposed a six-month deadline to the creation of an e-bank. When Harrods elected to enter e-tailing, three months was its time budget to getting everything up and running.

Hyper-Intensity of Competition

Once in, strategy formulation needs to happen dramatically faster than in traditional businesses. During the last decade, the pressure of competition moved traditional businesses away from a simple aim-ready-shoot idea of strategy formulation that performed heavy analysis before deciding on strategy and only then carried out actions. Today, most firms have moved to the higher tempo of ready-shoot-aim as they seek to try new ideas out quickly, and analyze them later. However, in the e-business world, the tempo is dramatically faster still. E-business is about shoot, and keep shooting, as action becomes strategy and results are your analysis. The CEO of eBay was not kidding when she remarked that she rethought her strategy *every day*.

Some of this need for strategy adjustment comes from the unexpected opportunities that emerge. Aquarium.com,[10] a small Canadian retailer of specialist aquarium supplies, went on the Web to serve its local clientele and was overwhelmed by a flood of orders

---

[10] Now part of pets.com.

from Japan where the items they sold were not readily available, and looked awfully cheap in yen. The Mighty Ducks ice hockey team had a similar rush when its goods became a fashion trend in France, yielding a deluge of business from French teenagers. Some opportunities come from the unexpected penalties of success. AOL's well publicized problems with the capacity of its network were matched by E*TRADE when it went down for several hours leaving day traders hung up and possibly litigious.

More hyper-aggression comes from the need to continually defend your space. Yahoo, hardly one of the most graphically interesting of the Internet portals, was at least a first mover and had generated a loyal following. As competition heated up, Yahoo was forced to react. It hit on the formula of adding free services (it made the bulk of its revenue from advertising), so raising the content of its site, and coincidentally raising the investment bar for its competitors. In pursuit of this strategy, it developed or acquired such capabilities as local sites in different countries, games, classifieds, chat rooms, e-mail-for-life, Web site creation, calendering, to-do lists, and so on. All this was aimed at providing a convenient experience so that a person's e-life is locked into Yahoo and becomes too difficult to change.

Finally, some opportunity comes from the intense reaction of competitors in the real world. Part of Barnes & Noble's reaction to being sidelined in cyberspace by Amazon.com was to attack in the real world, trying to take control of Amazon's distribution system, and forcing it from pure e-world to a "clicks and mortar" world. A Canadian car dealer set the industry on edge by selling across geographical boundaries through the Internet. The reaction of his fellow dealers was violent as they took him to court in a case that is still pending.

Transparent Prices

In theory, Internet prices will be increasingly transparent, even to the point of showing customers how the prices of complex goods are built up through the value chain. Even worse, goes this logic, not only will people be able to find out prices by personal comparison, there will be whole sites that will be dedicated to price comparisons in specific product categories. A good early example was books.com,[11] which would go out to other sites to get price comparisons for you and

---

[11] Now part of barnesandnoble.com.

sought to match them immediately. Another is pricescan.com. This kind of price comparison and transparency accelerates the normal process of commoditization of products, moving them toward total competition based heavily on price.[12] The only good news is that e-business can be structured to operate at a lower cost and those with the skill, insight, and first-mover advantage can lock in those lower costs stealing a march over their competitors. Some evidence seems to back this up. On-line retailers do tend to be cheaper than conventional rivals, and they also adjust prices more finely and more often. This clearly places price pressure on the bricks and mortar suppliers.

However, as between on-line sites, studies indicate that price competition may not be as severe as theory would suggest. There is considerable variation in price even for identical products, such as airline tickets, which, on an exact comparison basis, can vary by as much as 18 percent. And this is also true of other goods. Hardly perfect competition. Retailers on the Web have all the tricks of their real world brethren with loyalty programs and other offers that make shifting suppliers expensive. Also, shopping on the Web is not entirely without effort. Research indicates that even shoppers who use "shopbots," computer programs that search many sites for the best deal, still usually buy from the market leader. The reason, apparently, is trust. Over the long term, as the Web matures, we can expect prices to come under greater pressure, commoditizing many goods even more completely. However, there will always be room for a canny supplier who can customize the shopping experience in some way.

Paramount Role of Knowledge

The Internet is a knowledge world. This grand-sounding concept is really very simple. Every time potential customers touch the Web site, they leave behind information—that they came, that they made certain specific inquiries, that they bought something, that they designed a product, filled in a survey, all kinds of information which the computer can capture and analyze. In the old days (1995!), collecting customer data demanded surveys, and they were expensive and slow. Today you can have it all immediately and largely free. The same

---

[12] There is no doubt that the Internet will push pricing in this direction, but as *The Economist* ("Friction in Cyberspace: Retailing on the Internet, It Is Said, Is Almost Perfect Competition. Really?" November 20,1999.) pointed out full price pressure has not yet arrived in all sectors.

applies to supply. Suddenly, the business becomes about analysis of information to create the insights, which will allow you to create something the individual customer will value and slicing the market into thinner and thinner slivers. This is a knowledge management world.

In this world you have two needs: to keep the information flowing in ever greater depth, and to find, and hold on to, the people who can take that information and derive insights from it—in short, create customer value. The management of human talent is a huge issue. Incentives and motivation to keep people is extremely important, and very difficult when people are in short supply. A recent US survey of webmasters indicated an average tenure of seven months. When Netscape went public, it sought to tether everyone to the deck with high bonus potential, a common approach in Silicon Valley. But, even in less hot-house environments, the power comes from having people who can convert information into product insights. Lose those people, and you have lost your edge.

Ubiquity of Communication

The emergence of the Internet as a viable mass communication medium in the mid-1990s changed the face of consumer communication fundamentally. However, the idea of networked organizations had been around for some years in the business world. Electronic data interchange (EDI) allowed individual firms to swap information by dedicated firm-to-firm links. What changed was the ubiquitous nature of the Internet connections; everyone could hook up to everyone else for very little cost compared with the old EDI. Suddenly, a firm could access the full field of suppliers and reap enormous gains. It was into this world that GE introduced its now famous e-procurement. Moving from a highly manual system that could only form relationships with a restricted supply set and operated slowly and expensively, to an Internet-based system with ubiquitous access by vendors to GE's needs, sped up procurement, opened new supply sources, and saved GE millions of dollars.

* * * * *

E-business has changed the strategic landscape forever, and its potential has barely been scratched. The differences laid out above are early insights into e-business, and are being fast supplemented. However, what we know already is that e-business is a deeply entrepreneurial space, with low—but fast-rising—barriers to entry on a large scale and where competition is presently in the white-hot phase. Should you wait for it to settle? Only if you intend to exit the business!

If you intend entering, how do you manage a major program to get you there? First, you need to follow the basic rules:

- *Know why you are doing it.* Is it strictly a response to competitive pressure? Are you seeking to get ahead of the competition? Where is your industry on the adoption curve? Do you want to be out front or a follower? Are you already late, and, if so, can you possibly catch up or do competitors have a lock on the sources of customer information? How much effort are you willing to expend?

- *Ensure key decisions are made.* E-business in its most intense form is a major shift in the way the firm does business. If the top team is split on the issues, those that come up—such as conflict between distribution channels when e-commerce sites compete directly with traditional players to sell to the consumer—will not be effectively resolved, the initiative will be slowed, and the benefits probably not realized. Strong governance of an e-project is critical.

- *Impose tight program management.* At the core, an e-world transformation is a technology installation, getting the technology platform in place. Every part of your business will have to be rethought. When you get into this environment, nothing is more important to financial success than tight control of the installation program(s).

- *Keep separated from the existing business.* The creation of a Web business is best done in a different space if only so that you can see the key aspects of the new business approach more clearly. However, where this sets up tensions with the existing business the separation should be short. Building links to the legacy parts of the firm will lower antagonism and allow people to believe that they can be part of the emerging future.

- *Use change management tools from the start.* Involving people, having different stakeholder groups understand the business case and the strategy behind the program is important to getting acceptance and eventually wholehearted support. Doing this requires careful thinking about who will be affected and devising ways of bringing them in—this is change management.

If you have met the above requirements, how do you measure the effectiveness of your e-business strategy and the process of transformation? How do you measure it against the critical success factors?

Change on the Run

E-Business

1. Own the customer interface—at all costs.
2. Be obsessed with speed.
3. Shoot, shoot, shoot, and keep shooting.
4. Build a knowledge force, and involve them intensely in strategy, and tactics, and hold on to them during the change.
5. Develop a long-term view, but get started on some project now—today.

Installing New Plumbing

ERP is dead, long live ERP. With the passing of Y2K, the primary driver for the urgent installation of enterprise-wide resource planning systems went away. However, that does not mean the need or demand for these systems has passed. Even in an e-business world, someone has to make the products, and the demand for data will be just as great. Indeed, as big e-world players with installed ERP seek to connect to their customers and suppliers in ever more tightly connected networks and swap ever more critical information, the demand for structured and disciplined data will increase. The same will be true of product development, customer management, and cost management, in fact all the modules of these huge systems. The big programs have been expanded to connect through the Internet, and so we can confidently expect installations of this kind to continue, supplemented by Internet-specific packages, to get at staggering financial gains. It has been estimated that Internet-based customer care can lead industry to gains in the region of $270 billion, Internet commerce to efficiency gains of about $60 billion, supply chain management nearly $450 billion, and workforce productivity gains of about $50 billion.

This total of well over $800 billion is probably low.[13] Indeed, based on Cisco itself, companies that are fully Internet-enabled can be up to 65 percent more productive than those that are not.

The CPR Story

case   Whatever the strategic reasons, installing huge systems has enormous impacts on the business, as it rips out the process core, and re-plumbs itself. The case of Canadian Pacific Railway (CPR) is illustrative of the scale and intensity of such a program. "You have to love adventure to do this kind of thing," says Jennifer Heath, who led the change management work in one of the most complete enterprise-wide resource planning system installations carried out in North America. "You need the sense of adventure to give you the energy to engage with such a huge undertaking, to stay healthy and enjoy the learning experience." Ken Porter, the project leader agrees and adds that sharing this sense of adventure and accountability for enabling change, is a critical requirement of the project management team and the steering committee.

In 1996, Canadian Pacific Railway, one of the largest railway systems in North America, adopted what it called the IT Breakout Strategy with the aim of leveraging technology and systems to significantly improve performance. This program subsequently broke into two parts: APEX (the program we are looking at here) was concerned with applications and processes for enterprise excellence in the areas for finance and accounting, procurement and materials management, engineering and mechanical; the other program was concerned with service excellence in transportation operation. Both happened at the same time and were joined by several other projects including some downsizing and outsourcing.

The APEX program became an installation of SAP, a comprehensive enterprise—wide information system. CPR installed all the modules of SAP, except for payroll, in the same program, moving it from a system project to a huge integrated change effort aimed at fundamentally transforming the way CPR operated. Approval to start APEX was given in early 1997, and to meet the Y2K deadlines, the installation work had to be completed by mid-1999. The level of effort was enormous. Eight thousand people were trained in new processes that had to be designed. Three hundred and fifty locations had to be addressed on a railway system scattered across Canada and the northeast and Midwest USA. New systems had to be created, networks built, dial-up connections made, and 5,000 computers with related basic software installed in locations where there was no

---

[13] Cisco estimates, 1999.

business requirement in the past and hence little familiarity with these tools. The need to put in the required computing equipment first meant visiting each location twice, doubling the normal workload on the team.

New processes to link to these systems had to be developed and deployed to people who had often used their own local or idiosyncratic approach and were totally unused to the data demands of modern systems such as keeping highly detailed track of time. The use of computer keyboards and the degree of discipline needed was a major shift in the way work was done in an almost fully unionized environment. People had to work in different ways, and often needed several training sessions to get the new approaches in place. This is still a problem today as people are moved around, and skills are dissipated. Getting the unions involved was critical, and major efforts were made by everyone to create a positive environment. Strong union support became a hallmark of the project in both countries, creating positive labor relations in a potentially difficult environment.

The deployment problem was initially underestimated and so big it had to be done in three stages: an initial big bang got basic systems such as finance and accounting in everywhere at once, followed by a mini-bang that deployed limited functionality at all locations, and a final phase that picked up the rest. The highly concentrated training task started with the basics such as how to use a computer, use standard software such as Windows and Lotus Notes, and conduct simple e-mail transactions. Only then could they move on to the SAP package itself. In every area, basic and sophisticated new work approaches were implemented; e.g., standard costing, MRP and DRP which replaced local, highly customized processes and systems, and to everyone's frustration, they sometimes initially proved less functional until they were modified to fit the business needs.

CPR is a complex organization that was previously deeply siloed. Within its ranks were groups that had rubbed along together for decades, some working well together, some not. Different groups had significantly different agendas, and different unions represented different groups. Like all such projects, this one faced the problem of a limited number of good resources—resources that were in demand for other projects. Project management had to contend with the resource constraint and also with a corporate history of missed deadlines, which would be fatal to a project like this. Teams of over 150 people were set up representing all the affected areas—finance, mechanical engineering, materials management, IT, engineering, change management, and so on, teams that had to be formed and made to work together. Simply passing on and reinforcing team skills was a major task. During the different phases of the project individuals were required to travel and to work incredible hours making it difficult to maintain the project's desired balance between work and personal life. The overlap of several major programs was to be a significant issue, and failure to keep adequate track of activities in these other projects was a source of problems for APEX. In addition, the downsizings and outsourcing created teamwork problems as people worked on programs that could make them potentially redundant.

Key to success was getting local management ownership for a successful implementation and for the realization of the benefits promised. The APEX team was there simply to support them, not to make it happen. From the start the aim was to avoid the tendency for the business to distance themselves from the development of the solution and then reserve the right to criticize. This was unacceptable. Yet getting this level of accountability from local management often proved to be difficult. Each site was required to have its own Site Transition Team, a highly successful approach which (led by a key person termed a Super User—an expert able to do the local training) worked its way through a checklist of activities to prepare for the deployment. Where this was conscientiously undertaken deployment was much easier. Where it was not, a much more difficult time was experienced. After project completion these teams (with their Super Users) were disbanded and have had to be re-formed to get at the ongoing issues of benefits maximizations, and training of new personnel.

The program was physically deployed on time and within committed economic returns—a major triumph.

So much for the facts, but what did Jennifer, Ken and her colleagues learn from this experience? First, to expect the unexpected. As Jennifer puts it, "It doesn't matter how much you plan, some things will not go according to plan, so get over it. This is not an argument against planning but for flexibility; you always have to correct course." Second, to bless a strong sponsor. This project was shepherded along by George Halatsis, the EVP/CFO, a person of great commitment and determination. "When we needed a decision or to get someone into the room, George was there." Adds Ken, "Without the speeding of decisions that this allowed, it would all have been much slower and behind schedule."

Third, the team learned not to point fingers at individuals. Suppressing the urge to blame and focusing on the process that had created the problem kept temperatures down and allowed for better working relationships. "We also measured our success with a balanced scorecard. We looked at cost and the work plan, naturally, but we kept a focus on benefits to the business, on the effectiveness, of our change management, on our own team effectiveness and on 'connecting the dots.'" This last point was very important. With many different projects happening in CPR at the same time, ensuring that this project did not duplicate or negatively impact other work was critical to success and to the project's reputation. "With so much going on, if we were not aware, we could experience significant push back. Change effects are cumulative, and there comes a time when people have 'had enough.' If we walked in at this point we were in for trouble...!" says Jennifer. Add to this the accumulation of stress, the fragmentation of CPR's culture into functional, professional, and geographic groups, and the need for hyper-awareness was magnified. Faced with the regular potential for this hightened push back, keeping up the team's can-do attitude was vital. Picking up the adventure theme, they went mountain climbing together, raising the levels of trust and the willingness to depend on each other. They even started using climbing jargon like "on belay" (to secure a rope or pin) when discussing the need to support each other at difficult points.

But, even with all this good thinking, the project still hit the inevitable crisis. Inevitable, because it always seems to happen. In this case, about halfway in, the project was slowly slipping behind, but no one wanted to acknowledge this fact. Faced with this reality of denial, Jennifer, Ken and the project management team set out to break the logjam. They started with the project team itself and got the issues out on the table—what was wrong, how much time was being lost, and what needed to be done? Full understanding was the goal. In effect, we needed to talk about the "undiscussables." Armed with the facts and some solutions, a process that took two weeks in a project that was already falling behind, they went to the steering committee. Jennifer comments, "This was a very pivotal meeting. It lasted two and a half days with our senior stakeholders and created some very helpful dialog." The result was the project getting back on track and even making up the lost time to finish on schedule. The message: expect problems, plan for it, and deal with it.

And then, suddenly, it was all over. There was a big celebration and everyone went back to their lives. But few were ready to go back. "The reality of projects of this kind is that the opportunity exists for tremendous development; to become more intellectually, emotionally, and socially fit. There are big highs and big lows, and you definitely know you are alive!" exclaimed Jennifer Heath.

* * * * *

Implementing a major ERP installation is a demanding process, requiring the rethinking of all of the key processes of the business, and reshaping the way people work, as the CP Rail example illustrated. CP was an unusually comprehensive case, but even single module programs demand heavy transformational thinking.

- *Know why you are doing it.* Building a business case for the change is absolutely fundamental. Major technology installations change the way people work, and though you can force them to a degree, it is very difficult to get the wholehearted assent you need if no one understands why you are doing it. It can't simply be change for change's sake, or you'll get employees rolling their eyes and cursing, "Not another management initiative...." Building the case for change and having leadership express it and stand behind it is the starting point of effective change thinking. Part of building this vision of the future is making a clear distinction between today's processes and the new ones—the "as is" versus the "to be." Allowing people to be part of the analysis can help get the new ideas accepted.

- *Ensure key decisions are made.* It is highly unlikely that your program will be the only one underway in the business, and any of these other programs may have a real impact on your work. This happened in the CPR case when parallel programs confused people or had an effect on teamwork. Connecting the dots—the links between programs—is a major activity. Moreover, every organization is short of good resources, and competing for top skills against other programs can be a major problem. It is not unusual for top managers to refuse to release people, particularly if they feel that their own projects are going to be affected.

- *Impose tight program management.* There is nothing more important in an ERP installation than the program management. These projects have become notorious for missed deadlines and cost overruns. An ideal approach is goal-directed project management that uses a long series of short-cycle deliverables to keep tight control. In this way the program cannot get too far away from you.

- *Keep separated from the existing business.* The business has to keep running. The separation in this kind of project is more or less automatic, as there has to be a changeover date when the new systems go live.

- *Use change management tools from the start.* The heart of change management in ERP projects is stakeholder management and training. People become severely unsettled when their work routines are reshaped, particularly if they face the possibility of losing their jobs. Communicating with affected groups is absolutely vital. Indeed, it is virtually impossible to overcommunicate.

In addition, we can identify other keys to making a major plumbing program happen.

Change on the Run

Major Plumbing

1. Keep the time frames tight, and stick to them.
2. Hire the best program manager you can find.
3. Understand the full scope of the problem including collateral activity, like installing hardware and teaching neophytes.
4. Build a strong coalition of interests and a supporting team, and hold on to them into any follow-on work, such as the customization and benefits realization.
5. Involve all the key stakeholders (including unions) intimately so they feel ownership.
6. Recognize that getting the system in is only the first step. A full program of system tuning and customization to realize benefits will be needed when the installation dust settles, so don't let your team go away.

Making Mergers Happen

The shift to global integration has set off a round of mergers and acquisitions at prices never before matched.[14] E-leaders will depend on merger activity for growth and mass that can protect them from being devoured. Embracing the basic skills of merger integration is a root skill. But mergers are fraught with all kinds of human and business problems. The focus in this section is strictly on the change

---

[14] See Philip H. Mirvis and Mitchell Lee Marks, *Managing the Merger*, Englewood Cliffs, NJ: Prentice Hall, 1992, for what is still one of the best expositions of merger behavior ever written.

issues that so often determine whether the originally envisaged gains will ever appear. Experience says the odds are not on your side.

Some years ago my 12-year-old daughter was on a camping trip. The group was portaging their canoes from one lake to the next, when she slipped off the path and fell into muskeg swamp. She had actually gone under before her friends and the guide were able to push paddles under her armpits and get her to float. She was rescued but with great difficulty, the pull of the swamp acting like an undertow dragging her down. That helpless feeling of being sucked into the morass is, from a change perspective, very much like trying to make a major merger work. That is not really a stretch. The fact still is that 50 percent or more of mergers seem to fail to meet their original value creation goals and so destroy value in the process. Of the rest, many contribute only moderate gains. No one intends them to fail, but once the firm has stepped into the swamp, it can seem as if there is no bottom—and no friends with paddles to buoy you up!

The Swamp Monsters

A 1996 PricewaterhouseCoopers survey concluded that the potential economic advantage of merger deals was only achieved in half the cases, and recent anecdotal evidence indicates that little has changed. Most damning was the fact that the operational benefits in lowering production, distribution, and operating costs were the least likely to be realized. Even market share gains may be temporary or significantly eroded by subsequent losses, the very benefits which, in most cases, were used to justify the deal in the first place. The pressures pushing merging firms into the swamp and chipping away at the value in the deal are many, and they put in an appearance even before the ink is dry on the deal. Eight of the leading problems are discussed:

- The Devil Deal
- The Disaster of Delay
- Stress, Distress, and Depression
- Milling Rumor
- Arrogance and Thin Skins
- Culture Wars
- Left Behind
- Poor Leadership

The Devil Deal

The loss of value can start right with the deal itself. Those of us who have bought something at auction know the feeling. Sometimes you get caught up in the bids. The adrenaline rushes, and all those carefully devised plans come to nothing as you pay far more than the item is really worth. Ego, simplistic strategy—growth can be gained fastest by buying it—and arrogance combine to put the adrenaline rush into hyper-drive. But, in mergers and acquisitions, such over-bidding has real consequences as the new owners try to recover their overspending out of the hide of the acquisition, often in order to keep the financial markets happy. Deep cost-cutting of perhaps the crudest kind may be ordered, and too often the fundamental value of the acquisition is compromised.

The Disaster of Delay

If the bid doesn't get you, the almost traditional delay in starting can. The tight rules insisted upon by the lawyers can create a long gap between the announcement of a deal and its consummation. However, the world doesn't stand still in that time period. The employees of the acquiree, and even some of your own people, fill in the silence with their own ideas of what is happening. Rumor builds on rumor, and bogeymen are everywhere. By the time the firm starts to integrate in earnest, it has a small mountain of speculation to overcome. Even worse, this preoccupation with the merger takes people's minds off their jobs, productivity falls, quality suffers, and the best people start thinking about protecting themselves by leaving. Value has started to leak out in myriad little ways.

Stress, Distress, and Depression

Mergers are major changes, and change brings stress in its wake: sickness, absenteeism, loss of concentration, aggression, or a strange passiveness. In one spectacular case of the merger of two Canadian breweries, suicide and fatal disease increased dramatically among employees. People go into shock and retreat defensively, as they sense their freedom to act is narrowed. Just at the time you need leaders out there leading they may have gone "into laager," circling the wagons, and setting strategies for surviving in the coming hostile world. The blunt reality is that in many cases there is heavy overlap in management and leadership, and jobs really are on the line. If this goes too far, a sense of fatalism sets in, a feeling of powerlessness steals over people. It is a sense that their fate has been settled elsewhere, a fatalism that may be compounded by feelings of guilt or failure. If this seems strange, remember that the amount of stress people feel is based on their subjective impressions, not on any rational, objective criteria. Moreover, it almost doesn't matter whether the change is good or bad, it is the degree of change which seems to be the key—people getting married suffer as much stress as those divorcing. Finally, stress is cumulative. This psychological implosion caused by stress strips out value directly.

Milling Rumor

Delay can stimulate rumor, but nature abhors a void, and any hiccup in communication will leave the field clear for the Jeremiahs and Cassandras predicting the worst doom and gloom. Nothing is so bad that it cannot be worse and with some justification. Most mergers are accompanied by significant changes to the way people work, from status loss to job loss. Even if these prove to be good in the long run, coffee klatch and watercooler chat is in the here and now. There is a kind of grisly thrill that comes from contemplating the worst—a delicious shiver. The contemplation of unspecified benefits is not nearly so gratifying. Rumor drives stress and depression as well as soaking up work time, and more lost productivity means more lost value.

Arrogance and Thin Skins

Mergers have winners and losers. Mergers of equals are very rare. Arrogance and an insistence on doing it "our way" projected by acquiring company executives can make the acquiree feel like a victim. This is even more likely because the acquired company staff is already feeling bruised, defeated, and angry, and is actively looking for any signs of triumphalism. Strange as this may seem, this arrogance may be rooted in fear. The executives of the acquiring company are also at risk. They may have an inside edge, but there is no guarantee that they will survive. They may indeed be obsolete themselves, particularly if they have bought a young go-getting firm. Fear can be sublimated into controlling behavior and an (unconscious) desire to denigrate or strangle the upstarts. Where there are educational, cultural, or racial differences this negative attitude can worsen. The impact on value is considerable. Fast-moving companies are slowed down. Energy is diverted into battles over method. People get sick of it all and leave or are pushed out as "difficult." All this translates to a weakening of the firms and a loss of value.

Culture Wars

Culture is the accumulation of the "way we do things around here." In successful organizations it is an outgrowth of the traits they had to display to be successful, and the processes they choose for performing work. Every culture has had to be deliberately grown or has grown up unheeded based on some common perceptions about life, work, and service brought by the founders. These evolve into "values" where they become set in concrete, and once in place, no one really thinks about culture. But put it under threat, and it becomes the most precious of commodities—a reflection of our identity. In a merger, culture is under threat big time. The reaction can cripple organizations. Fast, flexible businesses which are "no better than they should be" in the marketplace can be overwhelmed by bureaucratic acquirers that try to impose their ways of working.

A classic, if odd, example of this was IBM's "take-over" of its PC business. The early IBM PC had been bolted together by a merry band in Boca Raton, Florida. Hugely, if unexpectedly, successful, it found itself at the leading edge of a rapidly evolving business superficially similar to the mainframe business—they were both in computers. But, in terms of market demands (speed, innovation, flexibility, dispersed relationships), work methods (bolting together versus invent from scratch), distribution channels (captive sales force versus distributors) and personal perceptions of the original band, they were as chalk and cheese. The PC group's success was its own "enemy." As they became visible, they attracted the attention of top management who, with their mainframe perspective saw the PC as a "window on the mainframe" and the decision was taken to bring them into the fold. The nimble upstart was blanketed by mainframe thinking, slowing it down to a five-year development cycle, and imposing intense scrutiny on technology decisions. IBM is as nimble as most today having understood the issues, and dealt with them, but those early decisions almost buried their PC operations.

The loss of value in culture wars comes from the time and energy, which goes into fighting them, and the potential loss of competitive strength which happens when an inappropriate culture prevails.

Left Behind

The market doesn't stand still. Competitors know you will be distracted, and they will attack. They will approach customers with all kinds of stories, and try to steal your best people. Customers will worry about your stability or your commitment to them in the new world. And to protect themselves they may decide to use other sources besides just you, so cutting your share of business. If customer service or quality levels fall because of the reactions of your employees, customers are merely confirmed in their prejudices. Value can be lost directly and with great ease in the marketplace.

Poor Leadership

Executives under stress and middle managers who are distracted make poor decisions based on lower quality information. Time pressure rises with the number of decisions, and decision quality falls. It has been claimed that a merger requires 10,000 decisions—true or not, it certainly does need an awful lot. As they sense this loss of control, managers start to display ever more controlling behavior, demanding detailed action plans, and so on. Leadership decisiveness drops, and people notice it. This stokes their fears so they start to leave or retire on the job. A firm that systemically makes sub par decisions must lose value.

All these push you down in to the swamp. They exist to some degree in every merger. The change issue is how to avoid the full impact or recover from them if they have happened.

Fighting the Swamp

The longer you stay in the swamp the more difficult it is to get out.[15] Your clothes become soggy, your boots fill with slime, your muscles ache from the effort of staying in one place, your mind numbs, and you lose the capacity for rational thought. In the business world we can even put a price on that delay in getting out. You lose points of market share, your productivity collapses, and gross margins fall, you fail to cut unnecessary costs—it can all be calculated, and added up to a dismal total of daily profit and value forgone.

---

[15] For insights into how one firm manages a flow of acquisitions, mostly asset oriented with low blending, see Ronald N. Ashkenas, Lawrence J. Demonaco, and Suzanne C. Francis, "Making the Deal Real: How GE Capital Integrates Acquisitions," *Harvard Business Review*, January-February 1998.

The trick, of course, is not to fall in the swamp in the first place, or if you do to get out as fast as possible. Speed has long been recognized as a key issue in merger integration. But, it is only recently that it has become a key deliverable. Feldman and Spratt emphasize its importance in their book, *Five Frogs on a Log*[16] and liken it to taking off a bandage. You can pull it off slowly, and suffer a little pain for a long time or you can rip it off, take the hurt, and move on with your life. Their prescription favors the latter—get people moving and keep them moving so they are too busy to worry.

But how do you get speed? There are a host of tools for merging businesses, each of which can provide some boost. We examine six of these:

- Decide Your Intent
- Provide Effective Leadership
- Get Past Their Immediate Fears
- Create a Sense of Control
- Who Are We Now?
- Value: The Essential Difference

Decide Your Intent

It sounds almost too obvious, but how far you intend integrating the acquisition is the starting point. If you intend full integration with your own firm's approaches dominating, then just make that clear, and get on with it. There is no need to pretend to consult, which would be resented anyway as patronizing. Those who cannot take it can leave, brutal but effective. Similarly, if you intend to let them go their own sweet way, then leave them alone—strictly alone. Only if you intend to blend do you need to worry about speed.

Provide Effective Leadership

Every survey indicates that in periods of turmoil people look to their leaders to make sense of the confusion. If the leaders are equally confused, angry, alienated, or destructive then this is the message the

---

[16] Mark L. Feldman and Michael F. Spratt, *Five Frogs on a Log: A CEO's Field Guide to Accelerating the Transition in Mergers, Acquisitions, and Gut Wrenching Change.* New York: HarperBusiness, 1999.

people will get. The biggest weight falls on the CEO's shoulders. He or she probably negotiated the merger or at least approved it. If they aren't out front selling it people will wonder why not. The CEO needs his or her own vision of the merger, and what it is intended to do for the business, and they need to promote that view relentlessly with staff, employees, customers, suppliers, and any other key stakeholders.

But leadership involves more than one person. The whole leadership team needs to be pushing the same story. They need to have identified the critical success factors for the merger and be out there doggedly selling them—and living them. It is very easy for leaders to become distracted from the merger—in fact, most would consider the merger itself a distraction from running the business. When transition meetings start to be slid in between more "important" issues, gradually everyone loses focus. Leadership stick-to-itiveness is a major factor in merger success and speed.

Get Past Their Immediate Fears

There are top-of-mind fears, and then there are fears-in-waiting. As the merger moves on new fears will surface. The immediate fears are very basic. Do I have a job? Will there be heavy downsizing? Who will I report to? Will I lose my empire? Should I leave? From a customer viewpoint, will I be serviced properly? Addressing these questions quickly is not as simple as formulating them. Customers may well have negative experiences in the early days. Downsizing may come in clumps as management gets their arms around the new business. Deciding who to keep is difficult when many people are unknown—it takes time to research the skill base. Creating a new organization falls into the same category. It may be easy to work out the very top, but it can take forever to fill in the details. Besides, boxes are not enough. People want to know their role in some detail. Just pinning up a box chart may raise as many issues as it settles. Again, this takes time. Into this (further) delay comes the rumor mill, and the swamp laps around your feet.

The solution, of course, is to understand the list of issues, to set up transition teams to deal with them, and to communicate. The secret of success is communication and more communication. Communicate until you are sick to death of communicating. Communicate honestly and openly, and address tough issues in a straightforward way.

Develop a communications map of all the stakeholders and try to send messages which are as customized as possible. Remember the customers—your competitors will. Find a few big themes, and communicate them heavily enriching them as time passes. Never let them find out any company news in the public news media, always get in first. And use a mixture of media—face-to-face, internal newspapers, e-mails, speeches, direct mail, whatever works. The aim is to inform, to emasculate the rumor monster, and to keep the record straight. Even if you cannot speed decisions up, you can ameliorate the negative impact.

As these personal issues are solved, the solutions will trigger another wave of anxiety if the removal of uncertainty is combined with mass downsizing or major reorganization. Here the issue is more brutal. Everyone who stays behind wants to think that those who left were well treated—after all it may be their turn next! This can translate into heavy payouts. The cost can become significant, and if you later find yourself unable to afford the same level of generosity, it can trigger significant new worries. Your aim is to get the downsizings over with quickly, take out the right amount first time, and do it cheaply. That's no small task.

Understanding the list of fears demands research. Don't be afraid of focus groups. Ignorance of the issues will only make things worse. Research is your friend.

Create a Sense of Control

Once the immediate worries over jobs are dealt with, a second-order fear comes up, a lack of any sense of being in control of your destiny. This may be compounded by demonization of the other firm, particularly the acquirer by the acquiree, a sense of being surrounded by enemies who may have missed their first chance to get your job, but will keep trying by attacking your ways of operating, and so on. It is paranoia, yes, but history is on the side of the paranoid.

The only effective way of giving people a sense of control is to involve them, and the creation of more transition teams is the ideal way. The composition of the teams—a mixture of people from both organizations—forces people into proximity, and once there, dialog will help erase some portion of the demon image—or make it worse if the paranoid were right. Experts on mergers do not dispute the need for transition teams; the issue is the number and size of the teams. There are two camps: those who wish to be heavily inclusive and tend to want very large numbers of large teams, and those who are more decision-oriented, and prefer many fewer, and much smaller teams of key decision makers taking fast operational decisions closely supported by the top leadership team. The large side would argue that inclusion speeds implementation by lowering resistance. The small side would claim that big teams are hard to get together, come to compromise decisions, and are so slow that value drains out of the business while everyone is stroked. The evidence would seem to support the small side. Mass teaming rapidly becomes unstructured, unfocused, and unprioritized. However, if you have too few teams, all decisions find their way to the top, and the top team is overwhelmed, slowing the transition.

The solution is some happy medium. Start as soon as feasible with a few cross-functional teams of high-potential people and add to them when necessary. Using your high-potential line managers is important. It keeps them in the loop, lowers the probability of their leaving, and exposes them to each other. This exposure may have to be carefully managed using facilitation. The last thing you want is unnecessary clashes. Your aim is to get them to trust each other and start to arrive at joint decisions to which they can all commit. A classic facilitation trick would be to place two flip charts back to back, then have people from different predecessor firms write down their beliefs about the other firm. The charts are then turned round and the issues discussed. If that is too touchy-feely, have them list how they would attack a particular problem, then get them into discussion. The focus on line managers reflects a bias toward operational decisions rather than bogging down in important but not urgent support issues. Functional teams working together at their own pace can best handle these.

Who Are We Now?

In blended businesses, with aspects of both organizations in the final result, the issue of building a new culture takes on mythic proportions. Changing an old culture is like breaking a bad habit—you don't do it by focusing on the habit, and agonizing over it; you do it by creating a new habit to take its place. The equivalent in culture terms is getting into knots over the values of the business, and seeking to change those, rather than the behaviors which underpin them. Remember where culture came from: an accretion of behaviors tied to the work, the market, and behaviors displayed by the founders. Put under pressure for years, it hardens into organization-specific values. Your objective is to replace that old concrete with new concrete. However, before you act, do your homework.

Killing the fast-moving, flexible high-tech culture which serves fast-moving markets where being first is more important than being exactly right could mean eliminating most of the value from such an acquisition. If, however, all you wanted was their established core product, then take it, put it into your production system, and fire the lot of them. If it was the culture you wanted, then transfer development to the new acquisition, and fire your own people. The questions are purely strategic.

You have decided to create a blended culture. How do you go about it?

Start with the Work

When PricewaterhouseCoopers merged in 1998, one of the first tasks was to create a common approach to the audit. This thinking was then taken farther to all offerings of the business. Teams took the approaches of each of the predecessor firms, and selected the most powerful ones, or invented new ones. Although consultants are notoriously attached to their thinking, they did not try to bury the old approaches, they simply introduced the new, and promoted it relentlessly. The essence of a business is the work it does. This is the root of its culture. Change the work, and you change the culture. In a manufacturing firm this may translate to process teams developing new methods, fighting it out under intense time pressure until they come to a solution. Once they have created an answer, train, train, train. Promote the new approach. They may need facilitation to get past arguments about whose approach is best practice, but these can usually be overcome by either comparing them with a third party or exploring the business and operating reasons behind the approaches. The result is speed.

Model New Behavior

Behavior can be changed head-on but values cannot. If you want people to work in teams, give them team skill training, form teams, put in team-based performance incentives, and shower recognition on those who work, and take out those who don't. Oh, and by the way, start with the leadership team, and insist on the new behaviors. What the leaders do not model does not get absorbed. No amount of training can paper over leadership indifference or antagonism. Force new leadership behavior, and lo and behold, team behavior will appear. If you want to keep costs down, keep your own down first. Walk the talk is trite but so true. How do you know if the talk is being walked? Look at the critical decisions. How are they being taken? If this behavior is the new behavior you want, then you have got through to people. As behaviors change new values will appear, not the other way round.

Select the Right People

Be ruthless; look at everyone you have—from your own company and the one you bought, as if you were hiring them for the first time, which in a way you are. You may have been stuck with some fools as a result of the deal but you don't have to keep it that way. Look for people who display the competencies and attitudes you want. Promote them, fire the difficult ones after attempted remediation, and you will gradually build a cadre with the right stuff.

Symbols, Heroes, and Celebrations

These have always been the mythological levers—the flag for patriotism, the American Express agent who never lets you down, the company's annual picnic. Create your own new set of symbols. A new name for the joint firm? A new logo? New colors, new uniforms, new everything, and anything that creates a focal point. Create new heroes. Collect stories and publish them around the business. Shower those who model the new behavior with recognition so encouraging others to emulate them. Have celebrations of the positive kind, but also of the sad kind. Try holding a wake for the old businesses, celebrate their histories, their achievements, their people, then put them away in the museum, and start afresh.

Mass Involvement

We talked about teams and the need to involve people to give them a sense of control. How do you get people involved? One way is to take the strategic direction of the firm and push it through a series of workshops where the strategy is enhanced and expanded to operational detail. At the end of such a process, which could be fitted into the normal planning cycle, everyone has been involved and has built a sense of commitment to the new business. Strategic alignment is only one way. All training activities can be tilted to discussion of the new world. Use town meetings, any excuse, but of all of them a formal strategic alignment program is the most powerful.

Value: The Essential Difference

The literature of mergers is extensive, and few new things have been added in years. Speed, teams, prioritizing actions based on what is critical, all kinds of techniques for getting speed have been there for a long time. What has changed is the willingness to go for speed in the face of that Band-Aid sting, and the research support, and the aggressiveness with which the remedy is recommended.

Yet there is something different out there. Feldman and Spratt[17] hit on the concept of shareholder value. It is really such a simple idea—the best ones always are. The objective of a merger is to take two businesses worth so much on the stockmarket, and to join them so they are at least worth no less, and at best much more. Fail to do that, and the shareholder who could have held stock in both companies loses. It is not a complicated goal. Yet, we know that it is rarely achieved. Feldman and Spratt's insight was that if shareholder value is the goal then focus on shareholder value.

This "great simplicity" brings immediate clarity. The starting point for your top management team is to identify the value drivers in the combined company, which may include certain behavioral traits—culture. Put numbers against them, and array them by return. Then move on to the probability of success in different time frames—three months, six, a year, five years, whatever. You are looking for the classic 80 percent of value concentrated in the 20 percent of drivers, and have teams start working on realizing the identified value. Certain things happen immediately. Many infrastructure projects, which would have absorbed lots of leadership time, are seen to yield little or no shareholder value. Pass them on to the functions to solve in their own good time. Quick wins are achieved, which gives people the sense of progress. The awesomely long lists of actions to be taken are prioritized

---

[17] Ibid. (Feldman and Spratt, *Five Frogs on a Log*).

and shrunk, taking stress off management. The process of prioritization creates a focus for leaders to discuss the business, putting objectivity ahead of passion—though it may take outside help to do that. Team tasks are now very clear, and performance targets can be set in value terms. Everyone is expected to follow the plan. If they go off on their own projects and won't come back, then they have to leave.

When you start, you already have some idea of the value drivers—presumably, that was the basis of the deal—but chances are you are not fully informed. The search for shareholder value, therefore, becomes a learning experience. Leaders take their first, best shot to get going, then drive to ever greater analytical sophistication.

* * * * *

In the e-world, no firm can afford the loss of any market value. The effective integration of mergers is then a major issue. Unfortunately, as we have seen, some of the basics of successful integration are easily compromised. The deal and the delays can confuse the problem of formulating the business case and getting it across to the organization. Top teams can be compromised by new members and power struggles. Project management in a political drama may be compromised and weakened. Keeping the merger team separated when they have careers to look after and are worried about them can be difficult. All told, merger integration is very difficult; even applying change management techniques can be difficult if management has a "just force them" attitude.

Change on the Run

Making Mergers Work

1. Go for speed.
2. Prioritize actions based on value.
3. Keep task teams few and focused.
4. Sort out people and roles quickly.
5. Communicate, communicate, communicate.
6. Focus on work and the behaviors needed to do the work when trying to change cultures.

When Profit Collapses

In the hyper-competitive e-world, businesses will fail as they always have. Like they always did, leaders will seek to turn them round, and if they are e-leaders they will discover that the same basic rhythm that drove their predecessors will drive them—but faster. It took Lou Gerstner around two years to pull IBM out of its profit crunch. In the process he did all the right things, selling off unnecessary assets, reshaping the portfolio, cutting costs, downsizing people, reworking processes, reassuring the customer base, reworking the organization to deliver value more effectively. He built a cash mountain, raised value, restructured profit sources more toward services, and generally reshaped the business. However, years later he is still looking for new ways of driving new sources of revenue. Shifting a mega-firm is not easy—it takes time. No major e-business has gone belly-up yet, but it is just a matter of time before some major classic businesses bite the dust, as Encyclopedia Britannica did, in competition with the upstarts.

The Ancient Rhythm of Crisis Transformation

The collapse of a business model invokes crisis in a firm with a predictable response—an "ancient rhythm," which everyone dances to. It goes something like this:

- Leaving Home
- Refocus
- Realign
- Reinvent

Leaving Home

Oceans of ink have been spilled writing about how great organizations were blinded by their very success to the changes in their markets or to the potential of new technologies. Classic examples include IBM, which was gifted through its research labs, and total coverage of its industry with almost omniscience about where the world was going, yet still almost failed; firms in the property and casualty industry today that are feeling the impact of direct selling which has the potential of knocking the stuffing out of their classic distribution systems;

the US car industry, which could not credit that the defeated Japanese could build a car and redefine the way things are made; or the British, who clung to empire long after it was gone. The list is endless. The challenge of "leaving home" is to move before the crisis, a trick that is difficult to do even when the crisis is obvious.

Take the experience of Massey Ferguson, a major agricultural equipment company that had a near-death experience. The firm was spewing red ink, was saddled with a debt/equity ratio around 5:1, hundreds of banks were pounding at the door demanding their money, tens of thousands of employees were being let go, and the agricultural equipment market just wouldn't stop going down. The CEO made speech after speech telling the staff that change was needed if the firm was to transform. Despite this there was an eerie unreality to the whole thing. It was still unusual for a multibillion-dollar business to just die. Powerful individuals who were determined to retain their power base could still delay tough decisions on factory closures, notably in North America, well beyond the danger point. The firm owed so much to the banks that it was difficult to tell who owned whom. For a long time, the people leaving got good severance packages, and those who stayed saw themselves as the *crème de la crème* who would have no difficulty getting work outside—such is the happiness of denial. Experience was to prove them wrong. Many never made as big salaries again.

Blindness, willful or otherwise, is still prevalent in organizations today. Denial is still a basic human trait, and CEOs still give the survival speech, even though repeated too often it simply brands them as the source of the problem. If getting people moving there was hard, imagine a firm making solid profits, which is seeking to change before an impending disaster which only its CEO can see.

Refocus

Concentrated in the cusp between the old model and the new, refocusing is dominated by the realities of a failing business paradigm and dealing with the implied crisis. Profits are either collapsing, or are thought about to collapse. Old ideas are seen as worn out, yet people are locked into the past. Leaders need to break through basic assumptions while keeping the business afloat and generating the cash that is needed to survive and grow in new directions.

The top management of firms in intense refocus becomes obsessed with financial measures of success. Some years ago this would have been defined in terms of return on equity or assets or some other measure of capital productivity. Such measures are still used, but today the focus has moved to the concept of shareholder value as being more productive of ideas than the simple return measures. However, one thing has not changed; shareholder value thinking, like its predecessors, tends to push leaders into efficiency and cost-cutting activities as the fastest way of driving profits and cutting investment levels. As the firm continues to focus on shareholder value, and if it lacks the imagination to reinvent itself, cost-cutting becomes an obsession, which can have traumatic effects as the "fat" is cut out of the business, because that "fat" often focused on creating new futures. Sometimes whole industries—the dairy industry in North America, for example—can be caught in such cost-cutting, downward spirals. Gradually the whole industry comes to assume that it is impossible to innovate, and the industry is rapidly commoditized as everyone competes on price. This commodity trap is extremely difficult to break out of.

The overall climate of a firm in refocus resembles that of a hostile takeover. There is much uncertainty in the air and people are made tense and fearful by the certainty of job loss. If payoffs are poor, this problem is compounded. When people are fearful, their productivity drops like a stone creating worse profit problems and the need for more aggressive action. Whatever loyalty and affection may have existed are tested and often destroyed, so that people start to treat the firm as just a job. Again productivity drops. The rumor mill starts up at full speed and people constantly try to second-guess management. They are alive to the slightest inconsistency in communication and become expert at reading between the lines. The best people start to look for other employment, and the rest keep their heads down—on the often-true principle that this too shall pass. The finance department comes into the ascendant and deep distrust can start to arise between functions. Top management may be new or in disarray, power grabs are not uncommon, and the CEO (often new) is concerned mainly with retaining or consolidating his or her power base. All told, the depression that settles over the firm can be crippling.

The objective is to get past this period as fast as possible. Yet some firms get stuck in it as top management cannot find the strategic skills to break out of the cycle of destruction. This may mean changing key people. AT&T seemed such a firm under Robert Allen until he was replaced by C. Michael Armstrong, a former IBM executive who had had enormous success at Rockwell in the post-Cold War reshaping of the defense industry. Armstrong set about rebuilding the company. IBM under John Akers fell into this category until the board did the unthinkable and tossed him out to bring in Lou Gerstner, who forced, attention to the bottom line. Clearly successful at reduction, Gerstner moved the firm into the black, raised a cash mountain in the many billions, and drove the share price through the roof.

Realign

Realign is a period of rising hope in the business. The leadership has realized that it cannot save its way to health. All that the continuous squeezing is doing is creating corporate anorexia. Sales and revenue need to be built, preferably from new sources. Achieving this demands a shift in operational strategy, and perhaps the purchase of new businesses to develop market entry points. Developing a new strategy is only one step in realigning an organization. When the electricity utility industry was privatized, or the mutual life insurance companies went public on the stock markets, their leaders had to learn how to live in a private sector world—and learn abruptly. They were so big that they caught the attention of the financial analysts immediately, and there was nowhere to hide. Realigning leadership thinking is clear in those cases, but it applies in a more general sense. In a fast-moving world you cannot afford management which does not keep up.

Structure follows strategy. The old adage is true, and in a loss-stimulated strategic transformation, as the strategy is being created, the culture and structure are busily being analyzed to find where they may need to be adjusted. Organizational structure—who reports to whom—is the most visible, followed by role and responsibility definition. But realign also covers how firms operate, so shifts to empowerment, teamwork, and performance-based pay systems are needed. Realignment from a crisis will also mean rethinking underlying information systems. In fact, a complete rethink is needed of all the support structures of the firm. The aim is to underpin the new strategic direction, and lock the assumed competitive advantage in place. The risk, of course, is that the strategy is flawed, and the new strategic and structural alignment will simply drive you under.

Reinvent

Do not confuse reinvention with re-engineering—though paradoxically, Hammer and Champy claimed to be talking about reinvention when they wrote their book *Reengineering The Corporation*.[18] Confused yet? The downsizing movement of the early 1990s, and the claims that it failed in 70 percent of cases, tarnished re-engineering as a term. That kind of re-engineering is what we call refocus—trying to squeeze blood out of an old stone. Of course it failed. Squeezing something that is dry and out-of-date will never get you ahead.

Nor is reinvention following best practice. Trying to reinvent using incremental improvements from other people's insights will get you moving but it is unlikely to provide you with the edge that will mark you out. By all means use best practice as a stimulant for the possible, but in the end, there is no substitute for thinking out your own future.

So what is reinvention?

From a strategist perspective, it is finding the solution to a defined but very difficult problem. For example, how to provide each and every customer with custom offerings (or what feels like custom) while meeting or beating the cost base of a mass production supplier. In the literature, this is known as mass customization, and it is the economic model of the next hundred years suitable for winning in global, fragmented markets: the market of one concept.

Mass customization sounds very theoretical, but like mass production before it, it could not be more real. The mixed lines, short production runs, flexible supplier relationships, and the rest of the revolution that has swept through the car industry is mass customization at work. It was driven by our desire for a custom car but unwillingness to pay the traditional price. At another extreme, the modern coffee bar where you can get the beverage of your own specific taste is a form of mass customization. Other examples include the financial institutions that will encourage you to customize the services you get from them and the publishers who will produce course books for professors customized to their teaching needs. And, of course, the most famous, because it is the most complete, the Dell way of selling and creating computers. The ideas of mass customization have swept through every branch of an endeavor.

[18] Michael Hammer and James Champy, *Reengineering the Corporation: A Manifesto for Business Revolution*. New York: HarperBusiness, 1993.

Having examples does not guarantee a slam dunk. The power of the old paradigm, mass production, is still very great. Concepts such as economies of scale, capacity utilization, economic order quantities, and so on, which were at the heart of mass production, have not gone away. But they have changed shape and level of importance. Learning how the new principles apply in your case is of extreme importance.

* * * * *

Refocus, realign, and reinvention—the 3 Rs—are the keys to crisis transformation, and they work very well, whether the transformation is as large as IBM's, or smaller, like the work Heather, a respected executive, did in a major manufacturing company. Her great contribution was providing a structure and then using it to accelerate the change. She had been given the job of reworking a previously highly profitable business that was on a slide. She applied her version of the 3Rs, which she communicated to the organization as a structure for the transformation. She set up a series of steps. Step one (refocus) concentrated on improving the existing approaches and driving out cost.

There were some obvious things to do, which could be initiated immediately. As she did this, however, she was aware of the need to realign and reinvent. She got her change team together and they produced a view of the future, which they started to socialize through communications—discussing it with a wider audience and building it into speeches and training programs. She started to develop generic skills in her people, which she knew would be needed in the reinvent period—teamwork, leadership, and so on. And so it proceeded.

As she came out of the refocus period, she had set the groundwork for a new view of how to operate, which people came to accept. This did not eliminate the realign period; it merely raised the potential to shorten it. The reinvent period would take several years as new approaches were tried, but early on, the key elements of the solution started to emerge. As the nature of the work people would have to do became clearer, she was able press the HR people to start thinking about the performance implications and to start approaching other operations to think about the implications of cooperation and collaboration. Eventually, as success grew, confidence in the groundwork she had laid became evident.

Her way of thinking about and even communicating the change sped up the transformation significantly. People were much calmer and accepting of change and felt it was controlled. Ideas were embedded that had previously failed to get off the ground. The time gain was infinite.

Even given the ancient rhythm, you still need the basic techniques of a transformation.

- *Know why you are doing it.* If the firm is in severe financial risk, in theory that should be sufficient reason. However, denial will be rampant. The leadership solution is dictatorship. For all the advantages of teamwork, at times of deep crisis, the leader's role is to provide immediate and clear vision. Arthur Martinez may well have asked around, but he had a very clear idea of what needed to be done at Sears when it was bleeding and he did it quickly. He refocused the business on its core retail operations and even got rid of such venerable institutions as the Sears catalog.[19] Without firm direction in a time of crisis, the firm will wallow.

- *Ensure key decisions are made.* Linked to the prior point, the leader may need to surround him or herself with people who will take direction and drive to the solutions needed. There is no time at all for playing politics; a strong driving team ranged behind the CEO is needed.

- *Impose tight program management.* Program management will be important in the face of the tight time frames needed and will deliver the results creditors can live with. The program office needs to report directly to the CEO.

- *Keep separated from the existing business.* In a real crisis, the firm will have a transformation team that is looking after the ugly stuff of creditor management, particularly if there is any bank seeking to recover their loans. This will be kept separate from the rest of the business, but it is difficult to keep the rest of the transformation separate as it demands so much participation by leaders through the business studying and aggressively acting to cut costs, and so on.

- *Use change management tools from the start.* As with the separation issue, change management tends to lose some of its subtlety in the face of survival. However, the basic issues of communication remain with internal and external groups.

---

[19] Anthony J. Rucci, Steven P. Kirn, and Richard T. Quinn, "The Employee-Customer-Profit Chain at Sears," *Harvard Business Review*, January-February 1998.

The leadership challenges of a turnaround are stark—the firm must survive or die. The key emphasis is on taking really tough decisions that may affect the lives of thousands of people quickly. Indeed, over the long haul a firm may need two leaders, one to do the surgery and the other to stitch it back together.

Change on the Run

Profit Crunch

1. Be prepared to make really tough decisions—quickly.
2. Stop the bleeding of dollars and customers fast, then move on quickly to strategy.
3. Build corporate strategy first to get the portfolio right, disposing of noncore businesses and seeking entry to new markets.
4. Build operational strategy using high alignment and high involvement techniques to build commitment and lower tensions in the wake of downsizing.
5. Treat the breakup of the old business model as a major opportunity to think differently about the business—perhaps an e-business route rather than rebuilding the old world.

The Shift to Continuous Transformation

There are those who consider the lack of an immediate real or induced crisis a disqualification for being in a transformation. This is business as usual. Not quite. Jack Welch, the doyen of transformational leaders, admits freely that he inherited a fundamentally sound business, but he never stopped trying to improve it dramatically making it the second most highly capitalized firm, after Microsoft, in 1999. What he and others, like Jacques Nasser at Ford,[20] Shell International,[21] BP, Scottish Power, Daimler-Benz, and hundreds of other successful organizations have discovered is that the unforgiving market demands continuous reevaluation of the business's value from everyone. There are no more hiding places for any of us.

---

[20] See Suzy Wetlaufer, "Driving Change: An Interview with Jacques Nasser," *Harvard Business Review*, March-April 1999.
[21] See W. Warner Burke, William Trahant, and Richard Koonce, *Business Climate Shifts: Profiles of Change Makers*. Boston. Butterworth Heineman, 1999.

This theme of e-leadership and its need for continuous transformation drives the rest of this book. Crisis is important. One-off shifts to new forms of business like e-business can reshape a firm in a very short time. Mergers and new plumbing are huge events. But the reality is that when each of those events is done, continuous transformation is the name of the leadership game. In the coming chapters, the five critical success factors for holistic continuous transformation are addressed.

CHAPTER 2

ତ୍ତ

Drive Extraordinary Financial Results

S ome things do not change. Fail to make your numbers and your e-leadership is tainted, just as it was for all your predecessors. You can delegate human resources, marketing, production, information strategy, and even use outsiders to provide corporate strategy. You can and will delegate the details of managing the finance function. But in a world of astounding profit risk, you must be involved in the numbers. If your CFO is not providing you with high-grade financial analysis, is not enrolling the whole organization in focusing on improving cost performance, is not thinking in terms of designing costs out of the system altogether, then you are leaving money on the table and your profits are at risk. The choice of CFO is profoundly important.

The e-leader's problem is very simple. To satisfy the shareholders you must make steady improvements in value year-after-year. The financial markets apply a risk factor to assessing shareholder value, comparing your performance to your competitors, and the market's as a whole. Show profit or cash flow volatility and you raise a red flag. However, in a business environment of permanent white water, earning stable profits is very difficult. How do e-leaders create resilient profits and so extraordinary financial performance?

This problem is not new—it has been around for 20 years at least—as stable markets fragmented and the world opened up and globalized supply. In fact, it could be argued that the business response of the last 20 years has been almost entirely geared to moving from the industrial age model to the information age model of business development. Look at what has happened. In the industrial era, the essence of business thinking was to invest capital, go for economies of scale through volume in large, comparatively undifferentiated markets, stretch your competitors over a capital barrel, and win. Business risk was continued within the firm. Firms had high fixed costs, went for ownership in vertical integration, and tried to have actual legal ownership and control of the factors of production.

How the world has changed. Practically every management fad of the last two decades has been successful because it contributed to a revolution in this cost model. Even looked at in no particular order we can see a pattern. Virtual organizations, supply relationships, and vertical integration moving to supply ecosystems with strategic and IT integration reduced the risk on the OEM and dispersed it through the value chain. Lean production with *kanban, kaisen,* and other Japanese efficiency practices was aimed at lower cost and greater flexibility with dispersed risk through the *keiretsu* a forerunner of the e-business value network of linked suppliers. The shift in employee compensation to risk-based pay through bonus systems lowers the fixed cost of labor. The huge downsizings and rightsizings of the early 1990s were aimed at lowering the cost base and the breakeven point of firms. Even the soft stuff like teamwork and cross-functional cooperation allowed more efficient use of resources, greater flexibility, less risk, and lower labor cost. The obsession with process improvement lowered the basic cost base of a firm by up to 40 percent, cutting the breakeven and lowering risk. Even quality assurance was originally, and is still, sold on its ability to cut costs in the processes; to reduce, rework, and scrap, lower warranty costs, and so on, again lowering the cost base. Outsourcing may not have lowered cost directly, but it lowered the cost of management for higher service levels, as do shared services. Even quality assurance was originally sold on its ability to cut costs—through more efficient processes, reduced reworking of products, lower warranty costs and so on.

Big information systems are aimed at lower cost and superior data. Computers and computerized flexible equipment carry less risk by virtue of multiuse and lower capital costs requiring less debt. Financing approaches that push lease and other costs off the balance sheet lowered the apparent capital risk. Global supply arrangements lower basic costs, sometimes dramatically. Superior financial analysis has allowed accurate predictions of costs, greater ability to pinpoint issues, and faster reaction, so lowering business risk. So it goes on until we arrive at the pure Internet companies with trivial capital, lower financial risk, and staggering labor productivity and yet another dramatic potential drop in the whole cost base of industry. The shift of risk out of the business in all directions has been a profound change in the way we think about capitalist enterprise and a change in the direction of protecting profit from market turbulence.

Of course, risk has not been eliminated. The nature of private, commercial enterprise is the calculated risk. But it has changed shape. We still invest capital. We now have fixed information systems and factories with flexible but fixed capital. We have fewer people, but each iota of talent is more important. We have flexible supplier relations, but they have to be managed, and we have had to learn new skills in trust and openness. The bulk of our skill and competence is now locked up in computer systems that can be outdated, have to be managed, and can fail catastrophically. Capital needs are lower but the financial markets more aggressive. Risk does not go away, it changes shape. Indeed, the present obsession with risk management is evidence of a management learning curve as leaders seek to attain the visceral feel for risk in the new model that their fathers had in the old, settled, and deeply understood one.

So how do you achieve profit resilience? Clearly, by installing many of the items listed above and finding ways to mitigate the risk, say by building relationships based on openness and trust with suppliers. But also key is raising your level of sophistication when thinking about cost, understanding the transformational issues around upgrading that sophistication, and using the superior insights provided. The rest of this chapter addresses the five different levels of sophistication in cost thinking:

- The Traditionals
- The Process Thinkers
- The Super Analysts
- The Involvers
- The Designers

The Traditionals

Effective e-leadership is crippled in this type of firm. The level of thinking about cost is at its lowest. The traditional industrial age world was one of nibbling away at costs, punctuated by crash diets. Firms tended to lurch from crisis to crisis, settling their cost understanding in periods of stability. But in the e-world, such periods will be rare. Vestiges of this more primitive world still exist, but it is fast disappearing, along with the business environment in which it thrived.

This was the world of functional organizations, with silos, intense product focus, and attitudes. Cost-cutting focused on fixed and variable costs using an analytical framework of actual versus budget. It looked almost exclusively at the costs of specific products, perhaps with some analysis to reflect selling in different geographical areas. This was the world of classic standard costing where overheads were distributed to products based on the labor content, despite the fact it is often not a significant part of the total cost (as low as 15 percent in software). There was no process analysis worth the name, no benchmarks, no best practice. The world that supported this approach—long product life cycles, long lead times, little technology, labor intensity—has gone. In its place we have an obsession with speed, a need for flexibility, capital intensity on flexible multipurpose machines and lines, and massively greater customer service requirements.

This kind of firm had few probes into the roots of its cost problems and no effective disciplines for analyzing costs at the work level. There were all kinds of internal barriers to seeing the true cost of anything and only primitive ways of distinguishing between costs which drove value and those that were truly expendable. The underlying cost accounting approaches were simply unsophisticated compared with today. When crisis hit, it moved from the constant nibbling away at product cost to slash and burn as it swung an ax at costs it was ill-equipped to analyze. In crisis it was also subject to power struggles fueled by poor data.

case   Red McFarlane, a veteran agricultural market analyst, had been forecasting combine harvester and tractor volumes for Massey-Ferguson for many years. For some time he had been telling management that the equipment was getting more reliable, dramatically more productive, and expensive and that every ratio he calculated indicated that equipment capacity on farms in the developed world significantly exceeded need. Yet farmers kept buying, in part out of habit, in part out of lust for the latest, and in part for tax write-offs. What will happen, asked Red, if we have a downturn in agriculture, and people stop buying long enough for them to realize they didn't need a new machine every year? Of course, it happened, and equipment sales plunged. The firm started to cut costs, but despite Red's figures, no one could believe the industry would nose-dive by more than 50 percent, and stay down. As he left in a downsizing, Red had the sour satisfaction of being proven right.

The impact of this denial on the firm was devastating. Costs were slashed, but it was never enough. The firm could not get under the market volume collapse, and it continued to bleed. The banks—more than 200 of them—put the firm into "work out" as they tried to recover their loans, and management wriggled under a microscope. But, even worse, the cost-cutting generated intense power plays. Factories were closed and surplus assets were frequently sold—but not always. In one notable case a senior executive was sent to Italy to close a factory, but far from closing it, he disappeared. He "went native," as the British used to say of colonial administrators who stayed at their post too long and identified with the locals. He developed a new tractor line, and started to sell it in competition with the firm's main lines!

Cutting heads was based on an "everyone must suffer" basis rather than focusing cuts, and eliminating unproductive work retained functional fiefdoms. Cost-cutting slashed easy-to-cut areas like marketing and customer service, destroying customer relationships. Suppliers were squeezed at a time when their credit was keeping the business afloat. Process analysis was nonexistent, so cuts to the factories left old-fashioned production systems in place. After years of intense cost reduction, the firm was shattered and should have died. However, in the process of fending off the banks, management had so increased and dispersed the shareholding that they became the de facto "owner" as no one else could muster a majority—or cared. They held on like glue in the face of apparent disaster, but it still took nearly a decade to pick up the pieces.

Finance, dominated by CEO Victor Rice, a former finance executive, called all the shots in this crisis. The bank debt and work out ensured that finance held sway, and it was almost impossible to move without their permission. But they were focused on keeping the banks and other creditors happy and few attempts were made to generate a deep understanding of the underlying cost structure. Massey was a classic industrial age company. Its financial systems were sophisticated for the time, but not nearly real-time, and thinking was obsessed by a financial accounting view rather than a management accounting view. The management accounting was traditional using standard costing based on labor content rather than modern activity-based thinking. Process improvement was rare and largely prevented by the silo-based functional organization. Financial analysis was rudimentary with actuals and budgets being the basics. There were no customer value analysis and no value based management tools.

Modern organizations are better equipped with analytical tools, but they are not immune from traditional thinking. Even today, in deep crisis, methods tend to be crude, as are some of the solutions. There is no magic formula for judging how much you can cut—except the pain test. In short, you cut until you hit bone, then you deal with the pain. The best people to judge who to keep and who to cut are workmates. Create a team, give them immunity, and let them work it out. Cost cutting is a harsh measure. Working with a firm located in a small town, the team that was charged with cutting heads was moving very slowly. The VP Human Resources, who had herself carefully avoided giving up any staff, was getting antsy. Finally, she went out to see for herself and discovered the real problem—in a small town it is difficult to fire your neighbors. On her return, she set an example, and cut her own staff by 60 percent. The team took its time, eventually making the cuts, but they were marked for years by the experience. It is called survivor syndrome, a term most famously used to describe the deep feelings of guilt experienced by Holocaust survivors.

Leadership in a slash and burn world is about focusing on the future. People are going to get hurt. Your role is to pay as much attention to those who are left as those who are let go. There are ways of doing this. Any task that can get people involved in the strategic issue so that they understand it will mitigate the pain and make it easier to lay the people off, leaving less stress in the system. Speed is important. Do not hang around. Once you know the problem, act, and try to get all the pain over at once—so you can move on to healing. If you over-cut, you can hire the last few people back as contract workers. You will look heartless, and perhaps a little foolish, but it will be better than a death by a thousand cuts. The moment you think the cutting is over, move on to planning the future and involving people in that planning. It will bring focus and hope into their lives.

Put bluntly, the traditional world is a dead loss to an e-leader, but it has useful lessons. If you are stuck here, your primary objective should be to get out of this cost management environment as fast as possible.

The Process Thinkers

Process thinking is a root discipline of e-leadership. Without it, your firm missed the huge 30 to 50 percent drops in cost bases others got in the late 1980s and early 1990s. The uptake of process thinking in the 1980s, driven by Japanese quality thinking and the Toyota Method, was the first major opportunity to move to a significantly lower cost curve since Henry Ford introduced the assembly line and, with it, traditional management accounting approaches. As we move into the e-world, firms that have not made this first switch from traditional thinking still exist—unreformed utilities, protected firms such as some mutual insurance companies or government services—but they are well behind the game. Their challenge is to catch up—fast. There are five change challenges to introducing process thinking:

* Understanding the Journey
* Introducing Process Techniques
* Installing Process Thinking through Big Systems
* Achieving Outsourcing
* Making Shared Services Happen

Understanding the Journey

Firms that start down the process journey from traditional highly functional structures and command and control management approaches find themselves learning and changing their cultures dramatically.

The cultural journey starts with the emergence of the numbers from the iron grip of the finance department. For the first time, cost management moves out of the accounting silo and into the professional workforce and line management. By so doing, it dilutes the power of the finance function and engages everyone in efficiency and cost reduction—a major cultural shift. Finance still has an important role, notably in the development of financial data, but it is supporting rather than driving continuous change. In turn, focusing large numbers of people on their work efficiency changes their attitudes, so that they become engaged in the restless search for continuous improvement, which leads to continuous incremental change. People throughout the organization have to be empowered to make changes and become more business and process literate shifting the traditional roles of managers and subordinates. To live in this new world the managers have to learn new skills and move from pure administration to leading. To be effective in process improvement people need information. This leads to more open information exchange, so shifting the power in the business and again undercutting managers and finance people. Over time the relentless logic of process improvement reshapes the whole culture of the business.

The above is process thinking introduced slowly. At the other extreme, the installation of giant ERP systems massively accelerates the transformation. Firms that decide on such installations find themselves changing whole processes, shifting job roles and responsibilities, and demanding unprecedented discipline in information gathering in the workplace all in very short time frames. The impact of these big installations on everyone is so profound that it has given rise to a whole change sub-methodology with deep skills in involving people, managing projects, and training masses of people.

Once process thinking is embedded through either approach, the next stage of the journey begins. The deep analysis of costs linked to external benchmarking and best practice comparisons leads directly to outsourcing and its cousin, shared services. The firm moves from do-it-all-yourself to subcontracting specific work product. In addition to the inevitable downsizing that this creates, outsourcing often represents the first serious breaching of the legal and operating boundaries of the firm. This, in turn, leads to "webs" of relationships which have to be managed and which provide levels of adaptability encouraging continuous reshaping of the business to achieve superior cost positions. Over time, the firm moves to a more virtual format.

The journey for the pioneers of the 1980s was long and driven first through the quality movement and then re-engineering. The journey for firms starting out today has to be short and the change very intense. Either way, the effects are profound.

Introducing Process Techniques

When process thinking came into the business consciousness through the quality movement in the mid-1980s, it wasn't totally new. The ideas had been around since the 1920s, but it hit like a hammer in part because it returned to North America via Japan at a time when Japan was steamrollering the world. Suddenly, we could cut out steps, do things in parallel, concurrently, and simultaneously, and as we shortened the time work took, we not only got fewer errors, we got less cost complete with a perfect justification for taking the cost out—the work was not needed. So successful was the cost-cutting aspect of process improvement that it became the centerpiece of the re-engineering movement. Indeed, in most firms, re-engineering was synonymous with downsizing and cost-cutting.

From the point of view of driving extraordinary results, process analysis moved cost-cutting from the analysis of past costs to examining the sources of cost to give firms a far deeper understanding of their cost drivers. It took our eyes off the income statement and standard costs and placed them where the costs are—in the work. Soon, process analysis was followed by activity-based costing, benchmarking, and best practice—means of comparing one situation with others and spreading the most efficient ways of working to all areas of the firm. Cost improvements in operations now became heavily rooted in rational analysis, and, even more important, one-off cost reduction was abandoned for continuous improvement. Teams grouped around processes were empowered and required to analyze the process and find the root causes of inefficiencies and remove them, even if it meant eliminating their own jobs. Of course, for this to work they had to have an assurance of job security, an assurance that was followed through on.

The change issues in getting this kind of process thinking in place—such as focus on the formation of process teams working across functional boundaries, ensuring the support of all top management, the empowerment of the teams, and the rewarding of success on a team basis—are significant in old-style businesses. However after more than a decade of tackling these issues, they are now widely accepted as part of management science, even if they are not always used. The biggest stumbling block is always getting the cross-functional cooperation. This has to start at the top. If senior management encourages functional rivalries and power struggles, there is no way you can succeed. The only solution may be a wholesale execution of the leadership. This happened in a major car manufacturer some years ago when it was decided that the top team was the biggest block to change in general. Given top level support allowing cross-functional teams, the next most important issue is training in process analysis. This may include the use of process mapping software, training in statistical tools for measuring process performance, the teaching of such techniques as root cause analysis (the search for the source of a process problem), and the sensible use of benchmarks and best practice. Benchmarking and the search for best practice are two sides of one coin. Benchmarks are largely quantitative measures of effectiveness—for example, the number of days of sales in inventory, the loss factor on an electricity transmission, and so on. Best practice is process based, involving the techniques and approaches used to perform work often to get the benchmark performance. For example, how do you manage a just-in-time delivery system to minimize the inventory holding?

Teaching about benchmarks and best practice can have its humorous side. During a session on process improvement for a major and otherwise highly sophisticated client, participants were looking for best practice in the area of billing and shipping. The group considered that the best practice was probably L.L. Bean, the direct mail company. The next day the client's top management received a frustrated call from L.L. Bean complaining about the over three dozen people who had called to inquire about their system!

Installing Process Thinking through Big Systems

The late 1990s will be known in information technology circles as the time when the Y2K scare pushed major corporations into installing huge enterprise resource planning systems (SAP, PeopleSoft, Baan, J. D. Edwards, and so on), which almost without exception forced them to rethink their business processes. The return from installation in terms of cost visibility and the potential for huge one-step process improvement is enormous. From a strategic cost point of view such installations can drive a firm immediately to a significantly lower cost curve. Whether this yields competitive advantage will depend on whether competitors have already taken this step. That said, the work of rethinking, restructuring, and cultural change demanded by these systems is equally enormous, with the total costs far exceeding the software license fees by many multiples. The first round of installations in major firms is now over, and the bloom has gone off the concept. Attention has shifted to e-business installations, but the business need is not going to go away and we will see these programs installed in smaller firms. With the emergence of code able to link these internal information bases into e-business, these big programs will form a key platform for the future. Introducing such systems is a major transformation, easily diverted by internal politics and hubris making it difficult or impossible to achieve the cost gains.

case
A major monopoly, quasi-government energy organization ran into all the classic problems. The strategic reason for installing the system was the desire to access capital markets which require prompt, proper financial statements, plus a strong dose of pride—their logic was, if all the best companies have this system, they should too. People in the organization could more or less understand the capital markets argument, even though such markets were a foreign concept to them, having always been government funded. But the desire for modernity only served to muddy the business case when the implications for power bases, extreme discipline in data input, and so on became apparent. Why should we change so that some faceless analyst could be made happy? The organization was intensely functional with geographic silos under weak head office control placing barriers to the formation of the critical cross-functional teams. Of the six entities selected to get the program going, four were supportive, one indifferent, and one actively hostile, and the bureaucratic culture pushed the responsibility for the installation onto the shoulders of the contractor, making it difficult to institutionalize the new system. Even well into the program there is only a glimmer of understanding of how radically the change will affect information flows, power bases, and work patterns but in a highly charged organization with fiefdoms and command thinking, drama is inevitable. However, there is a strong suspicion emerging that there will be "too much" change, and that it may not be controllable, and those fears are raising the resistance level in the management ranks. Job security is emerging slowly as an issue, and insecurity is growing, which will be blamed on the system despite the well-known featherbedding of the last several decades.

Installing huge systems, a move that requires rethinking all work processes and information flows, is a political act. The demands on change management are significant, working with different stakeholder groups to build understanding and commitment to the changes, re-envisioning work and organization structures, and communicating with employees on programs which may take months or years to fully install—all these require heavy effort. However, it is not unusual for such projects to be seen as purely technical, and many fail to reach their potential because of this. In such cases, the traditional next step is a major benefits realization program aimed at getting at the advertised gains. Once again, if such wins are to happen, change thinking needs to be front and center.

Achieving Outsourcing

Outsourcing is a huge step forward in driving down the cost base, as it can now access the lowest cost sources of service. However, outsourcing is also a rite of passage for a firm. Not only does it require the admission that it is less than competent in some areas, but to get the cost advantage it has to commit to a whole new culture of flexibility and partnership. Breaking the boundaries of the firm, making these tentative first steps to focusing on where you add value, and depending on others with whom you need to form intense relationships is a major event. The continuous transformation implications are profound. The firm can now tap into world-class competence, and revise its choices, not quite at will, but certainly more easily than it could previously tear up parts of itself. There are still costs for change, but they are dramatically lower than in a fully integrated world.

Process analysis with benchmarking inevitably leads to the issue of outsourcing. There are some processes which the firm simply cannot do as well as others, whether for reasons of scale or skill. As you identify things others do better, or which are not core to your business even if you do them very well, then they are candidates for outsourcing. From a change point of view outsourcing creates a whole new range of issues beyond cost saving. The firm is suddenly dependent on a third party for a key service, say its IT services, as Kodak was when it outsourced its information technology to IBM. What happens if there is a disaster, if the outsourcee goes bankrupt, if circumstances change and the dramatic new directions are called for, and you are locked into an old supplier? The risks are very real, as are the crises they could induce, but so are the rewards—world-class capability in everything!

Outsourcing is a marriage with gains for both partners and an intention to stay married. Both of you will be putting investment into the deal, and you are both entitled to benefit. This is a learned concept. In the middle 1990s, one large and arrogant organization held numerous workshop sessions discussing strategic relationships with partners (outsourcing). The idea was to get them excited, have them invest, and then, if the idea was good, the company would dump the partner and do it themselves. This kind of bad faith undercuts any outsourcing attempt. The word gets around that you are not trustworthy, and suppliers shy away or up their prices for the extra risk. Trust is the basis of any modern supply relationship. Not to be trustworthy is damning and expensive. Making trust happen means instilling behavior patterns into everyone in the business; if you are the dominant partner in a relationship, you may have to resist the desire to throw your weight around in the interests of your reputation as a strategic partner. It also means that to make continuous transformation happen you have to be prepared to share strategy with your partners, a concept alien to traditional managers. The decision to look at outsourcing raises great stress in the business. Indeed, many public sector union agreements specifically outlaw outsourcing. From the union's perspective, the loss of union jobs in the main operation far outweighs the increase in jobs in the possibly non-union suppliers. Introducing outsourcing in such situations may be difficult or impossible. Of course, this does not apply to non-union situations, in which outsourcing grew at over 20 percent per annum in the late 1990s.

Making Shared Services Happen

In the mid-1990s, a group of Canadian banks decided that they shared a common problem, the high cost of back office, administrative services. The solution: they set up a single unit, jointly owned, which provided those services to them all. As organizations globalize, many of the local operations find themselves too small to carry the full cost of human resources, finance, information technology, and other support services. Their solution is essentially the same as the banks'—they buy services on an as needed basis from a central, internal department. Shared services have similar effects to outsourcing in breaking up the full function businesses of the past. Also, shared services are a stepping stone to outsourcing. For example, global information technology could be outsourced as a package, as could global accounting, or even human resources. This step may never be made but it always remains a possibility.

A shared service group is very different from a traditional centralized operation. The essence lies in the service contracts that must be struck. People in shared services operations have more in common with outside consultants than they have with their past roles as employees. They may even have to move to counting hours for billing purposes. Certainly they will have to negotiate quality of service and live up to that quality. In some cases the firm may even put them into a different legal entity such as a subsidiary.

The technical problems in introducing shared services are significant but so are the change problems. To gain acceptance you need to recognize the fears and concerns of each of those with a stake in the change. For example:[1]

- *Operating leadership* The operating leadership will be concerned about the disruption the change will cause to their operation and having to deal with a group that may be physically remote. To operating leaders it will feel like a centralization of power and responsibility and a diminution of their local power and personal status if those groups previously reported locally.

- *The staff people left locally* Staff people will worry about their careers. Will they be labeled as locals, failures, and see their careers crash and burn? What will their new role will be? Will there be a loss of job security? Will the change be just another flash in the pan?

- *The new shared services people* These should be the winners and to a large extent they are. They will find their jobs intrinsically more interesting because of the potentially wider scope, but almost certainly they will feel less secure as they will be more isolated from the heartbeat of the main business. This will cause career worries.

Overcoming such fears and resistances involves examining each jurisdiction and business unit individually. There will be places where shared services make eminent sense, others where local services are more appropriate, and the great middle ground which will have to be decided on a case-by-case basis. Once a business case is in place, and it is decided who is in and who is out, the firm needs to lock in the structure and roles of the people in the shared services center. Structure is important, but role definition is equally so—without it you will raise as many questions as you thought you were dealing with. Without this clarity people will be nervous as they live with uncertainty and ambiguity.

Acceptance of the new approach will not happen without leadership support—from the very top. The business case must be totally compelling, and those who cannot support it or who conclude they

---

[1] For more detailed coverage of the change and financial issues in outsourcing, shared costs, and introducing the super analyst techniques see Thomas Walther et al., *Reinventing the CFO: Moving from Financial Management to Strategic Management*, New York: McGraw-Hill, 1996; and PricewaterhouseCoopers LLP, Financial & Cost Management Team, *CFO Architect of the Corporation's Future*, New York: John Wiley, 1997.

are personally going to lose more than they can handle must be removed as soon as identified. But even this is not enough. Local pride and parochial feeling will make the change take longer than you think; in fact a "softening up" process may be necessary on the firm as a whole to get them ready to accept the change. Time spent preparing the ground, communicating, gaining acceptance, and training people is worth it in terms of speed of implementation and smoothness afterwards.

The Bottom Line on Process Thinking

The shift to process thinking is still going on. It started with the quality movement, was reinforced by re-engineering, was locked in by big ERP installations, and is now being resurrected yet again by sixsigma programs. Sixsigma is a process analysis-driven technique that focuses on eliminating product and service defects. Started by Motorola[2] in the late 1980s, it uses statistical measures to quantify the incidence of errors. For the statistically minded, sigma is the term that labels a standard deviation from the mean: sixsigma is six standard deviations. For the layperson, this translates to totally trivial numbers of errors. The idea is simple: set a target and measure your way to it. Taken up by IBM and others in the early 1990s, the concept went quiet until resurrected in the popular consciousness by Jack Welch at GE. It is now credited in the GE annual report with significant and continuous gains in quality and cost.

Whether you use quality principles, re-engineering, sixsigma, or your own homemade program, the message is clear. Process improvement is absolutely crucial if you are to get to a lower cost curve, and if you have not yet faced up to the major—but solvable—cultural and structural changes you are seriously behind your competition.

The Super Analysts

If process thinking is a root skill for e-leaders, high analytical capability is less prevalent, despite the huge potential of big data systems. The challenge to an e-leader, whether the CEO or the CFO, is to overcome resistance and get this potential installed. Not so easy.

---

[2] Note: Sixsigma is a registered trademark of Motorola.

The theory is people should welcome incontrovertible, factual, financial evidence of cost problems, market opportunities, or profit opportunities. If you knew a customer or market was unprofitable you would act and fire that customer—right? So why not get the data? If you knew that a factory was irredeemably inefficient, you would act and close it—it only makes sense. If you knew that one capital investment decision yielded more shareholder value than another, you would choose the more profitable one, even if it was not your favored solution—or at least you would feel guilty about it. In the past, such cost decisions as these, which lead to changes large and small, would have been sources of argument, delay, and special pleading. No more—with modern tools they should be easier to analyze.

Indeed, of recent years, the finance area has been endowed with a startling array of analytical tools. These include shareholder value analysis, value-based management, activity-based management, activity-based budgeting, target costing, product life cycle costing, customer relationship, and life cycle costing. But installing these turns out to be a change problem with at least five issues:

- Map Out a Path and Build Support Gradually
- Do Not Ignore the WIFM
- Design with Care
- Hurry Slowly
- Understand the Long-Term Technical Investment

Map Out a Path and Build Support Gradually

All of these new techniques are exciting advances to cost management for the finance people. Although it is unlikely that others will understand or support them immediately, finance cannot move forward without their support and access to their data. Unless it is intended to pull in the big guns and mandate the change, it will have to evolve (albeit, rapidly):

Start Small

Pilot projects are, by definition, freestanding and may involve using a simple package to manipulate data, which is largely manually entered. If the pilot is convincing, move on to something more sophisticated. But to be convincing, the pilot will have to yield a sig-nificant insight, something really worthwhile—so select your pilot with care. You want something where you are confident you can yield a good result, and you are sure the organization will care. When you have succeeded, broadcast the results.

Build an Appetite

The pilot should yield interest, because to go further with any tool, management has to be convinced that the time and effort is worth it. Even if convinced they may not be willing to leap into a full program. The next stage involves expanding the pilot. In practice, this will mean using more sophisticated equipment and accessing increasing amounts of data. You and others are going to have to put in even more time. The aim is to intrigue people to such an extent that they will demand more and pull the implementation through. They will do this if, and only if, they can see value. Eventually it is hoped that this appetite will develop into a full-scale implementation.

Change Work Habits

Even if a full implementation seems feasible, it will not happen in a business sense unless the transformation changes the way people work. For example, to get full use out of the data people may need to work in cross-functional work teams throughout the business so that they can share their insights. If your implementation of high-grade data precedes this kind of cultural change then little further gain will be made until it is tackled. High-quality analysis needs to be seen, not as an imposition demanding more and more data on top of an already busy life, but as a key tool in the performance of people's work, and a way of making their lives easier. If this last point is not accepted, either bureaucracies will grow up to feed the beast while leaders go off and do the "real" work, or data quality will decline, and pressure to remove the system as a cost driver in its own right will rise.

Do Not Ignore the WIFM

All change hits the question "What's in it for me?"—WIFM. For a data analysis program to be successful it must become credible as a business tool, but before you can do that, you need to understand how finance is seen in the business. If it is seen as an exciting partner, one that brings easy-to-use ideas that materially help the business, then the installation will be easier. If, however, finance has a reputation as a heavy-handed, control-oriented imposition with little understanding of the business but a lot of interest in power plays, then there is an uphill battle ahead. A win may happen, but it will be grudging, and the program will be tarnished from day one. Be totally honest from the start. The aim is to have people learn new ways of talking about cost and their business in ways that are associated with financial success. If this is seen as a power grab by the finance department, it will be a fight every inch of the way. The ways around this problem are classic. Involve people and let them own the program. Demonstrate advantages, but do not try to dictate implementation. Let people play with it so they see the potential outputs—in short, let them own it and control the speed of uptake with you shepherding them along. Train, and communicate as much as possible. Provide "quick wins" that justify line management in supporting further development. Finally, do not oversell any tool. If it fails to deliver the promise, then failure is inevitable.

Design with Care

Regardless of the specific tool, data analysis can become a complex nightmare, pulling in data and work like a dry sponge. Take great care with the design, and have great clarity about the kinds of outputs you are looking for. Stick with major products, important customers, and markets, and only drill down to greater detail when specifically necessary. Remember, like everything, cost analysis suffers from diminishing returns.

Hurry Slowly

This book encourages speed, but sometimes it is better to move slowly and get acceptance rather than driving off a cliff. Superior data analysis requires many adjustments and an organizational learning curve. New intellectual constructs are absorbed at a pace the people in the specific organization can learn. Pressing them on people can push the project backward. Shepherd it forward but do not force-feed. For example, every firm has a multitude of business initiatives on the go—process re-engineering, product costing, pricing, and so on. If the new tools can be used as a decision support tool on existing projects, then it has a leg up for full implementation. Try to be sucked along behind another need.

Understand the Long-Term Technical Investment

There is a vision: modern tools used as the principal means of cost control, but this, in turn, has implications for information technology investments. To be effective in a systematic way, these tools, by definition, demand wide access to data from across the organization. Such information may be captured in a modern ERP or some such system, or it may be embedded in legacy systems, which do not connect with the new tools. If there is no intention to replace the legacy systems, there will eventually have to be investments in data warehousing. From a management point of view it is important that senior leaders understand the full implications, and potential costs, so that if demand for the insights these tools can bring rises, there is no shock or disappointment.

An e-leader supported by this level of numbers sophistication has a major advantage. It is worth the effort.

The Involvers

Imagine an army of analysts with deep operational knowledge, and hands-on experience of the actions that incur cost. Imagine further that tapping into that well of knowledge was practically free. How could you avoid using what seems to be a huge advantage? Yet most leaders do just that. They fail totally to involve their employees in cost management except under highly structured conditions, such as formal process analysis. Even then, they usually only tap into a small group of employees. For the e-leader, driving for every fraction of a cent of cost advantage in the charge down the industry cost curve can be crucial; failing to involve all your resources is willful neglect. But this is not all. The really sophisticated e-leader realizes that the more you involve people so that they understand the issues, the more easily you can get them to adapt. This lowering of resistance to change lowers the cost of change, and in a world demanding continuous adaptation, this pushes your cost curve below that of your unreformed competitors.

The traditional world was one where financial information was held close to the vest. Only those who really needed to know were included in the inner circle. Knowledge was power. In the modern world of continuous improvement, high levels of public disclosure, empowerment of people, and a realization that "people are smarter than we thought" and can make connections between their efforts and the success of the organization, is leading to greater openness about financial information. E-leaders who favor this openness believe people are essentially rational. Show them why you are— once again—addressing a process because it did not yield the cost reductions hoped for, and they will come with you. Simply ordering it will make you look as if you have no idea what you are doing.

Getting people involved in cost management is a significant shift in management style, and there seem to be two, not necessarily incompatible, approaches emerging. The first, best illustrated by firms that take up *value-based management* (VBM) techniques, is top down. It seeks to impose a set of ideas about how the firm's market value is affected by actions, and then to enforce them through the performance system to push the value drivers, and stop doing things that swallow value. The second, best illustrated by firms that seek to *drive business understanding,* is more bottom up. This way starts by trying to educate people on the financial aspects of business. The aim is that they understand the basic language of finance and money, and having begun to make the connections between their own activities and the profits of the firm, they are encouraged to seek out and yield cost savings. The leadership philosophies behind these approaches are clearly different—the first more compatible with traditional command management, the second demanding greater belief in people. From a change perspective, introducing value-based management is a very different problem from moving to open-book management.

Introducing Value-Based Management

VBM operationalizes shareholder value analysis. Shareholder value is directly related to the way the financial markets calculate share price, being the value of future cash flows suitably discounted at a rate that takes account of the level of risk in the business. The role of VBM is to take that concept and drive it through the business, applying it to the expected cash returns from every action and investment decision, expressing each in terms of the value it would create for the shareholder. Without VBM, shareholder value analysis is an interesting concept—useful but not operational. The approach provides a means of directly comparing efforts on different projects. Should the firm spend time reducing its receivables or investing in new capital plant? Should it spend money on a leadership training program or a new machine? These seemingly unrelated ideas can be assessed through the amount of value they create in the firm. The aim is clearly to get people to focus in the right places. Despite its underlying simplicity, introducing shareholder value thinking and value-based management can run into resistance.

The basic reality of businesses is that they create value and destroy it, and VBM unmercifully reveals both value creation and destruction. If the fundamental drivers of the business change, a previously excellent performer can gobble up share price, until the problem is fixed. The classic example was IBM which destroyed many billions of dollars of shareholder wealth until Lou Gerstner turned it round, then busily recreated most of that wealth. This means that VBM can expose today's value losers to the distress of divisional leaders who will see their reputations and potential for promotion suffer. Where there are potential losers there is resistance. Even worse, by linking value thinking to other tools such as customer value and product life cycle costing, the likelihood of a business unit becoming a value destroyer can be roughly predicted. This puts intense pressure on the management of that unit. If there is no mechanism in place to develop a new business model that can return the unit to positive value creation, the leaders will see investment moving away and the unit being harvested.

VBM like all super-analyst techniques is data hungry. To get decent results the models have to be fed either as one-off efforts or as long-term data flows. Those outside finance can easily see this as an imposition, which can readily translate into resistance, particularly if finance has a reputation for control and aloofness from the business already. Resistance will come from all quarters. For example, marketing often sees the financial view as hostile to the customer view, whether it is, in fact, truly hostile or not, so that elevating the shareholder may seem to degrade the importance of the other stakeholders. The technical need may easily be blown up to seem overwhelming. Only addressing the WIFM (What's in it for me) can solve such direct or inchoate resistance. This means the CFO has to be able to show the benefit of the approach in clear decision making, as a single performance measure, as greater clarity in strategy, and as the link to the ever more aggressive institutional shareholder.

Driving Business Understanding

Leaders who fully inform their employees about financial matters are still rare, but there are now enough examples to indicate that it is not a niche idea espoused by a few sentimental idealists. Firms such as Wal-Mart have always shared information, but others are coming on board. Unfortunately, it is not an easy idea to implement. Business expert John Case[3] identified three major issues in sharing financial information and seeking involvement in such practices as open-book management where all employees have access to full disclosure:

- Information previously restricted to those leading the business has to be shared with everyone. This means all kinds of information including financial goals, budgets, income statements, and forecasts. Not only must it be shared, but it also must be understood. Hand in hand with open books goes lots of training in understanding financial data.

- Once information is shared, managers must be prepared to hold employees accountable for meeting financial targets. This means that the key drivers of cost and revenue which managers use must be shared and owned by everyone.

- The compensation system must reward people for the success of the business. This usually means a sizeable bonus plan perhaps supplemented by stock options. The bonus must be tied to easily understood measures of performance that need to be continually measured and presented in scoreboard format.

This kind of thinking gets at a specific issue of great concern in the world of transformation. Employees should be aligned with the interests of the firm through an intimate understanding of how their actions affect costs and a close tying of their gains—income, promotion, etc.—to achieving the company's cost goals.

case   This was illustrated brilliantly by Sears'[4] successful turnaround that was built on providing employees with real and meaningful cost insight. The Sears experience involved a total transformation of the business, requiring all the disciplines in this book, but of particular

---

[3] John Case, *The Open-Book Experience: Lessons from over 100 Companies Who Successfully Transformed Themselves.* Reading, MA: Addison-Wesley, 1998; John Case, "Opening the Books," *Harvard Business Review*, March-April 1997.

[4] Anthony J. Rucci, Steven P. Kirn, and Richard T. Quinn, "The Employee-Customer-Profit Chain at Sears," *Harvard Business Review*, January-February 1998.

interest here was their use of cost understanding. Sears developed an approach they called Total Performance Indicators (TPI) based on the idea that the way the customers and employees interacted was what drove revenue and so value in a retail business. They called it the employee-customer-profit chain. They then took a highly original step and defined "causal pathways" between such "soft" issues as improvements in employee attitudes and customer impressions of Sears' increases in store revenue.

They had this work done by a firm of econometricians using factor analysis applied to years of survey and financial data. The work indicated relationships which Sears now has enough confidence in to use for predictive purposes. Once in place, the firm undertook a massive, highly interactive education process to bring their employees to an understanding of the strategic issues facing the firm, the firm's financial structure, and the message from the TPI and causal pathway work. They tied this into the performance system and brought employees face-to-face with the implications of their skills and attitudes on the profitability of Sears. The program was highly successful and is ongoing.

The implications of this work for transformation are profound. Sears had recognized that successful turnarounds can be lost in the years that follow if managers and staff are not engaged after the problem seems to have been solved. By entering a high involvement process, which engaged first all the leadership and then everyone around the issue of how profits are created, Sears prevented the natural tendency to sink back into old ways, locked in their transformation gains, and set the scene for more gains still.

The Designers

Few things are more strategic than designing a business such that it has an inherent cost advantage over its competitors. Such e-leaders have moved their businesses to a lower cost curve that they can continue to improve. In the e-world, firms such as Dell, Cisco, Schwab, E*TRADE, and Amazon.com have all done this and the race is on by the mass of others to either emulate them in untouched markets or to catch up if they were the victims. But e-business is not the only route to design in cost advantage. Other firms, e-business and classic, have been restructuring the way they do business so that costs are automatically controlled; not only do they get the advantage of lower costs they also do not have to carry the cost of control—for example, expensive management.

The E-Business Story

Imagine you had set up a business so that you built to order and carried no inventory in the entire supply chain from beginning to end. You rarely, if ever, produced a wrong product configuration. You had outsourced all transportation, production, and logistics to world-class suppliers, whom you keep continually on their toes through relentless performance assessment. Meanwhile, you focus your own efforts on the things you do best—customer management, configuration development, and so on. At the same time, you can move more quickly than your competitors because you are not dragging around thousands of people. Amazing, but that is exactly what Dell,[5] Gateway, Cisco, and others like them are well on the way to doing or have already achieved. These are the economics of the e-world original equipment manufacturers (OEMs). And it doesn't stop there. Close supplier relationships, long-term supply contracts, deep integration into their customer purchasing systems, and high volumes going to a few production points make the logistics dramatically more efficient than the majority of competitors. Finally, to add insult to competitive injury, you get paid before you have to pay your suppliers, so growth actually generates working capital instead of forcing you into debt.

The impact of these new models is devastating on traditional suppliers. IBM, Compaq, and others are unlikely to match the Dell cost base without stealing some of Dell's clothes, which is exactly what they have tried to do. Meanwhile, Dell and others can put price pressure on the traditional competitors or allow them to create a price umbrella under which they can enjoy super-normal profits. Moreover, leaders with a traditional background find it difficult to replicate the structure and culture of a business model so entirely different. While Dell or Amazon.com, or any similar firm that starts from a direct sales or information technology base, was starting from scratch, the bulk of firms are trying to get there by chipping away at the established cost base of an existing business. Everywhere we look we can see firms trying to make the switch. They add Web sites to get into e-commerce and a low-cost channel of distribution, but they immediately hit conflicts with their existing channels and either have to back off or go in to contortions to be fair. The property and casualty insurance industry is a case in point where e-sales are in direct competition with established agents and brokers. Manufacturing firms are buying supply chain

---

[5] See Joan Magretta, "The Power of Virtual Integration: An Interview with Dell Computer's Michael Dell," *Harvard Business Review*, March-April 1998.

management software to try to emulate the smooth integration of a Cisco, but they cannot replicate the cultural integration of Cisco or Dell's suppliers into the strategic decision making of the "extended enterprise," and so do not get the same results. Firms are buying e-procurement systems by the yard as they seek to follow GE's lead and struggle with quality control issues when they do not implement the hard-nosed Dell supplier quality performance approach—where orders are tied directly to performance. They try to shift to an Amazon.com approach and lock up Web customers, but cannot afford the poor back-office performance that Amazon, as a pioneer, got away with.

And so it goes on.

The business model that the pioneer develops and which reshapes the rules of competition in an industry often differs significantly from hybrid models that the followers are forced into. The leader will usually have thought through the problem holistically or have had time to adjust and learn; the followers will try to bolt their response on to an unreformed business in a huge hurry. Dell is structured to be low cost, end-to-end, but many of its competitors leave the impression they added e-business to their basic business as simply another channel rather than the way they do business. Schwab created a cost base radically different from Merrill Lynch and, after being pooh-poohed by the traditional firm that was in love with a full-service concept, had the pleasure of a public retraction as the high-cost firm found its customers loved the lower cost of trades.

E-business is cutting a swath through traditional business, with most traditionals in denial at some level. The transformation problem of getting these particular numbers right is going to occupy all industries for many years. The jury is still out on whether traditional firms will be able to transform to the new ways or whether many firms are going to have to simply close up their old shops. This may be a little extreme, but the fact that it is being debated is indicative of the seriousness of the issues. The fundamental strategic reality is that the Internet and e-business have created a dramatically lower cost curve.

The Search for Self-Control

E-business, with its mixture of the virtual, customer intimacy, technical pyrotechnics in the manipulation of information, and speed of reaction, is going to dominate our thinking. However, many managements point out that not all businesses will be e-businesses, though all will use some of the techniques. Someone has to make things. Someone has to pick up the garbage. Someone has to deal in the concrete. The risk to all these businesses is that they will be outflanked and heavily commoditized. Take the example of a major US railroad. Fewer businesses seem further from e-business than shunting trains around. True, they can use e-procurement; install various supply chain approaches and even take bookings over the Internet. But, the strategic heart of their business is moving people and things right? They were Wrong! Oh, they still have to move people and things, but the emergence of a transportation integrator, BridgePoint at www.bridgepoint.com, has caused strategic horror. BridgePoint Inc. offers to take over the shipping of goods anywhere, choosing the best approach, striking the deals, and managing the process. The railway is now faced with a "customer" almost omniscient about transport and its costs and attached to no one. The potential impact of their pricing is devastating and barring buying them out or getting into the business themselves, there is little the railways or shipping companies can do. Even if they succeeded in suppressing this player, another will spring up. The pressure on cost will be intense. Their strategic error was in focusing inward on the trains, and not outward on the customer's total transportation problem.

The solution, as your business is commoditized, is to recognize that the game is to have lower costs than your competitor. He or she will then create the price umbrella in the market allowing you superior returns to go with your lower costs. But how do you do this? In most industries, particularly those that have been somewhat commoditized, most of the input costs are similar for most players. All buy their equipment from the same few makers, all have unions who seek to equalize wages, and all buy their fuel from the same utilities and oil companies. There are few places to get an advantage. One of those few places is the "cost of cost control"—management. The trick is to devise a business model where such costs are low and are automatically driven down.

case   Aetna Insurance was losing money on their life insurance operations in Canada.[6] A combination of intense competition on term-life products, a decline in savings-based policies in the face of competition from the mutual fund industry, and a high fixed cost base with a career agent force was making the business untenable to the point where the parent company wished to sell out. The classic short-term

---

[6] The original version of this updated story was told in Gerald Ross and Michael Kay, *Toppling the Pyramids: Redefining the Way Companies Are Run*, New York: Times Books, 1994.

response would have been to close out the agent force and move to a broker system, which is what a lot of their competition subsequently decided to do. However, though moving to brokers cuts the cost and makes the firm's costs variable, it also loses them any real control over their sales force. Brokers handle other lines to protect themselves from pressure from any specific insurance company.

Aetna's solution, like Dell's, was holistic. Instead of moving to brokers, Aetna created a franchise system starting with its existing agents. Aetna looked upon the franchisees as its customers and it went to great lengths to provide business services to them. As an example, an insurance salesperson selling several lines would receive many reports from each of his or her suppliers. This leads to administrative problems as they seek to sort it all out. What Aetna promised was to source product from wherever made sense and to ensure that the franchisee only received one set of information and that that information fitted into an accounting system. This would save the sales person time and accounting cost and simplify their lives.

Meanwhile the "manufacturing" part of Aetna, while committed to providing product was not committed to creating it. It developed relationships with several other insurance companies in lines it did not want to serve, and wove them into its total offering, releasing capital, and providing equal or superior product. The fact that the franchisees were not required to go to Aetna for their product (although most of them did anyway) kept the manufacturing unit on its toes.

The key to this approach was a total revamp of the whole system, including IT, finance, and human resource policies—in fact, a totally integrated approach. So successful was the system that brokers and agents from competitive firms lined up to get in. Meanwhile, its competitors were going to brokerage systems, losing control, and sticking with making everything as they failed to reform their manufacturing operations.

The results for Aetna were startling—steady rise in sales in a tough, tough market, and, more immediate, a drop of 40 to 50 percent in total cost, putting them on a low-cost base compared with their competitors without effective loss of control. Even better, the costs became self-managing, and from Aetna's point of view virtually 100 percent variable (their prior sales force costs were now bundled in with the franchisees' sales commission), and the franchisees kept close watch on them, eliminating a whole lot of Aetna management's role. As this happened, Aetna's profit became more resilient to market fluctuations as the fixed component dropped and the variable or contingent component rose.

The change management issues in this transformation were significant. The top management of Aetna in both Canada and the USA had to be convinced and brought behind the idea, which not surprisingly meant a business case. Once this was accepted, the agents and potential brokers had to buy into the idea. This was accomplished by involving key, respected agents in the idea development process. Other agents could be assured that their opinions had been covered, and the system was suited to their needs. Even with this assurance, the sales force would not have come along if a charismatic leader—Nick Villani—hadn't persuaded it. The sales operation was then split off into a separate entity, Equinox, and run for the benefit of the franchisees and Aetna together. The governance structure of the new entity reflected this.

Finally, the actuaries were faced with a new reality—conform or move on. Most preferred to conform in what was now a more exciting environment. Indeed, one of the big changes was the cultural one of seeing the salesperson as a primary customer. Up until then and still today in many companies, the actuary-dominated internal culture had looked down on the salesman as inferior and too well paid. One of the reasons other firms did not follow the Aetna example may have been that the cultural shift was too great.

The transformation of Aetna's life operations was hugely successful and one would have expected that it would have been rapidly imitated. It was not. However, when Aetna Canada was bought by Maritime Life in 1999, the Equinox operation was a major contributor to the significant price paid.

The three keys to obtaining the gains of a new approach are:

- *Aim at a quantum drop in costs.* Aetna achieved at least 40 percent drop in the early years, and other clients have had similar experiences. Compared with their unreformed competitors this put them on a different and lower cost curve.

- *Go at it wholeheartedly and holistically without the chains of established systems.* Aetna was faced with a crisis. Would it have made such a radical step if it had not been stressed? Probably not. But change it did, and not just a small change. It was a total rethink of the business to a new model. The reality is simple. Business models are systemic. To bolt something on to the side of an existing system could cripple both.

- *Recognize that such approaches require entirely new control systems.* The cost of control comes in managers looking over people's shoulders and in slowness in decision making. Modern business models need to react quickly and have cost control built in.

Aetna's solution now seems easy. Franchisees are small business people with a deep interest in keeping costs down, but any system can be designed so that those running it are rewarded for cost minimization through performance management, benchmarking, contract negotiation, gain sharing, and so on. Cost minimization can be designed in.

In the e-world, the potential to move to a different and lower cost base through e-business is enormous. The rush to do so is on and will dominate the next decade. However, whether an e-business or a more conventional one, there are ways to design in low cost. The starting point in any transformation should be to look for these opportunities.

* * * * *

The gap in cost management from the slash and burn world to the modern one of high cost management sophistication, built on intense data manipulation and strategic thinking, is enormous. The implication for the quality of the e-leader's CFO is, of course, just as enormous. The traditional era was the world of the scorekeeping controller—the man in the green eye-shade. Today, the sophistication of the CFO must match the tools he or she can wield, which means that, from a CEO viewpoint, the starting point in driving extraordinary financial results is the CFO him- or herself. Not to have the most sophisticated CFO you can afford is to condemn yourself to second best. But the best must go beyond mere technical brilliance. The days of the accountant in his cubbyhole are over. The CFO must be able to deal with and understand the business in many dimensions including the strategic. In a world of extraordinary financial results, the effective CFO is an agent for business transformation.

CHAPTER 3

Unite People Behind Your Vision

Myths and legends can be instructive even in an age moving at e-speed. The myth of King Arthur and the Round Table is one such. Once he was king, Arthur faced three leadership challenges, to hold his people together through the crisis of war, to engage them in the problems of peace, and to provide an outlet for the restless spirits. The first he did through the Round Table and the community of knights, all equal of voice if not experience and all listened to though the King reserved the final decision. In peace, he enrolled the whole community in the building and realization of the dream of Camelot, the perfect city where each contributed according to his or her skill. For the restless knights, he had the spiritual quest after the Holy Grail, the cup used by Christ at the Last Supper, and rumored to have been brought to England by Joseph of Arimathea. The Arthur of myth faced problems familiar to modern business e-leaders.

- How to live through strategic crisis and resolve it quickly in ways that allow for fast and flexible implementation.
- How to involve the whole community of employees in improving the business on a continuing basis.
- How to engage, usually smaller, groups of people at an emotional level so that they can perform well beyond expectations in difficult situations.

Different leaders solve these dilemmas in different ways. Bill Gates has imposed a cult of personality on Microsoft, being treated by those he has made rich as an idol. Jack Welch was a teacher with an obsession for communicating his vision to people face-to-face. The Donnelly brothers of Donnelly Mirrors, a hugely successful automotive parts supplier, built intense loyalty around deep religious principles. What they have all done is recognize that the essence of leadership is having followers and that followers who are engaged intellectually, emotionally, and even spiritually have more commitment, can be more empowered, and will implement actions faster than those simply following orders.

This chapter provides practical approaches for all three of those leadership challenges, insights of great value in the e-world of fast-moving change, where rapid implementation, swift local adjustments by empowered people, and a deep commitment by small groups to moving key activities forward are all crucial. The chapter will cover:

- Strategic Engagement—unifying thousands of people in a common strategic cause.

- Operational Engagement—unifying whole workforces in the search for operational improvement.

- Spiritual Engagement—unifying smaller groups around difficult to solve issues.

Strategic Engagement

Larry Willat's manufacturing firm[1] was being squeezed by government price controls but he could see more fundamental problems looming. His executive team could not. They figured that the government would change, and the business would return to normal, but Larry found this difficult to believe. He sensed that something more profound was happening to the industry. He believed that they would have to find a new way of doing business.

When Larry elected to start a strategic alignment process the pressure had just become dramatically more acute. The parent company had decided to dump this unprofitable business and had put it on the auction block. Potential purchasers had started trickling

---

[1] The original version of this updated story was told in Gerald Ross and Michael Kay, *Toppling the Pyramids, Redefining the Way Companies Are Run*, New York: Times Books, 1994.

through, but most buyers, scenting a deal, made offers too low for even a cash-strapped parent to entertain. Despite this very clear message from the owners that the firm had to get its act together, when Larry started the change process, he could not get real support from his top management team. Despite the for sale sign there was no feeling of urgency—no sense of a burning desire to change.

case   Larry's firm was "ideally suited for the 1950s" according to a culture survey done a year before lying untouched on everyone's desks. The history of the firm was one of extreme maternalism—don't worry Mother will look after you, was the prevailing feeling. Despite the fact that Mother was offering to sell her offspring to the highest bidder, the inertia of habit lay over the firm like a pall. The fact that no one had put in a good bid only served to confirm everyone in their opinion that nothing would happen. The problem Larry faced was threefold:

- strategic—the market was tough, and he needed a new business approach.

- financial—the firm's structure was overloaded, and any rational analysis pointed to heavy downsizing.

- cultural—he was locked into a slow-moving, command and control world of intense silos and almost no internal cooperation.

To make matters worse the top team was totally dysfunctional; their internal rivalries had raised back stabbing to an art form. Larry had tried to make changes but the team had merely polarized into the new and the old guards. The strategic alignment program was expected to solve all these problems. Eventually, it did. The firm made a dramatic shift in culture, returned to high profitability, and was taken off the market.

The journey to their new world was full of ups and downs. The aim was to find a new way of operating, get everyone behind it, and implement quickly. To achieve this, the program had to develop new strategic solutions, break down the top management problem, loosen up the organization, and create new working behaviors. Concurrently, Larry knew it had to allow for massive downsizing, without putting the business into so much trauma it would be dragged down. Indeed, the idea of a unilateral headcount reduction imposed by the CEO was a real option, but he did not feel he had the moral right to do that when the firm was for sale. Moreover, he had no new vision of the future to use as a basis for people decisions. The approach selected was high involvement strategic alignment, which meant involving the maximum number of people possible in the creation of operational strategy to build commitment by allowing everyone a kick at the can.

If the apparent theme was the creation of a new strategic direction the hidden theme was to kick off massive culture change. In a firm such as this, the process is such a departure from tradition that it sends an enormous signal to the organization that things are to be done differently. This is how it worked.

The program was workshop based. A series of sessions spread over six months started with the top team and gradually involved more and more people, sometimes in small groups, sometimes in sessions of up to 100 people at a time. The content of the sessions involved the creation of a vision, and the exploration of the implications of that vision for the firm and every part of it down to each individual. In the course of that exploration, people suggested real improvements in the vision, though the final decision lay with the top team. By massaging, and helping to invent the new direction for the firm, everyone felt a high degree of commitment. By the end of the series of meetings, not only had a vision been created, but it had been locked into a full strategic positioning, the capabilities needed to deliver it had been identified, and action programs put in place. The sessions were syncopated, such that the top team would work on an issue and then it would be passed out for other teams to refine or reject (if they had good reason). The meetings were spaced out so that homework could be done in between and the attendees had a chance to absorb what they had decided. As the months went by the strategy was honed, and the people started to buy in. They felt a real sense of ownership. However, to the top team, the emerging strategy was little more than a good idea and the modern ideas of how to behave were not real to them. They had bought in intellectually but they still felt no burning need to do anything—until the session from hell.

Larry had known all along that the underlying numbers were poor, and so, at a subliminal level, had his top team. As an issue it was skirted around and was a great undiscussable. The heavy denial they lived in had prevented them from taking the poor profit picture seriously. In this session their world came crashing down. Larry took them through the numbers, and introduced the idea of the new, tightly focused business approach in a significantly smaller firm. The shock was profound. The numbers said that at least one third of the people would have to go—in a firm with no history of mass downsizing but rather with a strong entitlement philosophy. The tension was so great that one participant had to go out to her car in the parking lot and scream.

It would be nice to say that they got past denial at that moment and moved forward, but they didn't. It was another two sessions as they challenged the numbers and fought for their individual corners before they finally caved in. The top management was in a bind. They were faced with the CEO with his inexorable logic of the numbers pressing down on them, and the upward pressure of a middle management that had been involved and helped create an exciting future. The pressure on them to implement the new organizational vision that would help the firm live with its smaller size was enormous and they gradually started to internalize the new strategy.

The process now moved from idea generation to implementation. The action programs were handed out to cross-functional teams who investigated them and started implementation. Everyone's performance contract reflected the new plan. With a solid plan in place, signs of immense internal support and motivation, and, with no real buyers, the parent took the business off the market. This released the CEO from his sense of moral obligation, and he got rid of the most unreformed of his top management and sidelined others to where they could do no harm. Others he sent on leadership programs. Those who were able to change their basic styles survived but the others did not. He sought out new leaders, some from outside and some from inside, and pressed them to model the new leadership behaviors. Larry himself went on to glory in the parent company. The dreaded downsizing took place in an atmosphere of sadness but calm. The people had understood the necessity and accepted it. The implementation leapt ahead. It had been scheduled to take four years in total, but it was completed in two, including the strategic alignment program. Maintaining that speed of reaction is as difficult as creating it, but six years later, the firm is still hugely successful in a tough industry, having implemented new systems and techniques smoothly thanks to the underlying, initial alignment Larry created. When everyone knows where he or she is going, it is much easier to get there.

Larry's experience with high involvement strategic planning is not uncommon. It can work in any industry at any time, and though it requires careful planning it can be scaled to fit firms of every size. Creating alignment requires significant effort and, for traditional businesses, new behaviors. The mechanics are set out below, but first a word of warning. Whether a firm achieves the continuous alignment which underlies transformation will depend heavily on top management attitudes. Involvement is a two-edged sword. Once you have started it, it immediately drives new behaviors in the business. To then back away is a very significant act, akin to pulling the carpet out from under your employees. So before you start, ask if you intend to stick with it, and even more important if your top management will support you.

Dave Hurley worked for a division of a major pharmaceutical firm, and had been hired based on his success in driving a profit transformation in a competitor. Dave's approach there had been based on high involvement alignment. When he tried the same thing at his new employers, the top management was horrified. Their philosophy was the antithesis of involving people and they attributed every problem Dave had to the fuzzy management style. Needless to say, Dave did not last.

Content and Process

There are two parts to achieving alignment—the content and the process. The content assumes you have a method of involving people and focuses on the tools and facts you will use to produce a strategic output, which will guide the company. The process is about the way you organize the alignment activity. The content talks to the destination and the method, the process to the way people are involved, physically.

Level Set

It is highly unlikely that everyone will have the same knowledge and opinions at the start of a strategy process, since each of us has our own viewpoint and prejudices. A level set is a technique whereby all those ideas and views are put on the table and the beginnings of alignment created. Classically done through confidential interviews with a nonattributable feedback, the same material can be brought out during a workshop using a facilitator, though this uses up valuable workshop time. Doing it in the workshop can also be less effective because people are often less willing to share their true concerns in a workshop setting feeling that they may be a personal risk. This activity is crucially important. If issues are not raised deliberately, they will come up anyway in an uncoordinated fashion and will divert discussion from key issues. If you are using a facilitator, he or she should present the level set as a story about where the firm is—holding up a mirror to the group and wherever possible using their own words. You may also expect the facilitator to provide a diagnosis after the feedback, which provides original insight into the problems the organization faces, and what may need to be done.

The discussion of the feedback is where a lot of learning happens. Classically, the group discovers they are much more in agreement than they thought. In Larry's case the tensions in the top management team were brought forward, and though there were some surprises in the details, there was agreement on the big issue. The level set should be delivered as the first item on the agenda of the first session of the top team. It may later be presented to each broadened group in whole or in summary. Each group may well express surprise that the top team understands the problems as well as they do. This is a common reaction. There is nothing to gain by keeping this feedback secret as copies will leak out anyway.

The Vision

At its simplest, strategic alignment is about defining a destination—the vision—and then deciding how to get there—the strategy and action plan. That does not sound very complicated, but there have been oceans of ink spilled discussing what exactly is the destination and how you define the tools for describing the way there. In particular, the concept of visioning has run through periods of favor and disrepute. The present state of play defines two philosophical groups. The first points to companies like Merck, Hewlett-Packard, Nike, Walt Disney, GE, and others, and focuses on a multilayered approach of explicit and implicit visions covering the core values of the business, some overriding purpose, and that something Collins and Porras[2] called a BHAG (Big Hairy Audacious Goal), a 10- to 30-year statement that will inspire people to get up in the morning. Some examples they quote: Walt Disney has strong values around imagination and wholesomeness, Hewlett-Packard around respect for individuals, commitment to the community, and making technical contributions to the company. Nordstrom has an obsession with customer service, Nike with extreme competition, Procter & Gamble with product excellence, and Sony with the elevation of Japanese culture.

These values should be good for a hundred years and should be complemented by a clear and vivid sense of company purpose. Company purpose does not include simply making money or maximizing shareholder wealth—which is a poor strategic guide at the

[2] J.C. Collins and J.I. Porras, "Building Your Company's Vision," *Harvard Business Review*, September-October 1996.

best of times—nor is it to be confused with specific business strategies which may shift continually. Company purpose is, according to Collins and Porras, the firm's raison d'être—why it exists in the first place. In Motorola people focus on Six Sigma quality improvements. In Walt Disney the focus is on children having fun not just watching cartoons. Dell may describe their purpose as making their business clients more successful. If you follow a root cause analysis, and keep asking why you are here, the end result almost always comes to some social good that complements the value set.

BHAGs comprise some achievable destination that can only be accomplished through dedicated and heroic effort. British Airways' famous goal to be the "world's favorite airline" when it could barely get a decent passenger rating is an oft-quoted example. Wal-Mart's desire to be super-large, Nike's intention to crush Adidas, GE's intention to be the number one or number two in every market they served—all these are examples of long-term goals to which the firm can aspire. All have a multiyear time scale and can be described succinctly or with great poetry. Land a man on the moon in 10 years, resist invasion to the last person by fighting on the beaches, are aspirational: America could have failed for good engineering reasons, and Britain could have been defeated had the Germans developed the new weapons of mass destruction a few short years away. Take these visionary components, wrap stories around them, and you have the beginnings of a long-term corporate culture. With the poisoned Tylenol scare, Johnson & Johnson reacted in line with its ethos and pulled all the product off the shelves regardless of short-term loss. This is now a standard part of the myths about that company. Like American Express, Nordstrom focuses on heroic efforts by front-line salespeople and service providers.

This is one school; another is more narrowly focused and operational. This group drives to some simpler operational goal, focusing on the products, and customer groups being served. There, vision will talk about being the leader in making the best widgets or serving a customer segment well. They are less concerned with grand vision than specific market guidance, less with general direction and more with specific strategy. They want a vision and a mission statement that provide immediate guidance. Life here is more mundane but not necessarily less insightful or valuable. Larry Willat's group rethought their entire strategy by focusing on the distributor of their product as their primary customer and deemphasizing the end consumer with whom they could get little competitive advantage.

This focus on the narrow and the operational is not necessarily incompatible with longer-term frameworks. It is quite conceivable for a division of Hewlett-Packard to have a narrow vision in the context of the firm's larger philosophy and most probably all do. However, for many firms the narrow vision is where they want to be. They cannot raise their eyes to the hills of grand creeds and value statements. The business simply does not hold that degree of personal investment for the people there, or their needs are so pressing they cannot see the grander world. They cannot conceive of a BHAG, because they do not have any confidence that their business will survive. British Airways is not going to disappear in the next year or even decade, but Joe's small business very well might. The basic rule of any change situation is to start where the patient is. If the patient is bleeding to death then get them to an operational vision as quickly as possible and stabilize them. You and they can always come back to larger visions later.

When putting together such a narrower vision, focus is everything. There is a school of vision writers—even of narrow, operational visions—who want to develop statements that cover the needs of all the stakeholders. This is a big mistake; focus exclusively on the customer. Vision statements, particularly narrow ones, are change instruments, and one of the most compelling ideas in change is "a flag outside" around which disparate groups can cluster. The customer is the *only* true flag and the uniformly agreed source of income and worth to the firm. Build your vision exclusively around the customer and treat the other stakeholders as constituents that have to be addressed by a change strategy not as part of the vision. In this world, the vision is tight and customer-focused, and the mission lists the offering and approach.

Discussing Strategy

Strategic alignment processes, by definition, involve discussions of strategy, ideas that are traditionally the province of top managers or strategy specialists. However, the essence of most of the powerful strategic ideas is easy to grasp. Segmentation, competence, positioning, basic finances, and so on can be made very complex or very simple—the alternatives are usually in the hands of the facilitator. The issue is to decide which ideas are most powerful, and what tools you want to leave in their hands. At GE, the relentless drive of Jack Welsh was not from fad to fad with the latest idea driving out the earlier one, but a steady accretion of tools[3] for making decisions. Some of the ideas you want to get across will be resisted, but if they are strategically important stick to your guns.

For example, positioning a business in the marketplace demands making decisions about which customer groups you want to focus on. Making selections is extremely important for the proper allocation of resources and to ensure that the image you want to project is clear and unambiguous. People hate dropping customers—after all, look at how much effort went into winning them in the first place—but focusing means paring down to a core of preferred customers. A firm which serves no one in particular is one heading to commoditization, probably the exact trap you are trying to get out of. In the world of competencies, people hate to recognize that they are not best in class. Special interest groups will see recognition of low competence as a step to outsourcing and try to divert or resist the logic by decrying the relevance of the ideas. They will wriggle and protest, but do not give in.

From Vision to Reality

Regardless of the specific structure of the vision, it needs to be translated into actions people can do. Once again there is a plethora of terms and approaches, but they all come down to something very simple. Take the vision and decide what the firm must do to achieve it and the items needed to achieve those competencies. The last 20 years have seen the intermediate step focus different ways. In the 1980s we focused on critical success factors, but by the end of the decade we were into critical success processes in reaction to the quality movement. Competence thinking came along, and people shifted to key competencies. Today the thinking is around key capabilities. The words change but the issue remains the same. Less mobile has been the shift to action, though many have been the discussions about what is a strategy. Definitions can help but in the end getting to the action statement is all that matters because this is where the game begins. All the planning in the world makes no sense if you don't lock it into performance. Actions need to be agreed upon, responsibilities assigned, and people genuinely held accountable as individuals or teams. The action program should drive compensation.

---

[3] Peter M. Senge, *The Dance of Change: The Challenges of Sustaining Momentum in Learning Organizations.* New York: Currency/Doubleday, 1999.

A Series of Workshops

All strategic alignment processes are workshop based. The purpose of the workshops is to discuss ideas and analyze the business. The number of participants in a workshop will vary. The early ones with the top team may have as few as 8 to 12, but as the team is broadened it may be 25 to 30 in a mid-sized firm. In very large firms, this first broadening may take you straight to a team of a couple of hundred. As you move to more mass involvement a common number is 70 to 80 in mid-sized firms and more in large ones. As the process rolls out, groups of 200 plus are not uncommon. Each time you move up a size the facilitation approach has to change from the very intimate to the more intricate.

Off-site locations are recommended. You want the participants to be totally concentrated on the issues. You will want to control phone calls, and make attendance absolutely mandatory—the only excuse is a death in the family. Whatever is discussed is confidential so that people will open up. The discussion stays in the room, everyone's opinion is equal and valued, and once decisions are made people stick by them. You must get a commitment to a series of meetings in advance, because it takes some time for a process like this to catch hold. Even worse, the group may think they have solved everything in one meeting.

Progressive Involvement

The early sessions will be for the CEO and the top team only as they grapple with the problems of the business, fill gaps in their own knowledge, and become comfortable with widening the process to involve others. The second series will involve a wider group with the top team at its core. Key potential members of the top team should be added. Mavericks, stars, and people with the power to stop things happening also need to be brought in. In the third expansion, a much wider group will be involved; each person will be selected because they are responsible for some key part of the organization or have particular insight. At the fourth stage, the program can either go on to progressively larger groups or it can be broken down into small group meetings by function, by market, or whatever makes sense based on your structure. Even very large meetings tend to break down internally into smaller groups from functions and other areas.

Role of the Top Team

The leadership team is central to this transformation. As in Larry's case the CEO's immediate top team can be extremely dysfunctional. In old firms, where people have known each other for years, there may be rivalries or hatreds that can profoundly affect the way the top team operates. That top management team may be turned over by a new CEO to introduce new blood, or it may go through a power struggle. Where only part of the top team is changed and a small number of new people are brought in there will be considerable tension between the old and the new guard. You have two options. You can ignore the tensions in the top team, treat them as normal, or where they are addressed treat them as human issues of teamwork rather than as strategic problems. Or these tensions can be seen as key strategic issues that have deep implications for the way the firm operates.

The solution in Larry's case was to use the alignment processes to force the top team to work through the business problems that faced them all, to develop a clear vision of where the firm had to go and the implications of that vision. As this vision is developed the implications for the firm are identified, and tensions are brought to the surface where they can be resolved. Not doing this lets them fester. This tension in the top team is one reason that many new CEOs replace existing executives with their own choices. This idea of having people who depend on you is as old as the hills, but it can often simplify getting the top team to work together. However, it doesn't always work, and personality conflicts can occur in the new team.

Confusion and a failure to align with the strategy by the top team will have devastating effects on the rest of the organization. Rivalries will prevent cooperation, the strategy will be decried or ignored, and those seeking power will attempt to widen the gaps. Solidarity in the top team is an absolute requirement if the firm is not to be partly or fully paralyzed. A top team that will not work together or align, if put into a broad alignment process, may face one of two situations:

1. The alignment process will fail as power struggles overwhelm it.

2. The top team will be shamed into acting properly by the reactions of the rest of the organization as the true strategic issues unfold.

It is difficult to decide which will occur, but in social interactions on this scale the top team may well be the nut in the nutcracker. The CEO with the big vision puts pressure on from above, and the people are applying pressure from below.

Broadening the Top Team

Most top teams containing the heads of the various functions and product groups are too narrow a selection for strategy formulation in an alignment process. The team needs to be widened to include key players inside functions and operations, some rising stars, and various mavericks who are prepared to speak their minds (and often say the unsayable). In practice, anyone who can effectively promote or stop the implementation of the strategy should be included.

Widening the group can be traumatic for the top team as they see it as a dilution of their power, and in a way it is. They may well resist broadening or insist that it is done politically correctly with representation from all quarters regardless of the individual's potential contribution. If faced with this kind of demand, resist to make the point, then give in. It is better to have more people than fewer, and the rest will eventually squeeze out those who cannot contribute. The selection of people to be part of this broadened strategy team has messages for the rest of the organization.

Those not selected may need to be reassured of their worth, and those selected not puffed up beyond their worth. The initial broadening of the top team should move it to a manageable number, say, no more than 30 in a for-profit firm. If the group gets too big the process of discussion becomes too long and complex. This is not to say that larger numbers cannot be successfully facilitated. Indeed, it is common in not-for-profits with their flat structures, and in extremely large organizations, for the numbers to be a lot bigger. However, larger numbers are more difficult to manage.

Widening Involvement

Further widening of involvement needs to follow the logic of the firm itself. In a firm with a strong functional structure, which is not intended to change, the subsequent layers of involvement should be within functional groups, with each function building its strategy in the context of that for the whole firm. In firms with cross-functional groups, say around markets, it is best to progressively involve using this structure. Mixed approaches can be made when people can be gathered together in the same place. They may look at the strategy first from a cross-functional and then from a functional viewpoint or any other variant. Natural work groups can be very powerful, where the people who need to work together meet to discuss the issues which affect them. When you are dealing with large numbers, say up to a thousand in a particular area, which usually means very large numbers of people each with narrow concerns, it is better to run advisory sessions. Here, people have their say, but there is much focus on strategy formulation and more on getting ideas out.

It is important to remember that the way strategy is evolved and the structure of the involvement will have profound effects in locking in organizational approaches. A functional structure may become more functionally rigid and a cross-functional structure more cooperative. There are all kinds of variants. The key is to ensure that everyone has a chance to be involved at some point. The biggest risk is that if the involvement is not done effectively, some people's voices will not be heard and they will feel that they are being manipulated.

Advisory Sessions

Overlaid on this basic expansion can be very large sessions or town meetings that are less oriented to capturing strategic issues than to bleeding out discontent, catching ideas, or dealing with organizational problems. The great advantage of such meetings is that they provide a separate set of forums for irritating local issues as, work hours, factory safety conditions, difficult personalities and conditions of employment. If these issues found their way into the strategy sessions they would derail the process.

Meeting Rhythm

The meetings are held in syncopation. The meetings of the top team, in its original form or broadened to include others, should be held about six weeks apart. Less than this and you haven't had enough "soak" time to think about problems. More and you have forgotten the issues. After the first round, these meetings may be held less frequently—say, once a quarter. The next big group (say, 80 or more) may meet together only two or three times. They should meet after the top team has come to some strong conclusions and when there is some real thinking to discuss. Such big meetings need to be fed a "strawman" proposal to knock about and not be asked to create something from scratch.

Smaller functional team meetings dealing with local detail can start after the first big group meeting as there will be enough agreement to drive their thinking and provide context. Big working sessions of 200 or more, processing the mass of the firm, will happen after there is enough agreement on content. The advisory meetings may be held fairly early as they are used to communicate inclusiveness and not to do strategy work.

Homework, Studies, and Pitches

Data can be collected between sessions and individuals or teams given assignments to come up with ideas. However, this can be very dangerous. All people in organizations are used to decision and pitch meetings, at which an idea that was worked up off-line is brought to the executive group for approval. Such sessions take on a ritual air, and little of substance is ever discussed as participants are already polarized between those for and those against the proposal. The essence of alignment workshops is open, free, and creative discussion, and to let it descend to pitches for ideas is a disaster.

Managing Discussion

The workshops are for group discussion of the issues of the business. The basic method is to understand an idea (probably delivered as a very short lecture/discussion), have a small group discussion (perhaps two to five small groups), then to come back, share ideas, and come to some overall plenary decision. This works. However, that said, there are lots of firms where the senior people cannot stand this approach. They despise the process and find it extremely uncomfortable—particularly if they are essentially action-driven Industrial Age people. The reality is that properly worked this approach is very fertile. If the executives get away from it they may drive straight back to the pitch and propose mode. Few new good ideas will appear and the opportunity for everyone to internalize the strategy will be lost. The only viable alternative is to use very strong facilitation in plenary groups. Achieving this demands a very strong facilitator who can bring some content to the session, otherwise the whole thing collapses into the writing of lists on flip charts.

The selection of facilitator is absolutely critical. A poor facilitator will walk you through the process. A contentless facilitator will write down your ideas with no knowledge of whether they are any good. However, a content-based facilitator, who will have a strong strategy background, can drive immeasurably further. Such individuals are hard to find, though most of the consulting houses have them and there are many in private practice. However, persist. If you can find one he or she will be a winner for you.

Genuine Openness

Strategic alignment processes may make major changes in the way the culture of a firm operates. In cultures already tending to openness, they can massively accelerate it, and (particularly if combined with information technology and collaborative tools) make the organization much more democratic. Secrecy and executive privilege based on it, tend to be destroyed. Rarely, however, will people demand a right to make every decision, but they will make their voices heard more. In cultures that have been fear driven, enclosed, rigid or secretive, strategic alignment processes can be used to open them up. However, do not expect a rapid drive to democracy. People will have been brainwashed in a specific direction, and they will be slow to change. Many may not wish to embrace the new freedom, particularly if it is accompanied by the need to show more initiative or by the threat of job loss. Strategic alignment processes are, by definition, open and not everyone loves them, particularly those who are control-oriented or autocratic by nature. If this is the case, a strategic alignment process used by such a person will be an attempt at manipulation and, hence, worse than doing nothing at all.

Timing of the Process

Every organization has a planning process, even if it is rudimentary and driven solely by the budget cycle. For example, every firm has a rhythm to its sales year, perhaps starting with getting going in January, spring planning, the summer doldrums when people are away on vacation, and the late year-end push looking for strong total revenues. You are often left with only two short periods when managements are willing or able to think strategically—the spring and the early fall. Any strategic alignment process needs to take this timing into account and run its sessions and data gathering with them in mind.

Give It Time

Involvement takes time, but the rewards are enormous in terms of alignment. These include the ability to allow dispersed decision making (now that people understand context), to tap into experience, and to dramatically speed up implementation. Properly done, it also yields performance measurement. All organizations have planning processes that take several months of elapsed time, and the time needed for involvement-based processes is no longer. Strategic alignment has a Japanese flavor, in that it focuses on getting understanding and agreement up front with the implication that the action program that follows will be undertaken much more quickly. This is, in fact, what happens. As we saw in Larry's case, a reduction of 50 percent in implementation time is not impossible or unusual. Plans are also implemented much more effectively.

CEO Comfort Level

No alignment process can succeed if the CEO is not prepared to do it. The reality is that many people who have fought their way to the top are nervous about opening up to the organization as a whole. They prefer to develop strategy and pass it down through the organization. Indeed, many think that is their job and that it is a sign of weakness to do things otherwise.

Other CEOs are totally comfortable with opening up to the organization. This can be particularly true when the CEO is new and can use the process to find out more about the business. Then it is acceptable to be ignorant. But the comfort level dealing with openness is a matter of personality and taste.

If a CEO decides to go ahead, there are some ground rules for effective management of the process.

- *Keep quiet*—in sessions, allow others to work on the issues. If the CEO continually tries to impose his or her ideas the people will pull back, and the process will be a farce. This can be very difficult for control-oriented CEOs.

- *Commit to a full process*—cutting it off part way through sends a message to the organization that this was never real and that their ideas were never wanted.

- *Reserve judgment*—those who are working through the issue may need time to come to reasonable conclusions. They will get there, but in the short run the full range of prejudices, silly ideas, brilliant thoughts, and impossible insights that may or may not work will come out. Cut off discussion too soon, and the people will never commit and the CEO will be back at square one.

- *Attend the sessions*—there is nothing more demoralizing than the CEO not turning up. Nothing really gets decided, people miss the opportunity to send key messages to the top, and the whole process is diminished. Strategic alignment takes time, and if the CEO cannot commit to being there, perhaps it should not be done.

Lock into Performance Appraisal

Once the strategic discussion is over, it is important to lock the results into the performance management system in a formal way. If this is not done the actions will be swept away by the pressure of day-to-day business and will not be implemented. The technique is very simple. Ensure that everyone has a summary of the output of the strategy session and that their role is clearly spelled out. You then need to check back regularly to make sure action is taking place.

One of the most effective ways to communicate the results of the strategy sessions is to capture them on a single sheet of paper. It is always more effective than thick volumes of material too daunting to read and the process of getting the ideas reduced to fit onto a single sheet forces clarity of language. Your facilitator should be able to do this. Similarly, time needs to be set aside on a regular basis at the top management level to assess where the firm is on its plan. It is absolutely certain that unless this step is taken little will happen.

Communication

You may wish to tack a communication program on the back of this process to keep the organization up-to-date with what is happening. However, remember that content will not "settle" for some time, and to communicate too early can leave you locked into solutions you may later wish to change. Moreover, in a true high-involvement process a lot of the communication is taken care of by the process itself. However, that said, there is a need to quieten fears, particularly in the early stages, and opportunities for speeches, departmental meetings, and casual conversation should be made to supplement more formal communications. If the firm has a communications department, it should be involved.

* * * * *

Strategic alignment processes are commonly used at breakpoints in a business's life, when the strategy needs to be revived and transformational change is necessary. Moreover, initial alignment is just that, initial. A firm needs ways of locking in the alignment permanently, so that continuous operational improvement and rapid small-scale change is possible.

Operational Engagement

Achieving ongoing engagement of large numbers of people over long time periods requires a significant change in culture in many organizations. Success requires high levels of business education, an ongoing commitment by management to involving their staffs (behavior which itself has to be locked in place), a willingness by employees to be involved, and a compensation scheme that supports involvement. Two examples will illustrate this—the renaissance at Sears and the open-book approach at R. R. Donnelley & Sons.

The Sears Story

case   When Arthur Martinez took the reins at Sears in 1992, the firm was in
need of a radical overhaul.[4] He succeeded brilliantly—in the short run.
He refocused the image on women ("the softer side of Sears"), created
new lines, shifted to specialty stores, closed others, and of course, most
spectacularly, he shut down that icon of American rural history, the
Sears catalog. Combine this with a re-engineering of the business,
shifts in store hours and staffing levels, and opening up to all credit
cards, and he set the stage for spectacular results in 1993 with a shareholder return of 56 percent!

But this work was the result of a narrow process of involvement.
Driven by a relatively small group from the top, it barely touched the
lives of the other 300,000 people working in the business except to
tap into their energy. Martinez realized this, and kicked off a process
of involving his senior management—initially 65 and later 150
plus—known as the Phoenix Team. The approach was classic: team
meetings with off-site homework, and task teams working on key
issues of customers, employees, finance, innovation, and values. The
task teams conducted research inside and outside the business, collecting ideas, benchmarking data, and doing surveys and setting up
focus groups of customers and employees. A vision was developed by
another task team, building a compelling image of what Sears wanted to be—a "compelling place to work, shop, and invest." The other
task forces delivered other parts of the puzzle. A values statement
emphasized "passion for the customer, our people [who] add value,
and performance leadership."

The goals were customer-centred: build customer loyalty, create a
fun place to shop, hire and retain the best employees, and offer the
right stuff at the right prices. The employee group decided on involving and empowering employees, so that they could realize their personal goals and develop skills and capabilities. Finally, the finance
group focused on margins, asset management, productivity, and revenues. All this was great stuff, and by involving the top players, it was
pretty well guaranteed that they would be committed to the output.
But in the end all those items were just wish lists. They needed to be
locked into the business and made real.

Total Performance Indicators were a key step along the way to
this reality. Shopping is an experience, and essentially an interaction
between the customer and the employee in the context of the store. TPI
provided the quantitative link between employee activity, such as

---

[4] Anthony J. Rucci, Steven P. Kirn, and Richard T. Quinn, "The Employee-Customer-
Profit Chain at Sears," *Harvard Business Review*, January-February 1998.

polite service, and financial returns. By hooking changes in such soft concepts as service to revenue increases and to value gains, TPI provided a scientific connection (the indicator was created by econometricians using heavy-duty statistical analysis), which verified intuitive ideas (good service creates loyalty), and provided guidance for the investment of time and dollars. TPI, the vision, and other work had produced high alignment in the top management team. By 1995 the problem was how to involve and build commitment in the 300,000 employees, some 70 percent of whom were part-timers. Moreover, half the people showed little understanding of the financial structure and dynamics of the business or industry. They completely misjudged the returns in the business, assuming that Sears kept 45 cents out of every dollar that went into the till, when the reality was two cents. Sears embarked on a major program of education and involvement by holding town hall meetings that used a tool called Learning Maps.[5]

A Learning Map is quite literally a cartoon-like drawing depicting a set of complex ideas, such as the changes affecting the retail business (shown as a journey over many years with stops and incidents along the way), and later how a firm like Sears makes money. The aim is a mass raising of understanding of how the business works. The idea of linking that to town hall meetings so that action plans could be developed directly out of the learning was original to Sears. The maps and meetings are still used throughout the firm from top to bottom for structured discussions led by managers. In these meetings they search for practical solutions and ideas to improve the business. The approach is perpetual and part of an ongoing process of engagement with employees. There is really no reason ever to stop them. The issues in the business are constantly evolving, new people are constantly joining. TPI, town hall meetings, management involvement, all drive alignment into the business, and because of the heightened awareness, lower the barriers to continuous transformation.

Sears, leadership was a key component of the change. Making sure that they were aligned was very important. In 1995 Sears started development of a leadership model that covered all the parts of the transformation. This model, which listed 12 key leadership skills, became the basis for promotion, and when linked to 360-degree assessment was the basis for leadership improvement. Sears University, in Chicago, has put through over 40,000 leaders, pressing home these ideas, and raising awareness of the transformational issues facing the retail industry, again smoothing the way for more and more change. Finally, for the top 200 leaders in Sears, rewards are

---

[5] Learning Maps is a trademarked service of Root Learning, Perrysburg, Ohio.

based on the TPI, so that long-term executive incentives are based on nonfinancial as well as financial performance, a concept that has been pushed down to managers through the organization.

Sears has used a number of strong tools—involvement, performance measures, education, incentive compensation, and performance appraisal—in imaginative ways to lock in the gains from the initial transformation and alignment. The change problems were there—getting people to take things seriously, to lower the sense of threat while demanding more from people. Of course, Sears was helped by the fact that the crisis it had just been through was still fresh in people's minds, but the degree to which they have embedded alignment has been impressive. They are not alone.

R. R. Donnelley & Sons

case   R. R. Donnelley & Sons, America's largest commercial printer, instituted an open-book policy in 1995.[6] Open-book thinking promotes the idea of sharing all financial information with the employees, and the heart of such a program is a scorecard that shows how the firm is progressing. The scoreboard used by R.R. Donnelley & Sons is based on shareholder value creation and allows individual value-creating activities. The scoreboard is distributed every month by e-mail and supplemented by scoreboards created for individual departments. But Donnelley has gone beyond passing out results and expecting specific improvements to involvement of employees at every level in the annual budgeting cycle.

Donnelley's approach is based on pioneering work at Springfield ReManufacturing Corporation (SRC), the role model for open-book thinking. SRC's top leadership creates the strategic priorities, and sales staff the sales forecasts, then employees are involved in translating those into income statements, budgets, and the whole paraphernalia of financial projection. Where necessary they do research and look for cost and other solutions. Through this approach everyone starts to get a real feel for the numbers. During the year they meet regularly to assess performance against plan and to project the next few weeks. This information is passed up and down the company so everyone who wishes to be informed is.

Donnelley launched this in 1996 and used it to spread accountability for financial results through the business, which is a major challenge in any management system. A well-designed reward system helps. In this open-book world, rewards are directly pegged to

---

[6] John Case, "Opening the Books," *Harvard Business Review*, March-April 1997.

numbers employees see on their scoreboard and which they understand intimately. Bonuses can be significant—for example, Amoco Canada pays out 16 percent of earnings in employee bonuses. As in the Donnelley example, alignment is locked in by economic literacy, involvement in the standard processes of the company, and a well-designed compensation program.

* * * * *

Spiritual Engagement

Taking an organization through a crisis and achieving strategic alignment, and getting people committed to ongoing improvement are familiar managerial problems. The techniques many have behavioral opportunities and pitfalls, but they are, at the last, processes. Getting spiritual engagement is very different. This is an area of human unity that it is difficult to be objective about. It has emotional and religious overtones, ranging from the furthest-out New Age thinking, to religious proselytizing, from California to the Bible Belt. It sounds like eminent sense to some and totally flakiness to others. Some claim that it is so facilitator-dependent as to be almost cultlike; others say it can be taught to anyone open to possibilities. There are those who swear by it and those who will not even read the next section. However, wherever you stand on the spectrum, the test is the same—does it work? Only you can judge and only if you try it.

The best way into the story of spirituality in business is through a fairly common experience many have had.

They were a really tough group. Forty-two IBM leaders in a room ostensibly to develop a strategic direction for their division. Forty-two independent-minded individuals each used to running his or her own shop with little or no interference from the center. Forty-two people who were not going to give an inch and had the axes of history to grind, preferably on someone else. Forty-two people not renowned for their creativity, faced with the need to do something different, which none of them wanted to acknowledge. Eight hours later, 42 pussy cats, claws sheathed, left happy and laughing, having given up most of their independence to the center in a new, creative solution, and feeling as if they had struck a good deal—for everyone.

The session had been tough, and no magic had been planned, just plain facilitation of some simple strategic ideas. But magic had happened. Asked afterward to pin down why the sea change occurred, the division president couldn't, likening the experience to trying to describe the taste of strawberries—impossible. Nor could anyone else. But what everyone observed was that by the early afternoon everything seemed different. Agreement overtook discord, alignment came out of nowhere, and minds seemed to move onto the same wavelength.

The group was never the same again. The meeting entered folklore and those who were there recalled it vividly. Once created, alignment became frayed by the usages of time but never went away. The sense of common purpose remained. The creativity of the solution proved to be real. Afterward, still no one could describe the taste of strawberries!

There could be rational explanations. The division president could have been a charismatic figure who gave a rousing speech to the assembled multitude and swept them along. He wasn't, and he didn't. The group could have been under threat of imminent destruction and pulled together for the common good. They weren't. Someone could have appealed to their sense of loyalty, support for the firm, love of the greater good. No one did. They could have become caught up in some common hysteria when someone had a great "aha." No one did and they weren't. The solution simply emerged.

This could have been one of those freak events—the session from heaven, which was bound to happen sometime. But that doesn't alter the fact that it happened and that it was not a unique event. Most facilitators who have been around a while have had this experience to some degree. It was the session from hell that simply turned around.

So where did the creativity come from and how did the alignment appear? Could the experience be repeated? Enough rational people believe it can be for several consulting firms of high repute to offer services in this area.

Group Commitment, Transcending Self

Transcendence of self is at the heart of forming a spiritual connection with others and is a staple of most religious practice. The transcendent individual who has become one with their God/the Universe is a staple of many religious experiences. Saints, shamans, mystics, psychics, and gurus all exemplify some out-of-this-world experience in which they pass beyond the mundane to a transcendent state. This manifests itself in deep conviction to the point of martyrdom, or an ability to predict the future, perform acts of impossible strength or endurance, or simply to see into the souls of others.

This transcendence in enlightened individuals is proven. People can put themselves into trance-like states through meditation, prayer, or drugs. They do remarkable things well beyond the capacity of mere flesh and blood. Somehow, from somewhere, they are receiving a source of psychic energy denied the rest of us. Indeed, our modern rationality would tend to shy away or reject it.

If transcendence of self can be observed in the mystics it can also be found in the common man or woman. What is esprit de corps, but a willingness to put the group—such as the military regiment—ahead of self? Self-sacrifice is, indeed, the ultimate expression of the greater good transcending the self-interest of the individual. Patriotism, love of school, friends, family—the idea of people putting the needs of others and the group ahead of themselves is a staple of fiction that has its roots in real life. Even the dismal science—economics—has a flourishing literature in the economics of altruism.

To explain all this do you have to believe in God? Is this simply the God-squad promising something to business as a means of proselytizing on behalf or religion? Perhaps, but although many of the practitioners in this area are religious practitioners of different faiths, faith in a god is not a necessary condition.

Creating Commitment to a Group

There is no fully defined methodology for achieving states of connection with others and a group, but there are four approaches that point to ways into the field:

- Processing Intention
- Sharing Common Experience
- Engaging the Heart
- Channeling Energy

Processing Intention

This is the mundane approach to getting individuals to commit to a group endeavor, based on the idea of linking an intention to do something with your own best interest. The formation of an intention is the starting point for every creative activity whether as a group or as an individual. The path between intention and action seems to have a distinct pattern of increasing commitment. The original intention has first to be accepted intellectually as feasible, as personally satisfying, and instinctively right. Only then will the rational mind allow our emotions to be engaged. Once the mind has finished its due diligence, we can engage our emotions, which provide the thrust behind the physical manifestation of the idea.

Let's take an actual example. The intention to write this book was formed some years ago, while working with clients struggling to get change to happen. However, writing a book is a hard grind, so the idea could have stayed in the realm of intention forever—like most people's intention to get fit or become fluent in a foreign language. The fact that it broke through to a real book was partly because the idea of becoming an author touches something inside—in change parlance there is "something in it for me." Personally, it may meet a need to communicate one's experiences—whether others wanted to listen or not! Intellectually, it may allow one to promote certain ideas that could have business value. Having tested the idea and talked about it with friends and family one starts to become emotionally engaged—a level of commitment that is vital to completion.

The same process happens with groups of people. An idea is mooted and an intention is formed but nothing happens as it cannot provide the WIFM (What's in it for me) at any mental or personal level to the participants. This may not prevent the leadership trying to move the idea forward through compulsion or calls on people's emotions but the cogs are not meshed and the idea will collapse under its own weight.

We have all seen this happen. Every vision and mission statement that ever was simply posted on the bulletin board falls into this category. People are not engaged, they do not relate, and they cannot raise the requisite emotion to move forward. Indeed, cynicism and skepticism usually fill the void in their emotions. It is this need to engage emotional energy that underlies all the recommendations to involve people in strategic thinking and change activities. Only by processing the intention can they find the emotional connection.

From a process point of view, the shift from formation of intention through personal, intellectual, and instinctive acceptance to the engagement of emotion is straightforward. It can be satisfied by fully and genuinely engaging people in the formation of the original intention, by providing them with the opportunity and time to absorb the intention mentally, and then helping them commit emotionally. Many such processes finish with commitment ceremonies where people "swear" to the idea, but skipping from intention to commitment will not work. When next you see a poster on a wall covered with signatures showing "our commitment to quality," ask yourself about the process that went behind the signature.

Achieving mental buy-in takes time, particularly for groups. Fast, single-session meetings to find solutions to complex business problems such as strategy formulation almost never stick. People require "soak time" to process intentions, bounce them off others, and to bring those others along. Give them the time to own the intention, and you will see very fast implementation. The classic of this kind of intention-to-creation cycle is the Japanese socializing of ideas, but it can exist in any organization, and it can be speeded up. Experience builds on experience. The more people are involved, the more they understand, the more committed they are—the effect is cumulative. The result is a culture that has sufficient shared goals to allow people to process new intentions more quickly. The speed this brings to action is the competitive advantage of culture.

Sharing Common Experience

Conventional team building approaches can forge an underlying trust and the basis for individuals committing to a group. Going on Outward Bound programs and living under hazardous conditions which force reliance can drive connections at a human level that assist in resolving problems in the business environment.

A major accounting firm in New Zealand takes all its recently qualified accountants and puts them through an ordeal together. The group is taken at the dead of a moonless night to a rugged, rocky wilderness area of dense forest with rushing streams. They are left there to find their way to a specific point on the other side of the forest. The path is absolutely dark and simply entering the forest takes courage. Getting through the test requires teamwork as the members encounter all kinds of obstacles. This rite of passage into the firm is intended to drive home the interdependence of team members—an experience that they will refer to for the rest of their lives.

Engaging the Heart

There are several pieces to this concept. The idea the practitioners tout that the heart is the seat of the spirit is old—indeed venerable in literature and religion. The association of love with that organ is a staple image of our culture, based mainly on the heart's physical reactions to emotion. At a physical level, the heart apparently directly affects the waves of the brain; if one is reactive, only lower brain function occurs. We are assured by those committed to this thinking that if the heart and brain are entrained, coherent brainwaves are generated leading to peak performance.

By linking together cultural beliefs and the claimed physical evidence, practitioners come up with the thought that by focusing on the heart as the actual or symbolic center of spirit and emotion we can bring focus to our minds and open ourselves to ideas and the forming of intentions. Techniques such as meditation and yoga are inner self-management techniques aimed at producing a balanced mental and emotional state that allows the individual to access a wider and more objective perception in the moment—the perpetual present.

The method is, at its most minimal, a stress-reduction technique in which negative emotions are consciously shifted from the mind to the "heart" through visualization, and the heart beat is used as a meditation metronome. Once the mind has started to settle, positive feelings are recalled, and the heart is asked for a solution to the stressful situation. The process clears an emotional space where solutions can come through.

The technique is focused on individuals but it can also be done in groups where many claim that it does create commitment.

Channeling Energy

This is the only one of the four methods for creating commitment that has a direct spiritual link. Diane Houston was the leader of a dysfunctional group in a global communications firm. The difficulties the group had working together had prevented them from realizing the synergies that were possible. This was because the issues required significant participation not only in designing goals, objectives, and strategies, but also in the effective cascading of the objectives to front-line staff. The dysfunctionality blocked all that. Working with a deeply committed facilitator, in the course of one meeting the group moved to common goals and strategies with effective roll-out, and the team was operating as one. The output was remarkable. Not only were all the work objectives achieved, but Diane's division displayed the highest employee satisfaction ratings in the global organization that year. The team has been working together for a year and a half, and there is no sign of the old dysfunctionality.

We are all familiar with the phenomenon of psychics. Indeed, so familiar are we that consulting them has become big business. The idea of someone or something who can channel the energy of the universe and "see" into the future either directly or through the agency of some tool such as the ancient Chinese text the *I Ching* is well accepted by a large part of the general population. Even without scientific proof there is sufficient anecdotal evidence for many to believe that there are individuals who possess such hypersensitivity that they can function in this capacity. This hypersensitivity or higher state of consciousness may come naturally or may be developed deliberately.

Typically, such people describe their role as acting as a channel for energy which they often believe has a divine source. They can "see" energy patterns in groups of people, both positive and negative, and sense the human and environmental emotions which are the generators of such energy. These psychics can apparently sense things that they had never been told about and that they could not have otherwise known.

Groups who work with such facilitators start out conventionally by laying out the issues as they see them and reaching some kind of agreement on the problem—a clear intention. As the problem is apparently unsolvable at the level of consciousness the group is working on, the facilitator takes over calling for (divine) guidance. The energy to "see" a solution, we are told, flows through the facilitator and realigns the group energy patterns. The result is that the group moves to a conclusion.

For this to be successful the group must be open and trusting of the process. If they are resistant it simply will not work. Nor will it work if the group has other motives that will confuse the message being received by the facilitator. Moreover, it is crucial that the project is seeking honestly to do its best for everyone involved. This has nothing to do with how "divine" the project is—increasing profitability is fine—but a lot to do with how "rightful" (morally correct) the project is. Finally, the intention must be clear; in *I Ching* terms the question must be carefully thought out.

For the believer in such approaches the outcome is the result of the channeling of energy; for the skeptic it is the result of the clarifying of the intention or question. The arguments for the divine help lie mainly in the psychic capabilities of the facilitator who will commonly show levels of awareness that (it is believed) could not have been achieved any other way.

The Taste of Strawberries

Group alignment can be achieved in different ways from clever process design, through experiences, to clearing mindspace, and channeling energy. However, only the use of enlightened individuals to channel energy has the true, transcendent, spiritual aspect. The mysterious alchemy created by the facilitator shifts how groups look and feel almost instantly. Is the taste of this particular strawberry for everyone? No. Nor was EST or any other of the "Californian" approaches popular in the 70s and 80s. But does it have a place in the pantheon of effective approaches? Most definitely if only because it seems to work in a pragmatic business world that is the only true test.

* * * * *

Consulting experience using alignment techniques indicates that it tends to be restricted to leaders with a belief in transformation through people; who believe that there is nothing more important than getting close to the employees, leaning on their insights, selecting and developing them, and managing them through change. Research[7] indicates that this is about 37 percent of leaders. Of the other leadership types, some may use it spontaneously but are less likely to use alignment techniques. Those obsessed by strategy tend to be too sure of their own insights to use alignment techniques. The experts with their focus on the technical aspects of the business may not even think about it, and those heavily into control and procedure are largely unwilling to take on the risk of opening up to the organization with the resulting chaos that they then see. In these latter cases the tendency is to develop a direction and communicate it. The fact that they fail to communicate and certainly fail to connect with the people is lost on them. This does not mean that all is hopeless. There are other alignment approaches, notably the alignment achieved through enrolling leaders and the forced alignment of value drivers imposed through budgets discussed elsewhere. But for those e-leaders who cannot, emotionally, trust the high-involvement process, the door to intense commitment is firmly closed.

[7] C.M. Farkas and S. Wetlaufer, "The Ways Chief Executive Officers Lead," *Harvard Business Review*, May-June 1996, 110-112; see also C.M. Farkas and P. De Backer, *Maximum Leadership: The World's Leading CEOs Share their Five Strategies for Success*, New York: Henry Holt, 1996.

Harness People's Experience

The obverse of leadership is followership. Inspiring followers and harnessing their skills, experience, and emotional energy are the essence of leadership. Harnessing psychic energy is relatively easy in the midst of a crisis where there is clearly a shared problem and people look to the leader to lead and unify behind him or her. However, outside times of crisis, how does an e-leader encourage people to bring their experience to the table on a continuing basis? Finding an answer for your organization to this leadership question will be central to its survival in the e-world. The globalizing, converging, innovating, e-business-dominated e-world will demand rapid, continuous adjustment, punctuated by periods of euphoria and crisis. Having the mass of people in the organization willing, ready, and able to contribute to continuous transformation will be a major competitive advantage. The penalty of failure is, at the least, under performance—at the most, it is extinction.

If we look at the history of great, household-name firms that went into decline—IBM, Sears, Kodak, Xerox, Westinghouse, Massey-Ferguson, Daimler-Benz, even such institutions as the Eaton's and Marks & Spencer department stores in Canada and the UK (Eaton's, a 100-year-old Canadian retail institution, went bankrupt as this book was being written)—the problem at root was the same. Through a mixture of leadership hubris, lack of openness to stimulation, an inability to process their own experience, and often excessive focus on today's profit, the previously magnificent, thought-leading firms had lost the ability to learn and react to that learning, thus accelerating the damage competitors had started. All these firms had full knowledge of what was happening in the market; nothing stopped the spread of ideas, but their culture and the way their leadership thought stopped the transformation of knowledge into action.

Tapping people's experience to transform is not a new idea. Tom Watson, the founder of the modern IBM, had the THINK tag line decades ago, and he did not just mean the top management. Argyris and Schon[1] provided theoretical groundwork by distinguishing between solving today's problems and focusing on how problems were solved—the former making today better, the latter changing the way the business thought permanently. Peter Senge's *The Fifth Discipline*,[2] put flesh on the concept of learning organizations. In 1990, Senge's insights hovered between the idealistic and the apparently obvious, with only the broadest thinking about how to make them real. He and others talked in reverential terms about the release of human potential and gave learning an air of mysticism. His list of insights—systems thinking, personal mastery, mental models, shared vision, and team learning—was the first of many such lists to appear in the next decade. Today we have much more experience with what it means to have a learning organization, with a literature building describing specific success stories, but we still do not have a comprehensive theory.

It could even be argued that the term "learning organization" has contributed to that lack of comprehensive theory on how to harness experience, by linking the new idea of organizational learning with the old world of training. There is a strong element of training in the learning organization, but at heart it is not a training problem but a leadership problem for two simple reasons. First, learning is a social activity. Whether you are learning in class, through face-to-face discussion, reading books, or watching videos, you are interacting directly or indirectly with other people and their ideas. People learn from people. Indeed, as R. D. Laing[3] noted, people define the circle

---

[1] C. Argyris and C. Shon, *Organizational Learning: A Theory of Action Perspective*. Reading, MA: Addison-Wesley, 1978.

[2] Peter M. Senge, *The Fifth Discipline: The Art and Practice of the Learning Organization*. New York: Doubleday, 1990.

[3] R. D. Laing, *The Politics of Experience and the Bird of Paradise*. Harmondsworth, Middlesex, UK: Penguin Books, 1967.

of their lives by the tangents of their interactions with others. It follows then that anything that encourages interaction between people encourages the spread of knowledge and ideas and, so, learning. Anything that reduces that interaction dams the spread of thought and reduces the potential to learn. Leaders who preside over highly controlled, heavily hierarchical, deeply structured businesses with intensely applied measures and rules dampen interaction. Those who build networked, collegial, open, low hierarchy businesses where information and ideas flow freely stimulate interaction and learning. This has nothing to do with training. Indeed, this idea has been captured in the concept of the boundaryless organization where great effort is made to break down walls inside and outside the business. Part of the brilliance of Jack Welch of GE was recognizing this need and driving toward solving it over decades.

Second, in business and the world of organizations, learning that is not translated into action is irrelevant—"academic" in the business-pejorative sense. This is reflected in David Garvin's definition of a learning organization as one "skilled at creating, acquiring and transferring knowledge and at modifying its behavior to reflect new knowledge and insights."[4] Pushing for action is an executive task not a training one. This is not to say that training is not important. People who lack the intellectual tools to think cannot contribute effectively, but it does say that harnessing the experience of the people is a leadership challenge of making people ready, willing, and able to contribute, and it cannot be delegated.

This chapter is about how e-leaders can create organizations in which people can contribute their experience. This is a big subject and for convenience the chapter is divided into two parts. First we look at the leadership challenge of creating an organization conducive to harnessing experience.

• The Leadership Challenge

Then, we pick up a specific aspect of that challenge, encouraging people to a deep understanding of the business, and how that can be done through electronic games:

• The E-Game Frontier

---

[4] David A. Garvin, "Building a Learning Organization," *Harvard Business Review*, July-August 1993. p. 80.

The Leadership Challenge

"The top management team must stimulate the organization, not control it. Its role is to provide strategic directives, to encourage learning, and to make sure there are mechanisms for transferring the lessons. The role of leaders at all levels is to demonstrate to people that they are capable of achieving more than they think they can achieve and that they should never be satisfied with where they are now. To change behavior and unleash new ways of thinking, a leader sometimes has to say, 'Stop, you're not allowed to do it the old way,' and issue a challenge."[5]

The leadership challenge breaks into three parts:

- Creating the *Willingness* to Contribute
- Getting People *Ready* to Contribute
- Making People *Able* to Contribute

Creating the *Willingness* to Contribute

The willingness to contribute has to come from inside people. You cannot, over the long term, force them to contribute; they will only do it if there is emotional, psychic, or financial advantage to them. The leadership solution is threefold:

- Develop a Shared Sense of Destiny or Vision
- Enroll People's Hearts and Minds
- Provoke an Inner Urge to Improve

Develop a Sense of Shared Destiny or Vision

A shared vision is central to giving people a sense of a shared destiny. Without it there is no focus, indeed a lack of vision is harmful; if you don't know where you are going, don't be surprised if there are any number of opinions on how to get there. Sharing a destiny gives focus to people, helping them understand where and how to apply their experience and contribution. The leadership problem, of course, is how to get people to buy into a shared destiny.

---

[5] John Browne, head of British Petroleum, quoted in Steven E. Prokesh, "Unleashing the Power of Learning: An Interview with British Petroleum's John Browne," *Harvard Business Review*, September-October 1997. 158.

The classic problem of any vision is how to communicate it in ways that will make people want to implement it. Simply posting the vision statement on a bulletin board will not do it, though in these enlightened times it is still a source of amazement how many managements think this is enough. A number of ways of passing on a vision and developing a sense of common purpose are mentioned in this book, including strategic alignment processes with high levels of genuine involvement. This kind of approach engages people at an intellectual level and gives each one the feeling he or she has had a hand in the development of the vision, thereby creating commitment. However, after the vision has been created it still needs to be kept fresh and alive and elaborated in the hurly-burly of business life.

This is the logic behind the "Teachable Point of View" (TPV) and the idea of the leader as teacher as promoted by Noel Tichy.[6] In Tichy's world, every leader in the organization has internalized his or her own version of the vision, values, and strategy of the business. He or she is then expected to share that understanding with others. This multiplies the number of people promoting the business's direction many times and helps to communicate the vision in a direct and personal way not possible with more traditional media. This is made the more so when one understands Tichy's definition of leaders includes a much broader spectrum than the official management. Tichy's perspective was developed when working with Jack Welch of GE, who spent mythic amounts of time talking to his managers and employees, personifying the vision, and humanizing it, thereby making it more believable as an aspiration.

No matter how you create the vision, whether it is a huge stretch or something more modest, the vision problem rests with top management. Top teams which create visions then simply throw them over the wall to the organization or undercut them by public disagreement will never develop a shared destiny in their business. People will still come to work every day, but the lack of clarity and focus will make it more difficult for them to contribute.

Enroll People's Hearts and Minds

We have all met leaders we instinctively want to follow, their charisma becoming part of our own definition of leadership for good or ill.

---

[6] Noel M. Tichy and Eli B. Cohen, *The Leadership Engine: How Winning Companies Build Leaders at Every Level*. New York: Harper Business, 1997.

Charismatic leaders able to enroll people's hearts and minds are rare in business. Roger O. Goldman of National Westminster is one of these.[7] The vast majority of CEOs enroll people through deliberate approaches at involvement.

The secret to enrolling people is to involve them. What we help invent we own. It follows then that if you wish to enroll the whole organization, you have to involve everyone. We talked about vision creation processes above that are classics of this kind. Open-book management, the US Army approach to shifting behavior, the Sears, BP, and Shell major revitalization programs all sought to touch large numbers of people and engage their minds and emotions in thinking about the business. However, mass involvement can meet mass resistance to learning and the change activities it implies. Richard Pascale[8] reports a particularly interesting example of one man's determination to combat corporate drift by involving people in confronting their self-imposed limitations, which were preventing them from learning about and evolving the business.

Chris Knight was a three-tour expatriate when he came back to Shell Malaysia as chairman. He found a bloated, declining business in disarray facing aggressive competition. Although the firm was drifting and losing share to younger, more aggressive competitors Shell Malaysia was resistant to change. Complaisant in its position as the largest oil company, ultraconservative, and determined not to disturb the market, it led an oligopoly, which felt comfortable and safe—the perfect conditions for low learning.

case   For a year Knight tried to get his top team aligned—and failed. So he opted to try a different tack. He invited all 260 of Shell's managers to an event and involved them in a discussion of two major strategic proposals, which in Shell's terms were audacious. Also discussed was how the state of the organization was likely to affect the proposals. The dynamic of the meeting was a classic "nutcracker" on the top team. A substantial body of the middle and lower management started to form around the chairman with his vision so that the top team holdouts were caught in the middle—like the nut in the nutcracker—between an organizational groundswell and the chairman's resolve. One of the top team vented his disagreement, and two days later Knight fired

---

[7] Warner Burke, William Trahant with Richard Koonce, *Business Climate Shifts: Profiles of Change Makers*. Woburn, MA: Butterworth Heinemann, 1999.
[8] Richard Pascale, Mark Milleman, and Linda Gioja, "Changes in the Way We Change," *Harvard Business Review*, November–December 1997.

him, not for saying what was on his mind, but for not raising the issues earlier when there had been lots of opportunity. The shooting of this admiral was heard around, if not the world, certainly all of Shell Malaysia, and acted as a catalyst for Knight's ambitions.

The game was not over, but the door to change had been opened. Knight's next step was to force change through the rest of the organization by a ploy that had been used in Ford. He organized a series of one-day meetings at which salaried and hourly employees in small cross-functional groups worked on another controversial set of initiatives. Rivalry and bad blood would traditionally have stymied these. The technique he used involved teams from different functions exchanging notes—called "valentines"—which outlined their grievances against each other. The recipients then had to work out how they would resolve those problems, define an action plan, and choose a partner from the complaining team to work with them. In a plenary session the committed partners negotiated a solution in front of everyone, and in the process, all the distrust was aired and made explicit.

Involvement and alignment reversed Shell Malaysia's drift and opened it up to learning and further change. Enrolling people's hearts and minds is open to everyone. Complaisance closes the organization to learning about itself and about the business with direct business results of lower productivity and returns.

Provoke an Inner Urge to Improve

People will improve the business and apply their experience if you reward them for it. Children will keep their rooms clean if forced or bribed, but how much better if they do it because they want to, driven by an inner urge to improve. Provoking this urge is a leadership challenge.

Henry Mintzberg,[9] professor in strategy at McGill University in Montreal and author of numerous standard texts and articles on strategy and management, uses the image of a potter when describing this urge. The observation is that every pot the potter throws is an end in itself, but also a learning step to the next pot. The potter is always improving his or her craft—an image of continuous learning. The craftsperson image is accurate and seems to stand up in cultures such as Japan and Germany with intense craft backgrounds. It resonates less well in Anglo-Saxon cultures.

[9] Henry Mintzberg, *Mintzberg on Management: Inside Our Strange World of Organizations*. New York: Free Press, 1989; Henry Mintzberg, *The Rise and Fall of Strategic Planning: Reconceiving Roles for Planning, Plans, Planners*. New York: Free Press, 1994.

One way is to expose the organization to stimuli from the outside. Benchmarking, best practice, customer complaints, and indepth customer satisfaction analysis, particularly if built into the performance contract, can break the inherent tendency of organizations to look inward and provide the stimulus to action. However, that is not enough. If Toyota had used benchmarks as the sole approach to stimulating the evolution of its lean production methods, it would have failed or stopped early. This is the reality of pioneers—there is no one to push you forward except the pressure of your own vision. Generating this "oomph" is relatively easy in the context of a start-up. These are inherently exciting and the potential of personal riches can keep people there the 24 hours a day that is often necessary. But maintaining this excitement is much more difficult in large established businesses. This is one reason why continuous improvement programs fail to keep going. The glamour goes out of them as the goals are achieved.

The winners in the world of continuous improvement make many minor improvements which add up to a major gain to the bottom line. Gavin[10] quotes GE at 4 percent per annum cost reduction over several years and Allegheny Ludlum at 7 to 8 percent per annum. These gains are there for everyone to garner. The problem is that firms get bored or their culture gets in the way. There are few big wins and little glory in continuous improvement. Take the case of a major engineering company that had been racked by big projects for years, few, if any, making a huge difference to its underlying cost base. A new divisional president diagnosed the problem as the need for a multitude of minor improvements and got the organization started on a continuous improvement program. The whole concept collapsed in the face of organizational indifference and resistance. There was no glory for anyone in the proposal, and although no one ever outright refused, no one supported the activity either. They always seemed to find more exciting things to do. The leader left for pastures new, where she was hugely successful with the same strategy.

The key is to find a way to engage people in transforming their experience of the minutiae of the operation into cost savings. The starting point is that no one will do it unless his or her efforts are rewarded. Tying bonus systems into improvements in key performance indicators is a solution of this type. People will also not do it for control-oriented managers or where hierarchy crushes making an

---

[10] David A. Garvin, "Building a Learning Organization," *Harvard Business Review*, July-August 1993.

improvement. But what firms like Sears and other that have moved to open-book management have discovered is that basic business literacy is also crucial. Understanding the financial structure of the business and its underlying operational strategy helps people see improvements more easily. What does not seem to work as well as one would think is stock options. They work for top management, giving people a warm sense of ownership, but they are too far removed from the little things people can do and too much influenced by external events to encourage continuous improvement.

Other solutions include the power of leadership. Perhaps the power of a Jack Welch has been as much his ability to keep shifting the goal posts of vision and then to put in the personal time to drive it as it has any particular goal which has been set. Systems that have people drive specific indicators and receive significant and immediate bonuses are another approach, as is the playing of games. A team or number of teams are challenged to find an innovative solution to a real operational problem, sometimes alone, but most often in competition. The winning team receives a reward. The rewards from the game are small financially but large psychologically being the satisfaction of winning and are referred to as "pinballs," because the reward is getting to play again!

Getting People *Ready* to Contribute

People will not contribute their two-cents worth if they believe it will put them at personal risk. Why should they? The leadership task is to create an organizational gestalt where people feel their contribution is welcomed and it is safe to make it. There are four key actions:

- Build Leaders Who Do Not Stifle Initiative
- Build a Collaborative Environment
- Make It Safe for People to Learn from Failure
- Indulge in Open, Honest, and Straight Discussion

Build Leaders Who Do Not Stifle Initiative

The e-world of involved organizations, responding to fast-moving markets with continuous adaptation and transformation, is a chaotic one for control freaks. But, letting go is the only way of getting people to process their experience, learn, and act. Like bringing up children, the more you try to control them the more they resist you, take their resentments underground, and tune out. The aim is to provide a framework, help them find their own destination, and facilitate their getting there. And, just like helping teenagers find their feet and learn to become adults, the experience is both terrifying and exhilarating. Learning to let go is very, very difficult, and the mantra that the more you let go the more control you have, seems ridiculous. However, that is exactly what needs to be done. When the US Army teaches its masses of soldiers to take the initiative in war situations, the officers have to let it happen. This is particularly true in elite commando units, whose members must be able to act alone as well as in a group; can you imagine a member of Britain's renowned SAS sitting on his hands in a combat situation just because he had been separated from his officer? Would a Navy Seal?

case   Letting go of the hierarchy can be personally traumatic. The leader of a laboratory in a major manufacturing company was convinced that the intense control orientation of the product development process was a competitive disadvantage.[11] His aim was to break down its rigidity and to encourage people to greater creativity, to take more responsibility for their work, and to exercise initiative. He suspected that part of the smothering of ideas and initiative came from the heavy managerial load projects tended to carry. This existed because of the internal structure and traditions of the firm at that time; only an officially titled manager could approve work and carry it forward into the decision process. The idea that a deeply experienced professional, who actually wrote code and probably was the only one who understood it, could also carry it forward and recommend acceptance was "not on." It followed from this that a lot of managers were needed to fulfill the obligations of the decision process—even though they added no value to the product itself.

Recognizing that projects were overmanaged and that the managerial load soaked up dollars, the laboratory manager cut the management of a major project from thirteen to five as an experiment. The five recognized that they could not possibly impose traditional control on the 175 people working on the project. Almost immediately, they started to act like a single unit—a team, supporting each other in the leadership process, not trying to second-guess the experts and enrolling those experts as team leaders without titles. The professional expert was expected to meet with people from other plants and defend and

---

[11] Gerald Ross and Michael Kay, *Toppling the Pyramids*. New York: Times Books, 1994.

recommend his or her team's work. When managers from other plants not part of the project refused to meet with the professionals, the rule was to wheel in the nearest manager who would simply sign off and leave—whether he understood what he was signing or not. The new approach worked very well. Leaders led and professionals stood behind their work.

There was one exception. The manager with the most experience could not believe that this seemingly incoherent approach could possibly work. He was not prepared to trust his career and his project to others who were not part of the management structure. He also believed that without managers riding herd on the detail, ensuring that communications happened between different teams, and watching over time lines, the project could not produce a result on time. He kept trying to impose stringent control. At one level he was right. Projects do have to be managed, but the work being done here was highly imaginative and groundbreaking, rife with lots of iterations, not just knocking out another few thousand lines of code. People had proven over and over again that they could be trusted and the communications task that managers used to undertake was being done in new imaginative ways.

Experiences and ideas were flowing laterally, but the manager could not see them. In the end it was too much for him and, in a "come to Jesus" meeting he tried to take personal control of the whole project and effectively bully the other four managers into his control structure. They refused to follow him and he was isolated. The laboratory leader insisted that the group solve the problem themselves and, when it became apparent that they could not, he cast his vote by taking the manager out. The effect on this person was traumatic and he ended up literally in tears. He moved on to other projects, but soon after left the firm. The team came in ahead of their time line.

Fast development processes, rapid deployment of marketing ideas, making improvements in the production line all demonstrate that previously rigid environments are becoming more fluid as the business environment drives to speed and innovation. Leaders have to be able to let go. The new form of leadership in this high learning world does not require leaders to be the fount of all solutions. Those, and the commitment needed to make them happen, must come mostly from ordinary people. The leader must maintain the sense of direction, the evolving goal, and the pressure for a solution. Modern leaders must live with ambiguity if they are not to stifle rapid learning from experience.

Build a Collaborative Environment

Living with ambiguity and walking away from heavy-handed control goes further than the personal experience of individual leaders. If organizations are going to learn effectively they must reduce all the barriers to learning, starting with hierarchy and control systems. This is a real problem for some businesses, particularly engineering-based ones and classic bureaucracies, which are traditionally very tightly controlled. There, it may take a crisis and a determined leader to make the shift happen.

In 1992 British Petroleum was struggling under a mountain of debt.[12] After a spate of acquisitions, unfettered capital spending, and buying back a big block of shares owned by the Kuwait government, BP had sixteen billion dollars of debt. Within five years, it was down to less than half that. As an organization, it became more focused, more efficient, smaller, simpler, dramatically more profitable, and possessed of significantly less hierarchy; a drastic pruning of the management ranks had eliminated everyone between the chairman and the business units. The large head office staff groups responsible for extracting learning and communicating it had gone, dramatizing the role of the line organizations in driving learning. BP attributes its emergence as a recognized learning organization to the elimination of stifling control that came with this drop in structure.

The hierarchy issue is only one part of the structural problem of taking away barriers and controls that prevent collaboration. The other side of it is encouraging communication and collaboration in the population. Part of this comes from encouraging teamwork, getting people used to working with others from different parts of the business—setting up social links. Part of it is using technology effectively to allow people to communicate. Lotus Notes and similar collaboration tools are now well known, though they are often used as merely advanced e-mails. But technology environments can be created that allow the transfer of knowledge and that help in collaborative problem solving. An example is BP's Virtual Team Network.[13] BP's problem is that although much of its engineering experience is repeatable and reusable, those reusing it have to understand the geological and other circumstances to be sure of effective application. BP

---

[12] Steven E. Prokesh, "Unleashing the Power of Learning: An Interview with British Petroleum's John Browne," *Harvard Business Review*, September-October 1997.
[13] Ibid.

developed the Virtual Team Network to solve this problem. The VTM is a computer network that allows people to work cooperatively and share knowledge quickly and easily regardless of time, distance, or organization. Sophisticated computers allow people to work as if they are in the same room with their videoconferencing, electronic white boards, scanners, and group ware working across an intranet and the Internet. Started in 1996, it grew at a tremendous rate even though people had to pay to connect to it out of their own budgets—a phenomenon not that far removed from the origins of the Internet itself.

Make It Safe for People to Learn from Failure

Charles Handy,[14] the Irish business guru and author of visionary books on management, is of the opinion that organizations are structured not to be able to contemplate the results of their actions. Mistakes are best not talked about and successes are celebrated and either mindlessly copied or never repeated. The US Army's After Action Review[15] meets this problem head-on by teaching soldiers how to debrief and learn following action. Imagine one of the army's major training centers out in the desert where a very large-scale war game is played involving thousands of people. The teams who come to the center are fighting a resident force, which knows the ground and always wins convincingly. Part of the learning is how to learn from failure. As Pascale[16] points out, human beings are hardwired to react adversely to mistakes by blaming themselves, others, or fate. Day after day the trainers press home the benefits of learning from setbacks until it becomes second nature to see failures as opportunities for learning.

In the corporate world shooting the messenger or beating up on the honest miscalculation is fatal to innovation and learning. The celebration of failure is now an accepted part of management, particularly in product development. New ideas have a high failure rate and punishing those who try to innovate is foolish in the extreme. Indeed, the opposite reaction is called for. This is famously illustrated by the

---

[14] Charles Handy, *The Age of Paradox*, Boston: 1994.

[15] Former Army Chief of Staff Gordon Sullivan describes an AAR as a "structured way of facilitating learning from complex experiences that are often very ambiguous." R. Gordon and Michael V. Harper, *What Business Leaders Can Learn from America's Army*, New York: Random House, 1996.

[16] Richard Pascale, Mark Milleman, and Linda Gioja, "Changes in the Way We Change," *Harvard Business Review*, November-December 1997.

story of Tom Watson, founder of the modern IBM, who called in an employee whose high-profile failure had cost the firm millions of dollars. The employee expected to be fired, but Watson's reported response was "No way. We've just spent millions educating you!" True or not, this story was a key part of IBM's culture for decades before the gurus discovered the need to celebrate failure.

The problem of failure cannot be disentangled from the question of risk. To risk your own career is your problem, but to put your boss or coworkers at risk is an entirely different issue. Working with a highly bureaucratic organization, the issue of risk surfaced in the context of major market changes. People seemed to be paralyzed as they felt no mandate to take a risk. Prolonged discussion about the concept of calculated risk made no difference. The issue was not the specific risk, it was the fact that you had taken a risk at all, putting others potentially at risk. Breaking through this was similar to getting line workers to stop the line in the early days of the quality movement. They would not do it at first. Then some brave soul tried and nothing bad happened. Then many people tried some for frivolous reasons as people tested the boundaries of management tolerance. Only then did it settle down.

Indulge in Open, Honest, and Straight Discussion

Bringing disagreement to the surface the way Shell Malaysia did is the only way of getting at the root problems that disable organizations. Hiding things in the interests of politeness does not advance learning and merely obscures the problem. No organization is free from dissent, nor should it be—it is a part of the creative process. But, if it is not vented, people feel they have not been heard, that they are not appreciated, or that there are no go areas in the firm where you can put your career at risk. This is a cancer that suppresses creativity and in a knowledge world that translates into a direct loss of value— a major leadership issue.

The scene was a huge boardroom in the basement of a corporate headquarters. Gathered around the board table were the senior leaders of a major division of a global manufacturer, there to listen to and approve the business plans for the coming three years. Leader after leader rose and made his or her pitch, displaying a clear grasp of the issues with an impressive array of graphics. Marketing came to the podium and explained in detail how the division was going to make major gains in market share, pushed by a motivated sales force driving new products. Manufacturing explained how improvements in manufacturing techniques and the firm's new sales force program was going to drive wider margins. However, these higher margins would require higher volumes than projected by marketing and an assumption of significant investment. Development talked about a new product line that was not quite the same as that assumed by marketing in content or in timing of arrival. Finally, finance rose and showed their forecasts of sales and manufacturing productivity and investment based on projections of declining market share, higher wages, and an investment capital shortage. Then everyone sat back and the chairman began to thank everyone for attending.

Driven by total amazement, the consultant stopped the meeting, and amid puzzled silence and not a little resentment—it was close to the coffee break—pointed out the obvious. The presentations, apart from having the company logo on them, at best bore little if any relationship to each other and at worst, were completely at odds. How could they proceed without at least acknowledging this and preferably doing something about it? The silence stretched on and on. Finally, the division leader looked around the table and said, "You know, he is right." The sigh was audible. Everyone had sensed the incongruity, but no one was prepared to say anything.

They were suffering from terminal politeness—the inability of people to raise difficult issues—and so encouraging the business to fail. Terminal politeness is a form of conflict that occurs when an undiscussable subject has arisen and individuals are unwilling to take on a powerful individual or function. This reaction is also evident when a firm has become so dysfunctional that its normal processes of discussion have ceased to operate. In the case above, marketing and development conducted a dialog of the deaf, manufacturing felt put-upon by everyone and finance was arrogant and overbearing. Worse, the very system, which was supposed to deal with dissent, had itself become part of the problem. The firm had an elaborate way of resolving issues, which saw them progressively escalated to the top. However, as the firm had become larger, more complex, and integrated, with ever more interconnections, the potential for conflict had grown, overwhelming the process. Too many issues were now clogging the works and people tried to keep their powder dry until the internal disputes began.

The story was the same wherever one looked. Layers of hierarchy, thick walls between functions, and divisions that found it impossible to cooperate. Executives had become intensely power conscious and would stop any activity that eroded their position relative to their internal competitors or seemed to diminish their power—goodbye empowerment! The extraordinary level of action orientation had become almost grotesque as action became an end in itself and few people thought deeply about the business. As German novelist Heinrich Mann remarked, "Action people live only in the present."[17] The whole control philosophy of the organization worked against it. Based on the logic of checks and balances it encouraged paralysis and set up the potential for conflict. The business had become sclerotic while running at full speed, and it was doing nothing to heal itself—in short, it had lost the capacity to think and learn. Soon after this meeting the business went into crisis.

Discussing undiscussable subjects is absolutely vital if learning is not to be stifled, and there are ways to do this. Workshops designed to get at major problems should be preceded by a series of interviews with the participants and started with the interview results being fed back. This can be done in ways that capture the key concerns and expose them for discussion in a non-attributable fashion. Follow this with a facilitated discussion and the big issues should be addressed. Similarly, the lack of restrictions in open-book management means that issues that affect the financial results should receive exposure; this should ensure high interest particularly if everyone has a financial investment. Protocols can be used, like Intel's "constructive contention,"[18] which is used to bring out disagreements on questions of product development. The aim is to encourage open technical discussion. It is reported to be very successful, even though the final decision is in the hands of top management, because people feel that they have been heard and so are willing to continue to take part. The more jaundiced observers point to the fact the Intel always has another product in the pipeline and those who felt they had lost could always fight for their pet idea another day. Similar protocols exist in the US military to encourage performance feedback, in GE with its action workouts, and elsewhere.

However, sometimes protocols are not enough to get people to come out and raise issues. Graham Freeman was CEO of Ault Foods,

---

[17] Heinrich Mann, *Young Henry of Navarre*, translated by Eric Sutton. Woodstock, NY: Overlook Press, 1984 .
[18] See Andrew S. Grove, *Only the Paranoid Survive: How to Exploit Crisis Points That Challenge Every Company and Career*. New York, Currency/Doubleday, 1996.

major dairy company in the midst of a total makeover. The dairy business is very traditional and Freeman was not. He had just torn up the firm, fired many people, and broken up the entrenched power and seniority structure. He had also personally intervened to try to reinvent part of the distribution methods (introducing a box for holding milk called the H-crate). It was a total failure and the source of much muttering around the watercoolers and "I told you sos." In truth, it was a little thing, but enough to bring focus on leadership "incompetence" and inability to understand the dairy world. Graham learned the great truth that when you are in a downsizing period, everything you do is seen in a negative light. Instead of his idea being a quaint thought that failed, it was magnified into a major threat.

Recognizing this tension, he used it to his advantage. He needed people to follow him, and he needed to break down the traditional attitudes of subservience, muttering, and failure to discuss real issues. He had unassailable power but little respect. He would never be a dairy person, but he was a superb strategic leader. At the next meeting of his management cadre—about 600 people—he set out to explain some of his latest thinking. Suddenly, a character leapt to his feet and yelled out, "This is rubbish. Remember the H-crate." There was stunned silence and this highly traditional group looked around to see who the madman was. Graham responded by standing a little straighter, letting the silence build, then admitting that he had been wrong and was human.

The result was a watershed. People started to come out of the closet, talk, and be part of the change. The person who had yelled? He was an actor hired for the occasion.

Making People *Able* to Contribute

It is impossible to harness people's experience if they are not willing or ready. It is equally impossible it they are not able to contribute—even with the best will in the world. To contribute effectively people need skills and tools, which means leadership has to:

• Provide Shared Ways of Thinking About Business Problems

• Systematically Capture and Transfer Knowledge Around

• Encourage People to a Deep Understanding of the Business

Provide Shared Ways of Thinking About Business Problems

In order to discuss a problem people need accepted vocabulary, defined terms, and some kind of construct. To talk about the finances of a business, one needs the structures provided by accounting. To discuss engineering projects you need the jargon of engineering. To think through a problem of competitive positioning it helps to have Michael Porter's ideas on competition.[19] The fact is that reality is very complex and mental constructs are invaluable tools. The idea that people need shared ways of thinking about the world they live in is easy to understand, and all professional training in subjects such as engineering, accounting, finance, and even general management is really just passing on mental constructs that explain the world.

In the last several years organizations have started training employees in common tools that the whole organization shares and uses to analyze problems. Garvin[20] points to the quality movement as the root of much thinking in this area with its insistence on common tools—Pareto analysis, root cause analysis, statistical tools—being applied to hard data by people throughout the organization at every level. He quotes the example of Xerox Corporation's Leadership Through Quality Program, where all employees are trained in small-group activity and problem-solving techniques. At Xerox the latter consists of tools for creating ideas and collecting information, arriving at agreement, doing analysis, and action planning. All Xerox employees learn the tools with their common vocabulary and are expected to use them.

A similar story can be found in a wide range of organizations. In GE, one of the most significant contributions Jack Welch made was the provision of tools for thinking about and analyzing business problems. The tools were introduced over a number of years and through a number of programs and initiatives, but when a new tool was introduced the organization did not just ditch the old one. The new one, being purpose-specific, did not compete; it supplemented the earlier efforts. Over a number of years, the firm has built up a toolbox of concepts that are in regular use.

---

[19] Michael E. Porter, *On Competition*. Boston: Havard Business School Publishing, 1998.
[20] David A. Garvin, "Building a Learning Organization," *Harvard Business Review*, July-August 1993.

The use of common tools has an alignment effect in the business as problems are analyzed in common ways. This is effectively providing the people with a common business vocabulary which allows them to get past culture barriers across the globe. In the 1970s, IBM had an intense culture of training and providing people with common tools and a common vocabulary. This was so deep that Dutch behavioral scientist Geert Hofstede,[21] one of the great researchers of global cultural differences, used IBM as his model. He had worked with IBM in the early 70s and his thesis was that IBM culture was so intense that any differences in values and behaviors between countries must be due to national cultural traits. This intensity of tools and mental models worked to IBM's advantage for many decades. But it worked to its disadvantage in its crisis, because it lacked diversity of viewpoints.

Not all shared ways of thinking are analytical tools. The scenarios created by Shell's scenario planning approach are what Peter Senge called mental models, commonly accepted explanations of the future (in this case).[22] The Total Performance Indicators created at Sears are a mental model of the relationship between employee actions in the store and Sears financial results. At a more abstract level, ideologies are shared constructs about how society should work. Looking at the underlying, shared assumptions of a business can be enlightening, particularly when such assumptions are strategically restricting.

An insurance company had the underlying assumption that the policyholder was the customer. This assumption derived from an unquestioning adoption of customer-focus ideas. Millions of dollars were spent on advertising and product development trying to get what always turned out to be fleeting advantage. Yet all the time, everyone knew that their kind of insurance is sold by personal relationships between the agent and the policyholder, and, in fact, the company's customer was the agent. The shared assumption, once overturned, released energy and dollars to support the agent and market gains. Part of learning from experience is challenging long-held mental models.

---

[21] Geert Hofstede, *Cultures and Organizations: Software of the Mind*. Maidenhead, Berkshire, UK: McGraw-Hill, 1991.
[22] Peter M. Senge, *The Fifth Discipline: The Art and Practice of the Learning Organization*. New York: Doubleday: 1990; Arie de Geus, "Planning as Learning," *Harvard Business Review*, March-April 1988.

Systematically Capture and Transfer Knowledge Around

Every organization has lots of data on its operations. The basic logic behind the huge ERP systems, data warehousing, and data mining was releasing information captured in systems that do not communicate, so that it could be used to improve the business. But the issue of capturing knowledge goes well beyond shuffling facts and into the world of tacit knowledge. Tacit knowledge is contextual, it talks to; the insights derived from experience and the capability to translate them into new situations. Tacit knowledge has been seen as almost impossible to capture—it is simply too nuanced. Hansen, Nohria, and Tierney[23] studied different methods of knowledge capture and dissemination in high tacit environments such as the consulting industry and found two different camps:

- Those who were focused on the computer, codifying and storing information in databases where it is accessible to anyone.

- Those who see knowledge as tied to the person and only shareable through direct contact.

They believe that the wrong choice can have a significant business impact.

According to Hansen et al., consultancies focused on implementing standard programs, such as installing information technology systems, think in codification terms, identifying pieces of knowledge and treating them as "knowledge objects." All kinds of facts are stored this way: benchmarks, market segmentations, work data, schedules, and so on. Even some types of tacit experience are treated this way. A major training organization requires its associates to record their learning from different assignments in a structured way and then pass it around the globe. Such codification and database management is not an insignificant effort; it can be very expensive. One consultancy of this type has over 250 people who manage and feed the electronic repository.

The second camp includes the consultancies that develop business strategy as their primary offering and focuses on individuals conveying information to individuals. Uncodifiable knowledge is transferred at brainstorming sessions and one-on-one meetings, and through discussion the groups arrive at insights. To make this happen, consultants

---

[23] Morton T. Hansen, Nitin Nohria, and Thomas Tierney, "What's Your Strategy for Managing Knowledge?" *Harvard Business Review*, March-April 1999.

have to invest in networks of people who "know" and the firm has to actively foster them by moving people around, creating a culture of responsiveness to colleagues, and creating directories of experts.

The primary difference lies in the type of work to be done. Houses focused on the repeatable circumstances of implementation projects will do well with a codification strategy where the economics of reuse work for them and people can be taught by solving definable problems. Those problems, like selling into markets that require unique customized solutions, will go the personalized route, seeking insight into softer human and contextual issues and backing it up with mentoring approaches to people's development. Hansen et al.'s big message is "don't straddle." They noted that strategy firms came to grief with document-driven systems, which encouraged a cookie-cutter attitude to unique problems offending the client, whereas those implementers who could not replicate experience had marketing and production costs that were too high.

Encourage People to a Deep Understanding of the Business

When Sears started to involve people in the transformation of the business, it rapidly became apparent that very few employees were knowledgeable about the business, its competitive environment, and its financial structure. Sears' leadership came to the conclusion that without this knowledge people had no idea of how to contribute. Raising this consciousness in over 300,000 mostly part-time employees was a major and ongoing commitment to training in business literacy and the dynamics of the retail trade.

Sears focused on business literacy, but that is by no means the only type of problem. Imagine that you want to optimize a supply chain and people only know about their small part of the chain. You could be certain that they would focus on their sliver and that they would push all their cost-inducing problems on to others before or after them in the chain. If you wanted to introduce just-in-time inventory management, people could only benefit from an understanding of the whole system and how thinking systemically generates huge savings. Imagine that you are the CEO of a major utility that is being privatized and that you want your people to move away from being monopolists to understanding the realities of a complex growth strategy and their role in it. All these are holistic, systemic problems that are very difficult to teach people about using traditional methods. Lectures and diagrams can only provide a pale shadow of understanding about the complex dynamics at play.

But there is a solution. E-games bring the power of the computer to bear by creating deep and totally engaging experiences that make highly complex issues simple and intuitively understandable, without making them simplistic and trivial. The rest of this chapter addresses the problem of helping people contribute their experience by helping them learn and make sense of it in terms of business systems.

The E-Game Frontier

E-games have been around since the 1960s. Originally restricted to universities, they crept into corporate training in the 1980s with the emergence of smaller computers. They took their next leap at the end of the 1990s with the shift to networked games. Now rich, hyper-competitive business strategy games can be played globally across the Internet.

John Jenner's Journey

case   The year was 1981 and John Jenner had just been handed a major problem that was to launch him on a 20-year journey. John was an experienced manufacturing manager with a penchant for teaching and a senior educator at IBM's Manufacturing Technology Institute based in New York. The opportunity was to focus the minds of key managers and professionals who had the daunting task of moving IBM's operations systems to the next level, to keep them productive in a rapidly growing competitive marketplace. IBM's manufacturing systems that produced semiconductor chips, electronic packaging, information storage, and computing were the most highly automated complex manufacturing system deployed anywhere in the world. Very few IBM production executives had the experience to manage them. Indeed, most had been brought up on the relative simplicity of box assembly plants and were skilled in discrete manufacturing, not the flow concepts that semiconductors involved. Even worse, the intense functional alignment of IBM had prevented factory managers from developing a broad perspective on how the whole production system really worked, so grasping the new "flow" concepts meant introducing new cross-functional, team behavior.

John's mandate was to develop a training program to solve this problem. Educational practice at the time was straightforward—bring them into the school and lecture them, but John was convinced that

that well-proven technique would not work in this case. John's insight was that the problem the managers faced was not a lack of theory but a lack of experience in this kind of manufacturing system. They had no mental image and no intuitive feel for the dynamics of the system. They were probably collecting and looking at the wrong information and making inappropriate functional decisions. He was convinced that if he could provide them with a way of simulating the experience of running a semiconductor factory, in a safe environment, they would rapidly see the differences and develop an understanding.

The Manufacturing Operations Game

John intuitively felt the right way was computer-based gaming, a solution we are now very familiar with—for example, flight simulators—but which was new and innovative at that time. Business games had been around for a while in universities, but they were on mainframes, complex, algorithm rich, and academic. Worse from John's point of view, they were constructed for students to play over long periods. What he needed was a highly focused game, playable in very short elapsed times, which illustrated a few key principles, did not require huge budgets to make it happen, and preferably could be hosted on the emerging small computers. The solution was The Manufacturing Operations Game. John designed the game and begged, borrowed, and stole programming help in a skunk-works fashion, getting people to do things on the side and without budget, while development of the traditional course program proceeded.

The resultant game was graphically crude by today's standards—most of the modern tools were not available—but was state of the art at the time. It was designed to be used in the classroom with an instructor or facilitator on hand to kick off the experience, provide an initial explanation of what was required, demonstrate the mechanics, assist players during their game play, and conduct a debriefing. It involved teams of 12 to 15 players managing an existing and fully loaded semiconductor line. The pace and substance of game work was not sufficient to occupy more than 15 players and groups of less than 12 wouldn't experience the dynamics of team interaction. Only classroom space, trained facilitators, and equipment limit the number of teams competing. Groups of over 100 have been taught concurrently on many occasions.

Teams and individuals were assigned different functional roles and had to collaborate to produce a scheduled volume and mix of parts at the highest possible yield and manage the balance of material on the line. The aim was to play against the house and compete for a score better than that of other teams playing under the same conditions. The game was designed to proceed by days over a period of one production month. As they played the game managers were to learn the fundamentals of materials flow in complex manufacturing operations, learn the value of and practice the use of on-line status and projected information capabilities and, just as important, learn the advantages and practice of working in groups or teams. The game was a huge success. The participants—IBM factory and production managers—loved it and it contributed to a rapid rise in management quality in the semiconductor plants. Management quality improved across all of IBM's plants and so did profitability.

The game was highly focused, not seeking to solve all the world's problems. For example, it did not measure or exhibit product cost, because, when the game was designed, there were no manufacturing lines at IBM with dynamic costing and the game was designed to reflect the existing business. Two follow-on games, CAPCOST I & II, were designed to exercise the product costing connection by reflecting the financial implications of the manufacturing decisions. These latter two games were originally aimed at manufacturing managers but were also enlightening for finance staff who had little feel for the underlying sources of the numbers they worked with. These lessons of game focus and modularity became basic design ideas in all future games.

The manufacturing game was first introduced in the inaugural class of IBM's Manufacturing Technology Institute in November 1981 and is still in active use today. It has been installed at over 20 colleges, universities, and companies around the world and played by an estimated 10,000 people. It has undergone two technology updates but virtually no content changes since its inception. The US Senate Award for Productivity and the NCRYPTAL/EDUCOM award, the highest honor of the computer gaming world for education, were given to John Jenner for this game and others in the series.

The Distribution Game

The success of the manufacturing game was resounding, and participant feedback was the highest possible, which was also the case with others in the series. Games are intensely engaging and the participants teach themselves, drawing out knowledge from their own background and that of their teammates and reintegrating it with the addition of new ideas. This leads to high levels of learning and great student satisfaction. Based on this response, John thought he had moved the educational ball forward and his colleagues would leap on the wagon with him. But it was not to be—at least initially. He faced the classic pioneer problem. IBM would fund further work, but getting others interested in using this breakthrough was difficult. Part of this was due to a problem that dogs this area of education even today, though it has softened considerably—the word "game." Even changing the name from game to simulation or some such has proven impossible, as the concept has been in place too long, and the other terms carry their own baggage—simulations are supposed to be exact replicas of the world, which games are not. People associate the term game with the trivial, and the world of business is serious.

Students, however, love them when properly constructed and they are educationally effective—indeed for learning about holistic, dynamic business problems they are the only game in town. The stigma of the term game has been magnified with the rash of behavioral games that flooded the market in the 1980s and early 1990s. Based on the idea of action learning, these often truly trivial exercises suffered a major defect—the game facilitator could rarely link the game back to the real business world, leaving the players hanging. Business games of John's kind are not like that. They mimic the real world and students can make their own connections.

Facing this change problem of introducing an innovation, John developed a relationship with the Cornell University Engineering Faculty, and was able to keep the ball rolling, working with Professors Peter Jackson and Jack Muckstadt. Jackson and Muckstadt were attracted to the game idea for a number of reasons. The shift to small computers allowed easier access to programming, which meant that the games could be produced and amended cheaply and easily. The games were simple, yet able to display complex problems and most of all they worked with the student body. The pedagogical problem was how to teach a wide variety of students the principles of managing the dynamics of a supply chain that stretches from a supplier, through several levels of distribution, to geographically dispersed customers in a fashion that would engage their interest. Encouraged by the success of the Manufacturing Operations Game in their courses, Professors Jackson and Muckstadt developed The Distribution Game. It is similar to the Manufacturing Operations Game in that it deals with the difficulty of managing a multistage process in the presence of uncertainty. However, they changed the interface to move to a video game look and feel. That was in 1982 and although players could range from highly experienced supply executives to totally inexperienced kids in school, all students found the video format immensely engaging.

The game presents a meaningful challenge for the players by mimicking a deceptively simple system, where the problem is easily stated but defies exact analytical solution even for a small distribution network. In the process of game play, managers learn the fundamentals of material flow in distribution systems, demonstrate to themselves the value of information in reducing inventory requirements, discover winning strategies and see those strategies at the heart of advanced mathematical techniques. The game can be played in two modes: one in which the players are not given full information and must do a lot of guesswork and another in which all conceivable facts are fully available. The player discovers quickly that scores are better and inventories are lower in the full information version. Not bad for a game whose goal and rules can be stated in less than five minutes and a complete play of the game can be experienced in under 20 minutes.

One of the key problems facing Jackson and Muckstadt in teaching this material by traditional classroom methods is that it is both complex and boring to those who have not made it their life work—a deadly combination. The game solved this problem. As part of creating the 1982 video game look and feel, all relevant information is displayed on a single screen. System dynamics are illustrated with animation (trucks move across the screen to different destinations), game controls are simple (students type numbers into four different buckets to indicate their ordering and shipping decisions), and the scoring mechanism is easily understood. The players optimize the system by extensive experimentation in which they explore extreme approaches and gradually converge on a winning strategy. Not all experiential learning games use animation, but The Distribution Game owes much of its success to the power of animation to fascinate the player.

The Distribution Game was meant for the university world as part of a business course. It was therefore important that the facilitator/instructor could make learning points quickly and easily in the classroom to individual players. To achieve this a special-purpose chart, displayed in a corner of the game screen, presents an entire history of the player's decisions. The chart enables the instructor to diagnose player strategy and to explain basic inventory concepts and terminology. Further, the instructor can customize the game parameters to show how the winning strategy changes as the nature of the distribution system changes. It can be used to illustrate the impacts of just-in-time manufacturing and to show the high levels of safety stock required when demand variability increases. Finally, The Distribution Game has hidden features available to the instructor: there is an auto-play mode with a built-in optimizer where the machine effectively plays the game for you finding the best solution and graphical tools to illustrate key concepts in a winning strategy.

Like The Manufacturing Operations Game, The Distribution Game has demonstrated enduring value since its creation. It is in use at universities around the world and has been used with engineering freshmen, MBAs, graduate students in operations research, and supply chain professionals. Students may download it freely from the Web. Professor Jackson continues to get comments such as "I've played the game for six hours now. What is the best possible score? What strategy should I use?" Students ask to be taught how to win. This is truly "demand-pull" education.

The Manufacturing Systems Development Game

Back at IBM, John Jenner was observing another problem. The 1980s saw the breakdown of walls between functional silos in organizations and nowhere was this more important than the interface of product development and manufacturing. The problem was structural and behavioral. Each group had been stuck in its own world for so long they had formed inflexible ideas about how not to work together. The problem came down to how to tear down the walls. In the real world opportunities for engineers to participate in a new factory design are few and far between, but when they arise they are urgent and critically important. A game provides an opportunity to train engineers to effectively perform this critical ad hoc task by mimicking the circumstances and exercising the skills, attitudes, and behaviors that will be needed.

Another game was conceived. Called The Manufacturing Systems Development Game, it assembles a group of product and manufacturing engineers and sets them the task of designing a manufacturing system to produce a new product. To achieve this, they have to design a manufacturing system that will produce product which meets the specifications, delivers the volume and mix required by the forecast, and achieves the lowest average and individual product cost. Beyond the technical they have to craft a stand-up presentation and written report that will sell the design to game management. To make this happen they have to get all of the functions operating together and achieve a high level of teamwork necessary to produce a winning design. The game is intensely competitive, a feature of all the best games.

From a technical point of view the game is highly challenging, and it assumes that the players have played The Manufacturing Operations Game already. The game product is a family of first level semiconductor packages called multilayer panels, which are the next generation technology from the card panel, the single layer package in the manufacturing operations game. The players designing the new production system are allowed to scavenge the single layer card panel manufacturing system. These two products are simplified versions of real industrial products, retaining a challenging but manageable complexity. The economic trade-offs of product design versus manufacturability, timing, and economics between old mature processes and new untried high leverage processes, used versus new equipment, and choices in depreciation alternatives are all embedded in the game. The game assumes that even as they are designing the new system, product development continues resulting in potential engineering design changes. New product volume forecasts are given periodically as would happen in the real world.

Game teams of 15 to 30 players are assigned the roles of Product Engineer, Process Engineer, Logistics Engineer, Equipment Engineer, Information Systems Engineer, Industrial Engineer, and Cost Engineer. Each game team is headed by a player assigned the role of Manufacturing Systems Architect. These game teams compete with each other for the winning designs awarded by a group representing management. The management is made up of game facilitators and invited outside faculty and industry representatives.

Designed for a major business problem plaguing IBM and most other product companies at the time, this game is still found to be useful by several universities. At Cornell it is used as the capstone of an experiential learning (junior year) course in manufacturing systems. A monetary award is given by Procter & Gamble to the first- and second-place winners. From the point of view of technical excellence, presentation design, and delivery these student presentations are the equivalent of the very best work by experienced professional groups in the top companies today.

The Llenroc Plastics Game

Businesses are systems in which manufacturing problems affect development, supply chains, the customer, and the strategy of the firm as a whole. Professionals tend to be experts in a specific function and rarely have the opportunity to look down on the whole problem and look for ways of optimizing the whole system. The same is true of students who take their engineering electives and business courses often in vacuums with little to give them any visceral understanding of how it all fits together. Professors Jackson and Muckstadt, assisted by John Jenner and backed by funding from IBM, other manufacturing companies, and subsequently by the National Science Foundation, set out to address this problem by using experiential learning techniques.

The problem was how to develop a comprehensive curriculum which would deal with many different issues and provide hooks back into the underlying academic courses. Their prior experience had been primarily with single games devoted to single problems, with some but not deep continuity between them. To get the true depth they felt they needed they sought a multifaceted experience, which would carry over from one part to the next. Their solution was The Llenroc Plastics Game. Though the game has a strong manufacturing engineering bias it presents a wide range of other business issues that the instructor can pick up.

Llenroc Plastics is based on the experiences of a real organization, so there is immediate credibility to the story line and a natural realism to the details. It provides a comprehensive opportunity to redesign the manufacturing and distribution functions of a medium-size company. To succeed at this the players have to focus on the customer. They have to recognize differences in the customer base and opportunities for market share growth (customer and market strategy). They must identify practical and dramatic opportunities for improvement throughout the supply chain (supply chain management), manage inventories (for example, risk-pooling, which is holding safety stock in its most flexible form to minimize the effects of uncertainty).

Players must design a system capable of providing customers with a wide variety of products reliably with very short lead times and with minimal investment in inventories (operations engineering, operations research techniques such as optimization, simulation, and economic analysis) and justify capital investments using a strategic systems view (strategy formulation). To do this they have to work in teams to develop the teamwork skills of communication, cooperation, and coordination. Llenroc Plastics demonstrates the practical application of these techniques. Other courses in the curriculum provide depth in the methodologies.

The game consciously uses the principle of modular design. Each of the six modules has well-defined learning objectives and minimal dependency on others, and the modules can be played in any order. Some universities have placed the modules in different courses to provide a unifying theme across the curriculum. The modules cover a wide range of operational and system design issues. Module 1 is to redesign the transportation system for a regional warehouse, and Module 2 explores the inventory policies of a regional warehouse. Module 3 focuses on the design of a national distribution system. Module 4 considers the operational improvements of a bottleneck manufacturing operation, while Module 5 requires work flow and layout improvements of a non-bottleneck operation, and Module 6 develops a new approach to scheduling the facility.

The cases are integrated by a common concern to reduce cost and inventory investment and to improve quality and customer service. The modules illustrate the application of diverse tools of operations research. Module 1 uses economic analysis and routing and scheduling techniques. Module 2 requires probabilistic models of inventory dynamics. Module 3 is a complex problem of optimizing a detailed economic model of warehouse location. Module 4 uses simulation, diagnostic animation, and economic analysis. Module 5 is an application of just-in-time manufacturing techniques, and Module 6 uses scheduling techniques and linear optimization.

The Llenroc Plastics series features a variety of innovative software tools to engage the students and facilitate their analysis. The Transportation Game software initiates the students in the problems of scheduling and dispatching vehicles. The Warehouse Location Designer permits the students to explore dozens of distribution system network configurations and compute the profitability and service performance of each configuration. The Press Simulator is a detailed animation of a multimillion-dollar machine with a complex material handling system. Digital video is used to explain each component of the press system. The Cyclic Schedule Editor is a tool for creating and analyzing complex schedules in repetitive manufacturing environments.

Llenroc Plastics has been used successfully at over a dozen universities. It is a demanding experience both for students who play the game and for the faculty who mentor the students. But the rewards are great. As one student put it, "I worked hard, learned a lot, and had fun. These three things have seldom come together in my academic experience."

Change Games

The work done at IBM and Cornell in the 1980s was primarily about using games as vehicles for teaching and providing holistic experiences, which could be linked to other academic vehicles. They did address a business problem—that's where they started—and some behavioral issues such as teamwork and cross-functional cooperation, but they were largely sophisticated approaches to learning. In the 1990s, this began to be expanded further with other designers, notably Roger Shank at Northwestern University, creating instruction shells, which allowed the training of people in various competencies. These multimedia-rich vehicles were only one of a slew of computer-assisted training tools that appeared on the market, ranging from low cost and low functionality to extremely high cost.

For John Jenner and Peter Jackson the market had moved on to a different field, namely the intentional use of computer-based experiences to support critical transformation efforts in major corporations. This use of gaming is very different from computer-assisted instruction. The idea is to use the game to raise awareness of and break down resistance to strategic thrusts while passing on key skills and insights. Technologically, what made this possible was the explosion of multimedia tools, the emergence of networking technology that could support low-cost networked games, and a maturation of executive understanding of games as a business tool. What follows are two case examples of games produced in the last four years by Jackson and Jenner for a giant manufacturing firm facing intense pressure to reform itself.

The Pull Game:
Pulling Western Manufacturing into the Future

The Pull Game was developed for a major automobile manufacturer seeking to move their professional and union employees from traditional manufacturing to modern lean production. Led by Toyota, Japanese car companies long ago mastered the leverage inherent in integrated manufacturing; using such concepts as *kanban* and *kaisen* they reduced inventory and moved to just-in-time environments. In the process, they captured enormous market share. As these philosophies and methodologies became clear, Western companies developed their own versions and set to the task of changing the mind-set of thousands of factory floor operations personnel to dramatically new ways of working. The problem was how to explain the new methods in a palatable way that would not only clarify the advantages to the company and the workers but give them the skill to implement the new methods. E-games were ideally suited to this new role as the change vehicle. The old methods could be demonstrated running simulated factories, then the new methods could be applied. The advantages would be evident in the results. Participants could be convinced and retrained as well.

Structurally the game was very simple. Working in teams, participants apply skills learned on the job (old methods) to run the simulated factory. They are then introduced to the new pull (*kanban*) methods,
which they use to run the simulated factory. They compare the results
of using the traditional methods with the results gained by using the
new pull methods. The factory operations are replicated in miniature
in the game and presented as an animated graphic run by an embedded simulator. Game teams are created with a set of responsibilities corresponding to their real jobs on the factory floor. The production target for a set of parts is presented daily, and batch sizes are determined
and jobs scheduled by the teams. The teams set inventory policy.

Random events such as machine breakdowns, absent operators,
set-up delays, late arriving and poor quality materials, changed priorities, and so on, are presented and must be dealt with by the teams.
The game proceeds through several cycles using the old ways then
the new pull methods are introduced, and teams play several more
cycles using these new approaches. Production quantities, product
quality, product cost, and inventory levels are tracked and a score is
presented. Team results are compared to determine the most effective
team strategies and to verify the improved results using the new pull
methods. The delivery of The Pull Game is timed to the introduction
of new tools that support the new pull methods. Personnel who work
together are trained together.

The Thruput Game:
Using Multimedia to Deliver Abstract Concepts

The same client, having introduced *kanban*, wanted to deal with the
more abstract issues of *kaisen* or continuous improvement.
Kanban/just-in-time has a set of tangible mechanics attached to its
implementation, whereas *kaisen* or continuous improvement is less
tangible but no less important to competitive business. The operational strategy problem is that cost is increasingly tied to volume as
manufacturing systems mature through more mechanization and
automation, replacing the variable element of labor with a fixed element of capital investment. The only way to deal with this is to
increase the throughput or output of a given factory and to drive
down costs through continuous improvement in processes. This
game encompasses manufacturing response time, product cost, and
product quality, all key strategic issues for the firm.

With The Thruput Game, the players learn how to observe, analyze, plan, and implement corrective action to resolve line problems
that affect line throughput. They learn how the economic prioritization of problems enables the accelerated improvement of line
throughput and observe how the improved line throughput enables
compression (assigning more work as throughput is improved) that
drives added revenue and higher profits.

The whole factory floor is simulated and animated so players can
observe the major operations breakdowns. This provides a feel for
where the problems are but capturing these observations in a disciplined way demands information systems solutions underscoring the
need for effective information technology. The process of uncovering
line problems requires the parallel effort to capture incidents that
occur randomly during the course of the operating day. Typically,
these efforts start with manual records that prove inaccurate and
evolve toward information systems that are integrated into the design
of equipment. Mechanical/electrical sensors are designed to capture
the small time increments of disrupted operations. This game play
evolves through several iterations of information system design.

Any number of clever analytical tools can be plugged in to summarize and prioritize the information. When this is done compre-
hensively it often reveals that the sum of many minor incidents has
more impact than the major dramatic breakdowns which are easily
observed and are the usual topic at the next coffee break. While
information systems can accurately record the time lost through
interruptions of any kind, understanding what caused each interruption and how to eliminate the cause is much more difficult to do
within the information system. To find the cause and the solution is
detective work that requires the creation of game characters who rep-
resent people running the simulated factory. They have the answers
among them but which ones should the players interview and whose
responses should they trust? This multimedia legerdemain adds a
dramatic and appealing dimension to game play.

Improving line throughput requires players to make repeated trips
through the corrective action cycle, which consists of the following
steps: capture the incidents, analyze and prioritize, find the most
probable cause, and craft and implement a solution. Nothing new
here—it's the scientific method alive and well on the factory floor.

The delivery is in team mode. Teamwork is a natural requirement
of increased complexity of products and the manufacturing systems

to produce them. It follows that more highly integrated or tightly coupled manufacturing systems require more coordinated team efforts to run them. Business operations are forced to turn their attention away from individual effort and toward teamwork. If the mode of working is in teams, the mode of learning should be as well. Using a game as a change vehicle to replicate a defined methodology fundamentally changes the way operations are conducted. Used to train large numbers of operations personnel who are wedded to the old way of doing things, the game is delivered in stages. It takes players from today's process through the new process revealing the obvious advantages of the new process while providing skill building in the use of the new process. The same game is used in an abbreviated delivery to explain and sell the new methodologies to supervisors and executives.

The Engineering Factory Game

The Engineering Factory Game was developed as part of the same series of games teaching *kanban* and *kaisan* but is significantly more sophisticated. The games we have discussed so far have been focused on a person understanding something that presently exists. However, the beauty of the computer is that it can deal with things that are still in the world of imagination. The challenge placed before John and Peter in The Engineering Factory Game was different. Could a game be devised that would be an integral part of the manufacturing design system? And, more than that, could a wide range of people be involved such that they felt they had had a hand in the design and would therefore be committed to it? To achieve this in The Engineering Factory Game they decided to depart from prior game designs in a critical way. In those earlier games teams play against the house competing for a score but not interacting with each other during game play. The Engineering Factory Game differs from this by enforcing collaboration, a major problem in this still silo-oriented organization. This is done by creating teams from many functions and forcing them to contribute their specialist skills.

The Engineering Factory Game enables product designers to understand the whole design process of which they are a small part. They are given information tools not yet created nor available in their working world. They get to experience how their real world could be more effective if they had the right tools and the incentive to cooperate rather than compete. They participate in assessing the future needs of their working world. They become the pull force that drives their own working future. The methodologies and processes that have been refined and implemented to create integrated manufacturing operation are now applied to the world of product design. Designers are told that they can learn from their manufacturing colleagues, which is a bitter pill for some of them to swallow because they have traditionally seen themselves as superior. Labeling their world the engineering factory reinforces this message, as does the fact that a set of teams of players from different functions and professional disciplines has to interact dynamically as play proceeds. They contribute individually but win collectively, competing with other sets of teams. This added feature of cooperation takes games even closer to a real work ideal. Live interaction adds another dimension of excitement that further motivates participants to want to learn.

As they play they learn to improve the efficiency and effectiveness of the design process by scheduling work to meet work cell delivery dates. The whole work of a design process is a network of discrete work tasks called work cells. Players coordinate work with other design teams to improve the overall program delivery dates, select the most appropriate people for the design teams, schedule work to optimize deployment of people and reduce resources, adopt more efficient technology design tools, and use information efficiently. The game encompasses the design work required for several major design programs, offset in time but with concurrent design work across several programs at any one time. The design process for each major program is a defined network of dozens of dependent work cells. An embedded simulator enables work to progress according to given rules. Variability is achieved by given distribution functions. Players assigned to work cells supersede the rules to improve performance and efficiency. Work cells not assigned in game play proceed based only on the rules. This structure enables the number of participants and their game workload to be varied as they participate in a complete and very large set of design processes. This structure also provides the structure adaptable for remote network versions of the game play.

To meet their obligations the players may trade work with other teams to smooth workloads, transfer personnel to reduce costs, substitute better personnel to improve efficiency, and add overtime to increase capacity. Cooperation is carried out through e-mail features in the game. The scoring structure and weighting spurs cooperation.

The variability of the real world is emulated by random harmful situations including design rework, quality problems, supply shortages, system breakdowns, personnel losses, and so on. Helpful situations include opportunities to install new, efficient design tools by training personnel, design breakthroughs that reduce design time and such. As with the other recent games, The Engineering Factory Game is structured to enable users to customize rules, algorithms, narrative, and terminology. This was initially done to give users the ability to tailor standard games to their particular environments. However, it has been found that as the business problems and games become more complex, the need to make adjustments in order to balance the game play has become an important game design feature.

The Engineering Factory Game is a major step toward remote network games, where, in the not too distant future, individuals and teams of players will interact from different time zones playing from workstations in their offices. Learning may then become a natural part of their real-life work experiences.

Fastrac: Transformation and Corporate Strategy

All the games discussed so far have been focused on operations problems of varying complexity, dealing with instruction, behavior modification, and the introduction of transformational ideas. These kinds of operations are ideal for e-games, addressing as they do numbers-rich and holistic problems. Corporate and business strategy environments are more abstract and behaviorally complex. Business schools have modeled strategy environments since the 1970s—the New York Business School Game being an excellent example—but mainly with an operations strategy bias. The intriguing thought was whether grand strategy CEO problems could be translated into a game world at a level of effort and price that made it both customizable and cost effective in business transformation assignments. The result was Fastrac, designed by Michael Kay and John Jenner, a corporate strategy game shell whose modular construction allows rapid and competitive-cost customization. As with all the games in this chapter further information and a demonstration version of Fastrac called Change on the Run is available at www.changeontherun.com.

Fastrac builds on the learning from 20 years of game building. The players compete head-to-head across a network to build shareholder value. In the process they must manage their finances, transform the operations of their business, and fight in the marketplace. All the while, they must avoid being taken over or become the aggressor and take others over. The purpose is to involve people in understanding how businesses grow from the perspective of a CEO and the pressures and synergies CEOs must be aware of.

The basic shell is built for modification. The latest example is a major utility that wished to pass on commercial understanding to its mainly engineering staff. The game was adjusted to allow for a major acquisition/industry consolidation program and to display the different dynamics of different parts of the business. The game is played by three competing teams of about five players representing different companies and is wrapped around with other behavioral learnings.

The outgrowth of the game is the creation of a shared understanding of the strategy and environment facing the firm. The experiential nature of gaming allows a visceral understanding that cannot be achieved by speeches or e-mails or videos or any other forms of communication.

Twelve Lessons Game Developers Learned

Twenty years of experience in game design have provided a lot of learning about the do's and don'ts of games. This last section summarizes what has been learned and the principles being applied to direct current efforts.

1. **People bring their own history.** It may be thought that people working in venues other than those chosen for the game might not relate to it. Not true, because games enable things to be learned in lifelike situations and players draw upon other experiences to relate. In fact, games that are too much like the player's real world draw criticism since they are never exactly like every player's perception of their real world. The trick is to mimic their world, not to slavishly simulate it.

2. **Learn in groups.** Rather than the traditional computer-assisted instruction method of individuals interacting with the computer, group learning turns out to be much richer in game worlds. Not only does it contribute to an exciting and, therefore, motivating experience, but the collective experience of the players also creates a large knowledge base from which the players learn together.

3. **Get them into the game.** When delivering a game resist the temptation to give heavy, detailed explanations before starting. Lectures with more than the minimum information to get started are counterproductive when the idea is to learn by experiencing the issues in context. However, as the games grow to be more complex, you may need introductory exercises on the computers to learn the structure and mechanics before the game exercise can begin.

4. **Deliver a strong debrief.** Action learning skits often aren't linked back to real life, and people don't make the connection between the experience and their work. In e-games, this is much less evident as it is based on real life, a classic example being The Llenroc Plastics Game, derived quite literally from life. However, the need to drive home the learning does not go away. Methods of recap might include declaring the winners, asking them to recount what they had learned, or using the game as a lens to discuss their own business, how it is the same and how different.

5. **Games do not replace conventional teaching.** One clear example applies to analytical methods. While games can exercise analytical methods that have been learned, if a new analytical method is introduced in game play it may be used to some extent but will not be embedded in the minds of the participants. The purpose of games to illustrate holistic issues and dynamics is a totally valid solution, but coordination between traditional teaching methods and games will enhance learning.

6. **People are intensely competitive.** Well-designed games trade on the competitive nature of people by setting groups against the house and competing for game score or against each other directly. It works well and helps create the motivation that engages players to learn.

7. **Pace the game play.** For the game to be successful players have to struggle and finally succeed, therefore, tune the game so they start out behind the eight ball encountering lots of problems that drive them further behind. Then start feeding them helpful tools, which, if they work to master, will help them succeed. You want them all to get high scores so focus on helping the teams that are farthest behind. When they occasionally fail the risk is that they will blame the game and discount the learning.

8. **Complex current games require staging.** Complex games are packed with learning opportunities. These lessons must be fed piecemeal to the players because they can't absorb too much at one time. You can build as the game proceeds through several stages and get lots of complex issues across.

9. **Where possible customize.** When seeking to customize an existing e-game, such as Fastrac, it is relatively easy to change terminology, numbers, algorithms, distribution functions, and so on to fit the game experience to your circumstances. It is very difficult to change game structure, although a lot of flexibility is still available, but those who demand this capability seldom use it once the game has been rolled out, as there is a great advantage to keeping the game consistent from play to play. The facilitator knows what's going to happen and has the opportunity to keep enhancing the game play through consistent experience.

10. **Complex games are hard to tune.** Tuning—adjusting the numbers—is very necessary in order to make the game play properly. In this regard, games that are built to be customized are invaluable. Time spent on tuning is never wasted.

11. **Games can be so compelling that (college) students work at them to the exclusion of other assigned work.** This is a nice problem to discover.

12. **Keep it simple.** The overriding message to game developers is to keep it simple. When a game is created, it is easy to see what comes next. There is no end to the complexity that can be programmed, but if the game is too complex it won't succeed. We don't ask lecturers to add more material in the time allotted for classes, but we don't hesitate to ask the game developers to do so—and they comply all too willingly.

* * * * *

The e-games discussed above have been evolving over two decades, during which time the willingness of corporate educators to use them has risen considerably. This increasing acceptance is rooted in their need to teach complex ideas quickly to impatient employees—something the e-game excels at. However, we are still at the beginning of the world of business e-games as newer, faster technology allows the creation of ever more lifelike experiences. Will executives soon be playing games with the realism of a Nintendo 64? Quite probably.

The e-world is a learning world and the creation of an environment where everyone's insights and experiences are captured is a leadership problem. It is inconceivable to imagine a successful business—other than a monopoly—that would not be deeply concerned with harnessing the experiences of everyone in the organization. In the e-business, environment knowledge is paramount and the ability to create insight and to rapidly deploy it is a fundamental skill. The open, sharing environments of high-flying e-businesses will not translate in total to all firms, but no firm will be immune from dealing with complex, fast shifting markets and supply chains. Learning to facilitate constant adaptation and transformation is a source of competitive advantage and a critical leadership challenge, and something e-games excel at.

Galvanize Change Agents

The argument for having lots of employees able to lead change initiatives hardly needs making. The e-world will be obsessed with change. Fast-moving markets forcing strategy shifts, continuous process improvements, merger-integration tasks, new information technology installations, fresh e-business initiatives, and a host of other changes large and small will keep the problem of finding competent change agents high on the CEO agenda. After 20 years of a rising tempo in change, e-leaders are totally aware of the difference a good change leader can make, and recent PricewaterhouseCoopers' research indicates that a lack of skill in this area is one of the primary reasons change initiatives fail. Building a cadre of change agents and supporting them is an absolute must.

However, from the change agent perspective, taking on an initiative is to walk into a minefield of issues, many not under one's direct control—indeed, it may mean putting your career on the line.

* * * *

case   Paul fell into a classic trap. A deeply respected development executive with a long history of successfully completed development projects, he had lots of influence but at that time, no power. When he was tapped to introduce a new development process as part of his firm's transformation, he stepped forward and took up the challenge.

The result was a career disaster. The organization had established that slow product development was a major strategic problem—products were simply not coming out of the labs fast enough. This was partly a problem of entrenched developer techniques that were built for a slower world, partly of a performance system that did not encourage risk but heavily punished failure, and almost impenetrable walls between the silos of development, manufacturing, and marketing. This was made worse by a dispersion of labs, production facilities, and markets around the world. The business case was clear and unambiguous, and the problem and potential business returns truly enormous. Paul was crippled. Top management was in turmoil and he was never able to build the consensus he needed to get a proper mandate. When he tried to get explicit support he was brushed off with such classic power play remarks as, "Do you want us to do it all for you?"

Rather than wait, this action-oriented leader leapt at the task, treating it as another product development project and woefully underestimating the internal politics and resistances. His naive assumption that people would act in the interests of the firm as a whole, if encouraged to, proved to be optimistic to say the least! Moreover, he was doubly crippled as he was not able to generate a support team of peers who would share the risk and bring their budgets and insights to the table. They were simply too wary of the project. This lack of cooperation spread to other leaders whose people developed great resistance to the whole idea. Paul, in turn, interpreted the resistance as a not-invented-here syndrome when, in fact, it was rooted in deeper issues of power and fear of involvement. The more he complained the more they avoided him.

The climate then turned against him. Money he spent on consultants was used as a stick to beat him. As the organization was in a period of cost reduction and downsizing, all such expenditures were suspect, even though necessary. New top leadership coming in a year later saw no progress and looked askance at Paul who had had the baton. And so it went, one disaster after another. Gradually his reputation as a person who could get things done declined and his career went into limbo.

The message is simple. If the organization needs change agents, it must set out to create and support them. This means providing them with the skills and insights they need. This chapter is focused on the change agent and is written from his or her point of view and addresses the five keys to successful leadership of a change initiative:

- Getting Properly Set Up
- Defining the Problem
- The Dynamics of Change
- A Checklist for Undertaking a Change
- Managing Yourself

Getting Properly Set Up

Rushing into a change is a major mistake. Take time to set up the fundamentals and to understand the risks involved. Success in any change project starts in the planning stage well before there is any impact on the organization. Time spent on the fundamentals will not only make life easier, it will materially raise the probability of success. The four fundamentals are:

- Establish the Mandate
- Build a Change Team
- Set Up a Governance Structure
- Develop a Project Plan and Stick to It

Establish the Mandate

The key to any transformation from the change agent's viewpoint is the achievement of high level support. The basic rule is no mandate, no progress. However, having such authorization is never enough. The original strategy work may be the key source of your mandate, or it could be a fully defined business case that not only brings management along but also the rest of the organization. But a rational case is not necessarily enough to maintain your mandate. Just because you have one there is no guarantee that the organization will follow you or that management will stand behind you. You have to look to your own resources. A lot of the success of the change agent results from the personal power or influence he or she wields.

There are two types of successful change agents: those who derive their legitimacy from power they already have, and those who co-opt power and add it to any influence they may have personally. Influence is never a substitute for power. People will not move on

crucial matters if they do not believe that the powerful in the organization support what is being done. No matter how clever or
respected the change agent is, he or she is helpless without power
and a mandate that is consistently supported. Many large transformations are riddled with politics and a place where hope is a bed-
fellow with revenge, ambition shadows altruism, and everyone is
concerned with the final outcome. The change agent is at the heart
of all this and makes the perfect fall guy. It is better to know this
going in than to bemoan it later. This political meeting has enormous implications for who is chosen to run a change and how they
survive as they try. Paul's scenario, above, is very common. The
wrong person with the wrong political skills but high technical reputation is tapped for Mission Impossible and then not supported.
The message is simple: if your change agent does not have power,
help him or her get hold of it early. Do not wait, no matter how well
respected they are. Power cannot be ignored—if it is, its absence will
derail the project and wound everyone's careers.

So how does a change agent get power and an effective mandate?
Theoretically, the initiative did not appear out of thin air and was part
of some serious thinking about the business. Referencing the strategic
plan, should be enough. It isn't. Strategic plans are often compromis-
es, with many competing interests seeking access to limited resources.
The agent cannot get past this need to align leadership even when the
sponsor is the CEO. If there are competing interests, there are many
ways to sabotage a project using tactics such as delay and withhold-
ing resources. To get a project to work, the change agent has to build
a coalition of supporters. This may mean having to build leadership
support for the project all over again, on a leader-by-leader basis,
ensuring that there is something in it for all the key people. To lock
that support in, the project may have to be structured so those key
line executives own it.

Jack was the VP Human Resources of a major manufacturing firm,
and he was proposing a major change intervention driven out of
training. HR is in an ambiguous position in many organizations. It
has restricted and quite fearsome power in certain areas but if it
touches operations, its power rapidly dissipates into influence.
Training departments are even more poorly placed. A program, no
matter how innovative, driven from those two locations is a problem.
The pattern of resistance was predictable. Line leaders would quickly
plead their overwhelming workload, their people would simply not

have the time to attend, and, as for themselves, they would be out of town regardless of the date. Jack's response was to change the traditional pattern of training doing the developing and the line doing the rejecting. He created the program such that line people felt ownership with his people doing the work. He sold it on the logic of making it add business value. As a final twist, he had the program embedded in each line manager's plans. That is simple stuff when you think about it but all too often ignored.

Build a Change Team

No change agent can succeed alone—a change team is vital. After obtaining a mandate, the selection of this team is the most important initial activity.

There are two types of change teams: those which do the work and those which provide ongoing support and guidance.

Change teams that do the work will have to be selected on a basis of competence. You may, of course, have a team wished upon you, in which case you may have to work around any personal deficiencies.

Teams that provide ongoing support and guidance are often constituted in the form of an advisory group. In this capacity, they cannot make big decisions, but they can help you frame those decisions, lobby for them, and provide direct help if need be. This advisory group should include people with a direct interest in the success of the project, because it affects their part of the business or their careers. Look for people who can bring stable and legitimate budgets and people with them. Your unabashed aim is to bend the way they spend their money to fit in with the solution you are promoting. Change activities may well be over-resourced at first, often because of management ignorance, but once they get started they find their budgets eroding as top management steals resources for other tasks.

In the world of bending budgets, a classic is training. Training budgets exist, but often without detailed specification of the content of courses. If one can ensure that course materials and approaches for other programs reflect the messages you wish to put across then you have amplified the change dollars for your project. As an example, if you are introducing a new supply chain logistics approach and the training department is running a manufacturing program, then try to get a module inserted in the manufacturing sessions giving them a peek at your new project. This will cost you little and will advertise your project to a related constituency. Similarly, if your project needs IT support you want a senior IT person on your advisory team. You then have the chance to build rapport and squeeze your agenda into his or her plans. Again, change dollars are amplified.

The membership of both types of teams is a billboard to the organization. If you can attract the best, it tells the organization that your project—among the very many that the firm may be undertaking—is seen as important by those in the know. Look for a mixture of power oriented people and experts. The professional people in the business will assess the worth of anything you develop by the professional quality of those who gave it their imprimatur or actually created it.

You also need team commitment, which has to be carefully built, and the best place to start is with the initial planning of the program. Every change requires helpers. Picking a team and getting them to come on board is crucial as it spreads the political risk as well as opening up budgets and influence sources. The planning process for a change is often the best way of bringing these people in and getting their commitment.

Of course, there is no guarantee that your attempts to involve others will meet with success.

case   Paul found this out to his dismay as he tried to implement changes to the development process. He rapidly realized that his changes could not take root without shifts in the management system, which meant working with the HR department. At one time HR had had a global reputation as very advanced, but over the years vigor had declined and the function had fallen into disrepute with the line management. Paul got a very senior group together and explained the problem. Their response was delightfully smug. They had, it was explained, already dealt with this problem. Seeing his confusion, they listed the number of studies that they had commissioned and rules they had recommended to incorporate. The fact that none of these recommendations was widely known outside their group or that people were not using them was not *their* problem. They had been given a task; they had completed their task—tick, end of story! Nothing could get them to take things further. Implementation was simply not their problem, thank you very much. This firm went through a succession of senior HR VPs over the next few years, each one undermined by this entrenched attitude.

So you have a change team, a formal or informal group that is committed to driving the process along. Having a team is no guarantee that they will not slip away on you. Some leave for genuine reasons—they have left that job or the organization—and allowing for this is a key aspect of your project plan. Some kind of succession plan is critical. On a major technology project this may mean locking someone in for many years so there has to be some career benefit—such as a promotion, a new and valuable skill, or more interesting assignments—or it will be resented. Others simply retire on the job, turning up to meetings but contributing little. Keeping the team excited and enthused can only be done if the project is delivering value to the individual. The WIFM idea (What's in it for me?) applies as strongly to team members as it does to the people you want to change. The obvious solution is to keep them involved in the program, solving aspects of the problem, providing them with tasks to perform, having regular meetings, and so on. If you do this, it is important to acknowledge performance and help—people like to be recognized. Look for deliverables from the project that help them meet their other performance targets. For example, one of the activities in working on a major leadership project, was a leadership skills survey. This task could have been done in several ways, but the way selected provided the HR head with a 360-degree appraisal of all the leaders, something he had wanted for some time.

Getting a cross-functional change team to work together is the greatest contribution of an effective change leader. Without this cooperation the change equivalent of silo thinking occurs and each person pursues their own interests regardless of the activities of the others, perhaps even in spite of those other activities. Achieving an effective team may require formal team building help, through team meetings with a facilitator, or through more social activities. If team building is needed, find a team expert inside or outside the firm. Do not hesitate to get help, because the team is too important to mess with.

Set Up a Governance Structure

How decisions are made is important. Your governing group is the team that takes the key decisions and judges whether or not the project has been successful. They may be a specially constituted group or they may be the executive committee of the whole business. They may be judges, but they are also a part of your team with an interest in its success. They are a way of getting support from the very top, amplifying your results and concerns, and keeping you real. Forming such a group is simple if the project is central to the firm's success. High-profile projects attract high-profile steering committees often reporting directly to the executive committee, while low-profile projects have to struggle for airtime. Big technical projects usually have a steering committee of technical people with a few seats reserved for the key executive committee members whose areas will be most affected. Whatever your exact composition, keep them apprised of what is happening, give them the feeling the project is under control, and a heads up when things start to go wrong—in short, no surprises.

However, knowing who is part of your governance group is not enough. You need to look at them coldly and ask yourself what support you can actually expect. Not all leaders are created equal from a change agent viewpoint. Based on observations of leaders in change action, there are three basic types: stewards, transformers, and builders.

Stewards are stuck in the old ways and in improving them. They are experts at efficiency and may be young or old—stewardship is an attitude of mind. They may be good people in a stable environment, but they are not going to set the world on fire. In a crisis they are a disaster as their range of movement is severely restricted by their own experience or imagination or the organization's willingness to follow them. In such a situation they become besieged. They will go into shock and find it difficult to make decisions as life is moving too fast for them. Their responses will be of the cost-cutting kind as this is a natural extension of efficiency. Very occasionally, they can be moved to become transformers, but it is very rare. If you are stuck with a steward, do not expect support and understand that they may lash out under pressure. The best solution if you cannot get out of the assignment is to try to create relationships with a range of sponsors who may dilute the impact.

Transformers are the leaders who have made a conscious decision that the firm has to shift dramatically. They may not know how to do the details, but they will support those who do. These are the true leaders of change. Their biggest assets are an ability to set the bar high and push the organization over it. According to Noel Tichy,[1] one of the top gurus in this area, great transformational leaders have an ability to tell the organization a story about where it is going, what he calls the Teachable Point of View. Such leaders spend a lot of time with the organization passing on their point of view and making sure others share it. These are the leaders you want when the transformation is most severe and extreme leadership is called for.

Builders are transformers who have been stuck in quiet times. They keep the pressure on to change and they support their change agents—indeed, they are demanding. They almost certainly have a point of view about the organization, but that tends to be an extension of today rather than a new vision of the future. These builders may be old transformational leaders who have settled in and may be stuck on their one solution.

The blunt reality is that modern organizations have no place for stewards, but they still exist. The ideal leader is a transformer, though a builder is also valuable in slower evolutions. Given the transformer, what should a change agent be expecting from him or her and encouraging the leaders to do for them? Basically, they should be offering advice, guidance, and support in the difficult spots, help in taking tough decisions, communicating the importance of the project either directly or through visible support, and following through with active support when resourcing or other problems arise.

However, the leadership does not consist of just one strong leader, it is the whole body of leaders starting with the executive committee. If the top team is dysfunctional, the project is at severe risk. Major dysfunctionality usually expresses itself in political decisions, little or no cooperation, and discouragement of collaboration. As most initiatives are cross-functional today this can be fatal. If you are faced with such a top team and your project is high profile, then you have a major problem. The solution is to make sure the team is provided with alternatives and then pushed into taking decisions. If you let them off-load a key decision to you because they cannot agree, you are heavily exposed.

---

[1] Noel Tichy, *The Leadership Engine: How Winning Companies Build Leaders at Every Level.* New York: HarperBusiness, 1997.

Change on the Run

Recognizing a Transformational Leader

- Transformational leaders work with the hand they have been dealt. They don't moan about how things might have been different, they simply get on with the job. Indeed a true transformational leader may revel in the problems.

- Such leaders are grounded. They are self-aware and have a strong sense of who they are.

- They have a Teachable Point of View, a personal, viscerally felt vision of organization and what it can do.

- The motto is "who teaches learns." Transformational leaders spend a lot of time passing on their teachable point of view—in person.

- They set high standards for the organization and insist on their achievement.

Develop a Project Plan and Stick to It

Change initiatives are projects that are subject to the same logic as any other management activity. It goes without saying that a full plan must be created in as much depth as the size and complexity of the project requires. Budgets, responsibilities, people, timings, and dependencies need to be spelled out. The project plan itself should be goal-directed and not just a sequence of actions. Without this focus on outputs it is easy to get lost in minutiae. In particularly large and complex multi-initiative programs, a program office needs to be created to keep track of all the activity going on. A classic is a big information systems installation, such as an ERP program, where hundreds of people may be working at dozens of sites. For example, in a major ERP installation at an insurance company, 150 people in 20 teams were working on 30 different projects ranging from IT to HR to finance, and operations, and affecting the lives of 5,000 people. The program was so big and so political, it had its own HR person concerned solely with teamwork, career issues, and personality clashes. Merger integration, privatization, and demutualization can all be easily as complex as this. If you go this route select your project manager with care. He or she will find their biggest problem carving out resources, particularly good people. This will create conflict in the business with senior people. If the project has poor governance or a weak change team, the project manager will feel unsupported and may not bring up key problems until it is too late. Conversely, you don't want a project manager of such abrasiveness that he or she creates more problems than they solve. This can be a particular problem where passive resistance is high and people seek to destroy projects. Here, an insensitive or politically unaware manager can be a real problem.

Defining the Problem

The early stages of any significant change project need some data gathering and clarification of issues. The problem is not always what it seems and the change issues are usually more complex. You have been asked to introduce a new way of working—like Paul—and the technical issues are very simple, making the change itself look simple. We are all rational. Simply explain that the top leadership wants us to work this way now and all will be well. Wrong! The organization may simply be overwhelmed by change initiatives, or it may never have changed before. Its culture may be entrepreneurial and accepting of new ideas or it may be passive and resistant. If you have not understood the people and culture you are dealing with you have a major problem.

There are three fundamental questions to ask:

- How Ready Is the Business to Change?
- What Is the Culture?
- Who Are the Audiences?

How Ready Is the Business to Change?

There are two styles of change readiness questionnaires. The first is focused on some simple issues concerning the capacity to change. How willing are the people to change? What change skills exist? How loaded up is the organization with change activity? (One client claimed that "our organization can only change in odd-numbered years"—the serious point behind the humor was that all organizations have a change capacity and need periods of calm to absorb and integrate.) How competent is the management in dealing with change? In the case of a large utility, the overwhelming answer from the organization was that the top leadership was incapable of changing, unable to envisage a change, and had no support in the business! The starting point of this change was clearly addressing this issue. Where low capacity is identified the change agent needs to build skills, get clear prioritization, or change the strategy to building some early support in the business.

The second type of change readiness questionnaire is a little closer to a culture assessment. *Ability to Change and Transform* is a 60-question survey used by PricewaterhouseCoopers to assess the level of resistance to change. The kinds of questions asked focus on such issues as cross-functional cooperation, the degree of firefighting going on, the amount of authority people have, the clarity of strategic direction, and so on. The results give the change agent a feel for the level of effort. For example, if people say that cross-functional cooperation is very low and the project includes a lot of process improvement, then there are some clear preconditions with regard to team building that have to be met.

Change readiness questionnaires can be administered in quantitative form or through focus groups, the choice is yours. What a change readiness assessment will largely not do is tell you how to proceed.

What Is the Culture?

It is very common for organizations to undertake detailed cultural assessments and then do nothing with them. The psychologist's report sits on the CEO's desk or is discussed wisely by the executive committee and contributes nothing to the debate except to place an imprimatur on what everyone knew in the first place. Such surveys are of greatest value to new managements parachuted into older organizations. Part of the reason for this lack of use is that the technician who administers the culture survey is rarely the person who implements the change, and the change agent even more rarely has the skills to interpret the survey.

However, there is value in this kind of analysis at a high level. Out of many possible classifications we can identify four main cultures—power, role, support, and achievement. They are different starting points for a change. Each will provide different levers for you to pull—myths you can lean on or replace, ceremonies you can lock into or initiate, social networks you can tie in with, or heroes you can use or develop.

Power Cultures

Power cultures are classic command and control environments, run in a top-down fashion, and often by power-oriented people. People in power use control over resources to satisfy or frustrate others or control their behavior. Power in the organization is attached to position in the hierarchy, and people see leadership as the willingness to give rewards or punishment. Satisfied subordinates are happy with the type of rewards and punishment and like to be associated with a strong leader; dissatisfied ones leave. If this is the organization you have to introduce an initiative into, then you had better have the leadership totally on side and line up the rewards and punishments. It must be their agenda, not yours and that must be clearly spelled out. If the power is wielded benignly, this will be a paternalistic culture with fairness built in through systems and a sense of obligation. In very old cultures of this type, like many of the giant American companies of the 1980s and earlier, the internal rules and safety nets to prevent the abuse of power may create a huge dampener on change. Breaking through this may require controlled violence, perhaps a huge downsizing that snaps old loyalties. Where unions moderate leadership power, the organization may express its resistance through passivity, active union response, and waiting out top leaders. This is perhaps the most difficult of organizations to transform, and it is made even more difficult if large chunks of management and professional staff are also unionized through their professional groups. Where legislation protects the union and coercive tactics are not possible, the only avenue is involvement. Here the aim is to identify opinion leaders and involve them in designing the future. If they buy in because they own the result, then there is a good chance that the mass of people will follow.

Role Cultures

Role cultures include classic bureaucracies, where job descriptions define roles often in great detail. Power belongs to the role not the individual. A role culture may be a response to the prevention of abuse of power or, like much of government, be in place from the start. This is the world of order, rationality, and consistency. This is the world where tasks, duties, and rewards are carefully defined as a contract. The obvious starting point for change is to refashion the job descriptions and rewards. Involving people in changing them is crucial, but remember, a person's job description is their employment contract. If you start to break up the whole system, you will threaten everyone and be faced with massive resistance. Large systems of this kind can take many years to change, particularly if they serve some vital function, and the employees have developed an entitlement mind-set. These systems short-circuit innovation and people are rarely trusted at lower levels. This disenfranchisement confirms people in a 9-to-5 mentality, and as the controls become more pervasive, people cease to take initiative and the system has to put ever more stringent systems in place to effect control.

Support Cultures

In a support culture, people help each other beyond what is required. They communicate a lot about work and personal concerns, and caring, cooperation, and fitting in are important. People care about the organization and it looks after them. People value harmony, avoid confrontation, and value each other as human beings. This is usually seen in small groups, but it may have resonance in caring fields such as medicine. Introducing change here demands respecting the consensus approach, however much that may be overvalued. Indeed, in some organizations the consensus process may have been corrupted to become a stalling technique. Again, seek out the opinion leaders who carry the flame, bring them on side, and get them to own the problem of bringing the rest of the business along.

Achievement Cultures

These organizations are driven by a sense of shared purpose based on qualitative, intrinsic motivation rather than rewards and punishments. This is a world of high energy, a sense of urgency and authority established through expertise and individual contribution to the vision. People are empowered at all levels and channels of communication are open. The change here clearly has to start with the vision, which is the guiding light. Lack of clarity here can lead to confusion. Amending the vision will require involvement of many people to ensure it is accepted. In some cultures, the vision is based on the customer, and the route to changing such a firm is to show how the customer has changed and lead the new work approaches from the market.

* * * * *

Most organizations are hybrids of these four, and thinking through the interactions can be most instructive. It is not uncommon for role cultures to have power leaders placed over them if the outside stakeholders are looking to force change into a resistant bureaucracy. This sets up a dynamic of its own as the organization resists and waits out the leader. Meanwhile, the leader becomes more aggressive and harsh, and may tend to take out his or her frustration on direct reports for clearly failing to deal with the business. This may lead to churn at the top with the executives becoming isolated from the business. From a change agent viewpoint, in such organizations the sergeant majors are running the army and the officer corps is impotent to affect day-to-day operations. Change has to recognize the top, but the sergeants are where the action is.

The biggest change problems occur when the change aims at changing the culture itself, at shifting the balance among these four dimensions. Making a role organization into an achievement-driven one is an enormous stretch. You may be able to do small segments, but it would be a major challenge.

All the above said, there are other cultural overlays. National cultures differ[2] and professional groups—engineers, accountants, nurses, doctors, consultants—all have attitudes that grow out of the types of work they do and the deeply rooted traditions of their professions. Social classes—working, middle, and so on—are clearly important in countries such as the UK. Each of these and others can inform the change. Faced with a cultural survey, ask yourself what action it would lead you to, and how you would modify your approach.

Who Are the Audiences?

It is absolutely critical to identify your audiences. If you don't know who you are talking to and engaging to change, the project cannot, succeed. Without such knowledge you will find yourself applying one-size-fits-all solutions and wasting resources at the minimum and

---

[2] Fons Trompenaars, *Riding the Waves of Culture: Understanding Diversity in Global Business*, Barr Ridge, IL: Irwin Professional Publishing, 1994; Charles Hampden-Turner and Alfons Trompenaars, *The Seven Cultures of Capitalism: Value Systems for Creating Wealth in the United States, Japan, Germany, France, Britain, Sweden, and The Netherlands*, New York: Currency/Doubleday, 1993.

raising resistance at the worst. Such segmentation is, of course, only as good as the imagination behind it. Like market research, which is its closest analogy, simplistic segmentations will yield simplistic solutions. Populations may be cut many different ways—by the tasks they perform, or by function, classic demographics, organizational role, geography, professional grouping, attitudes, cultural persuasion, or promotional potential. Use whichever method provides insight into how they think and what they do. One group, for example, may be the opinion leaders whom you may single out for special treatment.

One outcome of this analysis is to identify the relative sizes of the groups. Working with the many hundreds of partners of a professional services firm the tendency was either to lump them together or split them by skill group. Far more instructive was to group them by client type, which indicated many differences in the ways they had to work. Suddenly it was apparent that the most sophisticated skills were only needed—in the short term—by a very small handful of partners and their staff. This meant that the program could be tailored to much smaller audiences, getting away from mass training, pinpointing work more effectively, and saving many dollars in training costs. Remember, in change as in marketing one-size-fits-all-fits-nobody. Spending time in understanding the audience is never, ever wasted.

The Dynamics of Change

There are patterns by which organizations and people adopt change. None of them are perfect descriptors, but they carry enough truth to be worth contemplating. Nor will any of these models give you direct information on how to actually change your business, but they help to understand the dynamics of what is happening. Change diffuses through populations all the time. Fads spread from epicenters and sooner or later every teenager knows about them. The same is true in organizations—understand the natural dynamic and you can flow with it. People react to change at an individual level in predictable ways, well known to psychologists, and whatever you may think, they will follow the pattern—you need to know it. People accept new ideas in different ways, and you need to know this too.

Three important patterns are:

- The Classic Mourning Cycle
- The Uptake of an Idea
- Idea Diffusion Through Large Organizations

The Classic Mourning Cycle

Swiss-born psychologist Dr. Elisabeth Kubler-Ross became the acknowledged guru of grief, with her groundbreaking book *On Death and Dying*,[3] followed by numerous other texts on the same subject. It seems a little extreme to take ideas from the literature of death and dying to illustrate reactions to change, but research indicates that the loss of identity and self-worth that can accompany changes in the workplace can be extremely severe.

She outlined a five-stage process people go through when confronted with a diagnosis of terminal illness:

1. denial,
2. anger and resentment,
3. bargaining,
4. depression, and
5. acceptance.

Denial

On hearing the diagnosis, the patient reacts with a shock: "No, not me." In the more benign world of business, denial may last for a long period and be shared by whole groups of people leading to significant passive kinds of resistance.

Anger or Resentment

"Why me?" is the question asked now. "Why my husband/child?" Blame, directed against the doctor, nurses, and God, often is a part of this stage. This outcry should be accepted; try not to judge it harshly. Remarks like "pull your socks up and push on" are rarely helpful. In the business world this is where we see the maximum resistance as people push back on the proposals or where the impact of downsizing or job realignment really hits emotionally.

Bargaining

"OK me, but...If you'll just give me five years, God, I'll ..." Bargaining of this kind takes place in the business world as well as people or groups seek to overthrow a decision. This is what Kubler-Ross calls a period of temporary truce.

---

[3] Elisabeth Kubler-Ross, *On Death and Dying*. New York: Scribner, 1969.

Depression

Now the person says, "Yes, me," with the courage to admit that it is happening; this acknowledgment brings depression. In the change world this can yield passivity and a loss of interest.

Acceptance

This is a time of facing death calmly. This is often a difficult time for the family, since the patient tends to withdraw into him- or herself. Work colleagues do the same thing and become uncommunicative. The family or work groups often go through all the stages along with the patient. The mourning cycle is mostly seen in downsizing situations or severe business collapses.

The Uptake of an Idea

The pattern by which people take up an idea has five stages:

- Ignorance
- Awareness
- Acceptance
- Application
- Integration

Ignorance is the state you wish to dispel. Awareness is getting them at least admit that they have heard of it. Acceptance means they think it is a good idea, but they haven't and won't necessarily do anything about it. Application means they have tried it and perhaps had a good experience but won't necessarily try it again. Integration means they have taken it up, and it is now part of how they do things. They can stop at any point along the way.

Ignorance is bliss—sometimes. Enough said.

Awareness is where the vast majority of communications programs get you to and where most old-fashioned change programs left you. The idea was that because you had heard of it you would be convinced of its worth and spontaneously integrate it into your everyday life. Some hope! It is here that resistance sets in, particularly if the initial awareness leads to the belief that "I will lose by this or I will have to put in a lot of effort." This is the best time to kill an idea, and as this is also the peak of effort by most change managements who leave the idea to fend for itself, the killing can be easy.

Acceptance is really tricky. "Yes, I really understand and accept everything you have told me, but I have no intention or ability to do anything about it. I may even believe it will make more money, but that's the shareholders' income not mine. It may make my life easier, but there are no guarantees in life." Acceptance is linked to compliance. "Sure I'll do this thing if you really want me to, but only because it's you." That sort of grudging compliance has no depth. "Sure I'll do this thing, but watch me screw it up." Malicious compliance is very common in passive resistant organizations. Just because they say they love you doesn't mean they mean it.

Application can see your whole change initiative stop dead—so near yet so far. "Well I tried it and I suppose it kind of worked, but there are all kinds of ways I could improve it or things it doesn't do. I think it has some limited potential. Perhaps you could take it back to the drawing board?" It is rare that you get, "Wow! How did I live without this?"

Integration is really difficult emotionally—on the change agent! "Well I've been doing things this way for some time now. I forget where I heard about it, but I have improved it a lot from the original"—even when it is precisely the same. "Let me tell you about it"—a new zealot is born. Never expect thanks. Never expect recognition. Indeed, if you have done your job well, they will have internalized it so completely that it will seem self-evident or their idea. If you can't cope with that reality, you're in the wrong game.

Moving people through this kind of sequence is *hard* work, demanding total commitment and total intellectual engagement with the process. If someone is resisting, it is for a reason. Resistance really is your friend. If they resist actively it is because you have hit a hot spot. You need to be aware of resistance all the time and think it through. Use a kind of root cause analysis, searching from the apparent cause to the deeper reasons. In quality improvement programs, after about half a dozen whys you have probably found the true reason. So they aren't coming to the table. Why? Well, that's what they say, but why? Well, if that's true, why? Never take surface reasons for granted.

Moving someone to accept an idea is akin to a catharsis. Once we are adults, it is rare for us to come across something that is truly new —we are usually replacing one idea with another. To make room for the new one we have to eliminate, adapt, or move the old one to another place. This is a catharsis. In the case of the zealot, the catharsis can be on both sides of the argument.

Assume you have a new idea. You have thought it through and it is a great and universal truth. You are filled with excitement and you start to sell it. As you go around you raise awareness. Some people demur, but basically everyone agrees. You push on to acceptance and after enormous intellectual effort, having people attend sessions and work with the idea, everyone agrees that it is the answer. But only a couple of people do anything about it. Why? Because all the rest are willful and stupid? No. That way lies defeat and dejection and the certain resistance of those *told* to do something.

In a recent actual case the root cause discussion showed that although the idea was correct, and would one day be universally so, today it was only true in some cases. It was simply ahead of its time. There was no immediate felt need. The solution was to continue to train and develop the idea, but acknowledge the timing issue and allow people an opt-out period until their market caught up. Paradoxically, as the pressure was eased, they became more willing to take up the thinking. Prior to the root cause discussion, the change agents felt angry, bitter, unappreciated, exploited, and worried. Change is tough on the emotions.

Idea Diffusion Through a Large Organization

There is a distinct progression by which ideas seep into a population. You have heard of the leaders, followers, and laggards idea. It is descriptive, but it doesn't provide much in the way of guidance on what to do. You may have come across predictive ideas that say that 2 percent are sycophants who will say yes to anything, 20 percent will get the idea immediately, 50 percent will follow, and the rest will never get it. Interesting, but to truly understand you need to combine all these bits.

First, back to the marketing world of leaders, followers, and laggards. Many years ago the Stanford Research Institute looking across a wide range of product and idea innovations in the US found that ideas are first adopted by about 5 percent of the population. These are prepared to live on the bleeding edge—for example, the computer nerds who are ready to go with unproven beta code in order to get the latest software first. They are then followed by another 15 percent. In the computer world this would be the heavy users who are looking for high productivity in established code or a new experience. This gives a total of 20 percent in all. At this point the idea is a "niche" thought, and it may or may not go any farther. Other evidence then seems to indicate that something happens that pushes acceptance and gradually the whole world takes it on except for a few resisters who prefer the old ways. Add to this an idea put forward by Arthur D. Little, the consultancy firm, that when a phenomenon reaches 60 percent acceptance, the economics of the old ideas and ways fail and become untenable. The old approach may then become a niche activity, perhaps the nostalgia item, such as the old Bakelite black phones that are now a designer item.

The specific example of the introduction of the Beetle will help clarify this process. When GIs returning from Europe introduced the VW into America, the concept of a small car was brand new to American culture. It was a niche idea accepted by about 5 percent of the population. Gradually, the idea gained ground that small cars could be fun and other European importers brought in their vehicles, all of different shapes and sizes and attracting different slivers of the population. Slowly, acceptance of the concept of small cars rose to the 20 percent range, with the mass of buyers of traditional US styles remaining unaffected and even scornful of these tiny vehicles. Then came the oil crisis of 1972. Suddenly, small was the way to go and in a few short years the whole American fleet was rethought and totally redesigned and large, boatlike vehicles were no longer produced. The nostalgia niche went into the second-hand, vintage car and car kit markets with fifties revivals.

Consider the economics of delivering ice in the days before refrigerators. It was profitable until the point when 60 percent of the households had refrigerators. Then business economics of ice delivery melted away. Similarly, when 60 percent of people had credit cards the cashless society did not seem so ridiculous. And so it goes on, a new technology or idea replacing the old.

As we move through the different stages of buying in percent 5, 20, 60, (never quite 100 percent) the change circumstances become different because the people involved at each stage of the change are different and so is the baggage they bring. A bleeding edge computer nerd is simply different from a late adopter who hates computers. The same is true in business. Those at the forefront of new ideas have power and influence; those at the back end of the process may be victims. If one intends to manage a change, the actions you undertake at the start of the cycle are very different from those at the end.

This is how it seems to happen:

- Building a Beachhead—to 5 Percent
- Expansion and Experimentation—to 20 Percent
- A Change Event
- The Scramble—The Next 40 Percent
- Victory—And the Last 40 Percent
- The Final Curtain

Building a Beachhead—to 5 Percent

The problem here is getting the idea off the ground. If you are using strategic alignment as your change vehicle, then getting the top team together with some other opinion leaders becomes crucial. They have the power and some leverage over the system, but they also have negative power. With their support it might happen, but without it, the change will not happen. For the same reasons, you need to get the professional opinion leaders to buy in if you are doing a re-engineering program. By all means get the power people in, but the professionals are the key. At this stage you may do some early pilots or models to be played with that are good enough to look like production models. Let the opinion leaders play with them, and own them, and love them. You now have your first group of converts. But whatever you do, don't get too attached to the pilot, for it will change in the coming stages.

Expansion and Experimentation—to 20 Percent

You can't keep a good idea secret. It will escape, and people will do with it what they will—improve it, refine it, scramble it, execute it, or simply distort it beyond recognition. How do you manage the next 15 percent—with difficulty? If you are using a strategy process, you can have a very deliberate program of involvement. If you are introducing a new approach to business—such as a new sales or marketing technique—you can rush out with a pilot version (a more mature version than you had started with but still not fully worked out) and hope that that way you can contain the experimentation. However, you will always have to recognize that maverick, unlicensed activity will take place. The solution? Recognize it, praise it, and don't make martyrs by crushing it. At some point bring it all to a head. Bring together all those you can find and start to distill their experiences, for example, through workshops, interest groups, or a formal competition. Get them involved in finding the true idea and its genuine variants (and there will be legitimate variants). Think in terms of a process of experimentation. Go with the flow. Recognize that the idea may never take over the whole system. It may just sit there with niche acceptance. Unless you push it forward or something happens, it will remain a "good idea," but not the new system. There is always a good reason for not moving forward.

The Change Event

There are four types of change event:

- Catastrophes
- Accretions
- Accumulations
- Willed Events

Catastrophes

In the most obvious case, some catastrophic event takes place and everyone sees the obvious solution. Take the case of the oil crisis; it was apparent that the world was different. If the crisis had been short-lived it would not have changed the American car industry, but it was deep and politically traumatic and the specter of oil shortages combined with rising anxiety about the environment. The conditions for an industry catharsis were right. In a company, the conditions might be a catastrophic decline in profits or the appearance of new competition.

Accretions

In the second case, there may be a slow accretion of changes. In a factory, for example, no one new piece of equipment may do it, but the steady shifts in tools and methods in a dozen different tasks may leave the whole production process looking suddenly different. You cannot point to anything in particular. The transformation may be credited to some program, but in reality it is probably a simple accretion.

Accumulations

In this case, we have an accumulation in the environment. You have been trying to get the sales force to work with their customers in a particular way, based on an assumption of what the customer will want, but people are dragging their feet. Then suddenly the word is out that this is the way to go. What has probably happened is that enough of the customers have now changed that the new approach is needed by a critical mass of the sales people. Having tried it they are now going to all their other customers and recommending it. The idea has gone over the top.

Willed Events

Willed events happen in firms that are making money but where the leadership believes there is a better way and decides they have to force the issue. This can still be very difficult. Take the audit profession. As accounting systems became more automated, customers became less willing to pay for an audit. They did not see the value. This was a clear external event, but no one in the audit profession took much notice, because the switch was happening too slowly. So audit strategists started to become more shrill about it and claim that the profession was in survival mode. This statement was broadly true, but not at that specific moment. People got very tired of this discussion and when the audit firms continued to survive, they simply became cynical. Indeed it was not until profits were in serious decline that the big firms took serious action.

It is like being the boy who cried, "Wolf." There are other ways of getting their attention. You could induce a mind-set change in key people through involvement in thinking strategically then hope they will carry the idea forward. You can bring in some zealots from outside, who are already converts to your idea and give them positions of power. You can make changes in equipment, structure, and so on that force the firm to work differently. You can threaten, cajole, and fire people who will not line up. If you are lucky you will get a change and the people will believe they have to move on, but this is a high stakes game. There is always the chance that they will resist you and the whole system will stop. Making change in the absence of a clear external or internal event that generates a felt need is very, very difficult.

The Scramble—The Next 40 Percent

The event has happened and the organization has recognized that circumstances have changed and they must adapt. Remember no one really *wants* to change, they are all doing it because they *have* to. In this period another 40 percent of the people come on board. The first few of the 40 percent rush in, scrambling to be there, and they bring with them all their prejudices and ideas from the past. They want this to be as easy as possible and this is a moment of great danger. Just when it looks like the battle is won, you get drowned by people taking your idea and dissipating it in every way possible. They will pretend to adopt it. They will liken it to some other idea and merge them to the detriment of the new one. They will not really understand the idea and substitute one of their own. They will claim that something they are already doing is the new idea—relabel it and declare victory.

If you are not careful you will have total destruction on your hands. To get past this, you have to be prepared with very structured versions of what you want doing. This has to be clearly distinguished from present practice and there needs to be a clearly marked migration path. Even that may not be enough if communicating the material is left to traditional training. Think about using modern, high-involvement experiential methods where you allow people to play with a simulation of the new approach, to catch people's interest. An example of this would be a computerized simulation of a new factory layout. Remember implementation can fail at any time.

In the early scramble, you awaken dragons. Up to this point you have had enthusiasts and volunteers or groups who have been given enormous support. In the scramble, the idea is thrown out to the crowds, and the surge of emotions and power plays can be fearsome. If the new methods involve new structures look for nasty infighting. If they involve one cultural group winning over another—say, sales over manufacturing or vice versa—look out for acts of revenge. Trade on the hope that this new method can bring to the people if they were shocked by the change event. Try to build faith, but remember the ideas will be under the microscope, and faith rapidly turns to cynicism.

There are occasions when counterrevolution sets in. Suddenly, the mass of the people are confronted with the reality of a change—they are actually going to be personally affected. If there are rabble-rousers with genuine differences of opinion, this is ideal ground for them. Indeed, it is their last best chance. If they don't act now the game will be over. Be on your guard and move fast. Acceleration through this point is your best hope of preventing the rumor mill from destroying you.

As the rest of the 40 percent come on board—if you have worked it right—they will be coming into a structured implementation. Although you will have some of the same problems they will be of a lower magnitude.

Victory—The Last 40 Percent

At this moment the new idea has won. Essentially it is accepted, and it is seen as only a matter of time before everything is converted to it. This sends a frisson of fear through the remaining 40 percent—they aren't on board yet. From your perspective you have to work out whether you care. In unmanaged changes, these people come on board or they don't. The performance system eventually catches up with them and squeezes some out. However, in managed worlds they can be a real change resource. They are the source of tension and examples. Tension because downsizing them can break up resistance. They can be examples: at the point when the new idea is in place, leadership may choose to set out stark alternatives. "Are you with the program or not?" Those who are not are encouraged to leave. This sends a clear message to the organization and will speed up the scramble. For those who are left you have to decide whether to hold on to them and help them or find a way of easing them out of the system. You will never get to 100 percent voluntarily. Also it is highly likely that by the time you get to this point a new idea will have come along and you will be off on something new! As a side comment, the size of this opportunity at 40 percent may seem large, but remember when traditional functional organizations re-engineered, headcount drops of 35 to 45 percent were not uncommon. E-business looks set to equal that number.

The Final Curtain

One of the realities of being a change agent is that the journey is so exciting nothing can ever match up to it again. Do you now go on to manage what you have created or do you move on to pastures new and perhaps a new change challenge? Indeed, there is the real chance that the organization will choose to ease out the person who changed them.

The dynamics of change are well attested, but they are only guides. Different firms will go through the changes at different speeds, and different individuals have different rates of taking up ideas. Indeed, it could be argued that in North America in the 1990s, the business population's ability to absorb change rose significantly as serious change became the norm. Downsizing, job change, retraining (indeed continuous learning for individuals), and the uptake of new technologies all point to an already flexible population becoming even more able to deal with discontinuities. In a world of high change, this has to be a cultural competitive advantage.

A Checklist for Undertaking a Change Strategy

Technical or professional people who give little thought to the change aspects of what they are doing run many change projects, and they almost always run into problems. Ensuring you have a clear mandate and support, that you build a team, get a governance structure, and set up a project office will get you going, but there are many other issues in a change initiative. The checklist of 14 items set out below is a quick overview of some of the bigger issues you will come across.

1. Understand the Scope

What are you supposed to be doing? This should have been made clear in the mandate discussion, but you need to be extra careful if you are to avoid scope creep where the original range gradually expands. Almost every project is subject to this, and the more successful it is the greater the creep. This happens for a number of reasons. Often the project leader will get carried away and widen the project. Leaders may scent competence and wish other work on a good change manager. Others seeing success may seek to attach themselves to your project to be pulled along in its wake. The project itself may evolve from something simple to something much more comprehensive. Whatever the reason, be wary. If the boundaries of the project change, you need to restructure your mandate, your budget, and possibly your team.

2. Start with the Audiences

Your audience analysis (often called a stakeholder analysis) is the primary tool for change. If you don't understand whom you are changing, it is almost impossible to move them, except by blind luck. Build a strategy according to the audience. How are you going to involve them and communicate with them? Be prepared to use a wide range of techniques from mass meetings to one-on-one discussions—whatever is appropriate to the audience. Identifying audiences will require significant interviewing to get clarity into the different groups. Also remember that audiences will change as the job progresses and the organization alters; the segmentation you started with may not be the one you finish with.

3. Find the Opinion Leaders

Who are the people who will amplify your message? Have them with you and you may well win, but have them against you and you will definitely lose. Plan to involve them. If possible have them help you develop the change approach so that they feel ownership. Remember that opinion leaders can be anywhere, not just in the traditional hierarchy.

4. Assess the Leadership Team

Who are the leaders, and what is their background? How do they interact? Why? Do you have to work around them? Will they support you? Does their support mean much? How much time will they devote to this? Where is it in their priorities? Are they able to lead and pass on a strong Teachable Point of View that defines the business, its future, and its values? Can the leadership be relied upon to put across a consistent message and to stick with it over time? Leadership is a precious resource to the change agent—use it wisely.

5. Understand the Change Vision

This should be clear from the strategy work that led to the project, but if you are not sure go back to those who created the strategy and get them to explain it. It may not be as clear as they thought. And if you don't understand, how can you pass it on? If the vision is narrowly construed, work out how it affects each of your audiences and develop materials for explaining the strategy and the project vision that are audience specific.

6. Build a Business Case and a Case for Change

You will need these to explain the change to the people. The business case will be more formal including quantitative analysis of the financial reasons for making the change. The case for change is more of a strategic statement of the benefits the firm expects to derive from the project. How will you develop the business plan or a case for change? Who needs to endorse it? Will the opinion leaders own it? Can it be easily explained? Is it rational or does it rely heavily on persuasion or force? The case for change may include benchmarks or best practice. These can be used to lever resistance, particularly when they are close parallels. Is there a "burning platform" that forces the change? Do you have to create a change event either to push people to leaving home or to push the initiative past the 20 percent of minority acceptance?

7. Select Messages of Serious Intent

One of the recognized keys to political revolution is the willingness to do violence. There come points in a major change when opinions clash and someone has to go. Fat organizations with entitlement cultures sometimes have to experience loss of employment to break them up and start to make them more competitive. Shooting admirals, encouraging those who disagree to leave, indulging in mass downsizing that breaks up old systems, reorganizing to do the same thing, may be done for other reasons, but they are also ways of demonstrating the seriousness of your intent. If overused, they can introduce catatonic shock and the organization may go into follow-orders mode or become destructive. Such behavior must have a valid business reason that can be made apparent to all. If you are going to be coercive, how are you going to heal the wounds of the people who are left? Consider high involvement. Busy, involved people are happy people.

8. Identify Compliance Levers

Change is a mixture of persuasion and force. Compliance levers are the heavy artillery. Performance appraisal and reward systems in the right culture should reflect the issues you wish to change, to focus people's minds. Changes in work rules, reorganization, new information technology systems, and certification processes can all help to focus attention. But they must be seen to be legitimate, otherwise they are simply coercive and will breed resentment that will outlive the change.

9. Select Involvement Processes

It is clear that involving people is absolutely the best method of getting change. Work out how to empower them to change themselves. Workshops, town meetings, team meetings, sessions large and small are all useful. How will you organize them and in what sequence? What messages will pass from meeting to meeting through the rumor mill? Who should attend? How do you deal with those who do not attend? Look for peer pressure opportunities or highly competitive situations where you can encourage people to rally round. Identify the touch points where you connect with the people you wish to change, such as process mapping sessions, training, speeches, social occasions, seemingly casual meetings, and the like. How do you manage each of these so that people receive continually reinforcing messages?

The mechanics of workshops seem quite simple, but the selection of the participants, the location, the facilitator, and the size of the group all contain pitfalls. Choosing the wrong participants can be a disaster. You need to get the people together who have an impact on the result. If that means cross-functional teams, and it probably will, then cross-functional it must be, even if this is not traditional. The same is true with multiple levels of the hierarchy. Off-site meetings are generally best, but if the venue is too luxurious it can send the wrong message. A poor facilitator can ruin your meeting or at the very least make it less productive than it could be. There are many types of facilitator, from those who will simply write down what you say, to those who push back. Find one you are comfortable with internally, from a consulting practice, or someone in private practice, and invest in them as they go up the learning curve. Workshop size is less important than choosing the right facilitation technique.

Although small workshops are organized very differently from events of say, 100, it is possible to run events for many hundreds of participants provided you use the right process. Check out your facilitators and what expertise they have.

10. Consider Pilots

The idea of a pilot is to try something out. This method is great for learning but limited in introducing the new idea. For example, you can run a pilot training session to learn how it works, but you would never leave it that way. For full deployment you need participant workbooks, facilitator guides, and the full panoply of train-the-trainer courses. If you use pilots, do so in a deliberate way. First, pilots are for experimentation, so collect the results; you have to have a way of pulling out the learning and cycling it back. Second, don't let the pilot become a vehicle for resistance; in many organizations the term pilot is shorthand for something we have no intention of introducing, but the boss has a bee in his bonnet about. Third, make sure people know the role of a pilot. People do not distinguish between pilots (an idea in progress), prototypes (a full-blown expression of the idea, which we will still tear down), and production models (an industrial, stress-tested version with all the bugs out of it for general use). These distinctions are obvious when working with hard goods, but when you are working with ideas, they tend to get lost and people confuse the pilot with the production model.

11. Make Training Effective

It is not difficult to make training effective, but the selection of appropriate techniques is crucial and can be seriously compromised if the training people are very traditional. There is a growing array of training techniques that can be used. Many have been around for some time, but not used effectively, such as action and experiential learning; the emerging uses of computer-based training holds enormous promise. Some of these are as boring as traditional talking-head classroom styles, but others are much more exciting and engaging. Training materials need to be vetted by opinion leaders so that they receive their stamp of approval. The names of the people involved are part of the course materials and a validation. Build the training materials, undertake feedback, and set up knowledge loops in the business. Pick good trainers—poor ones will butcher your painstakingly produced materials and waste your efforts. Beware of passing course delivery down the chain through train-the-trainer courses. Although it may be important to get a large volume of people through the program, you fairly rapidly start to enroll people with absolutely no knowledge of the subject outside the training materials, and if asked a technical question they are stumped. Your program is degraded and your precious message is diluted or lost completely. You need to be very aggressive about who trains. Look for real operating people rather than pure trainers.

12. Create a Communications Strategy

There are many ways of communicating from speeches, through internal newsletters, to e-mails. Tightly focused, multimedia communications will build awareness. In principle you cannot overcommunicate, but *do not assume too much power in communications*. People often don't read everything that crosses their desk. Actions speak louder than words in a major way and inconsistencies will be noted and encourage cynicism. A communications strategy needs to be created early and revised regularly.

13. Understand the Present, the Future, and the Gap Between

It goes without saying that a full understanding of the present state (where it is now—or "as is" in change jargon) of the organization will need to be created. This will provide one side of the gap which you have to leap. The other side is the vision of the future in all its dimensions (in the jargon the "to be"). If you are trying to implement an initiative out of the firm's strategic plan the future state should be specified in the plan. So if you are trying to make changes in the way the sales force operates there should be guidance in the original plans. If not, then developing that future picture is your starting point. In technology installations, a full vision of the work environment needs to be created. This analysis is crucial for explaining the issues to people and bringing clarity to the project. Creating such vision is an important change management opportunity, and you have choices. It may be developed by a small group and presented as a fait accompli. It could be developed as a strawman and discussed and amended in a senior group. It could be developed as part of a major workshop series that involves a wide range of people.

The resultant picture of the future state and the gap may be identical, but the result will be very different from a change management perspective. In the first case you risk being accused of imposing a solution and of developing a range of resistances—particularly in role organizations. Use a wider program and you will get greater acceptance. In general, the more people you involve the better for getting buy-in. Survey after survey has confirmed this for decades, but you may not be allowed that luxury, particularly in power organizations. Moreover, there can be cases where the organization feels so disenfranchised that involvement feels like an exercise in futility and as little more than manipulation. The vision is so central that erring on the side of involvement may be preferable, but don't expect it to work every time.

14. Measure Your Success

What isn't measured isn't done. The old management aphorism is particularly true of change projects. The measures of success should be part of the original mandate discussion. If you don't know what the leadership is expecting, you cannot readily deliver it. Try to be very specific. Set dates for completion, milestones, costs and resources to be used, time frames for interim check backs, and so on, and have measures of pure project management effectiveness. These should be reviewed with the steering committee on a regular basis. The financial and business returns expected from the project should be specified in the formal business case, but be aware of how the case was created and by whom. You can find yourself saddled with someone else's enthusiasm.

The project method you use should be broken down into very short time slots (think of tasks as short as five days, duration for some technology projects) and specific task deliverables set for each period. This prevents task drift. This approach is called goal-directed project planning and is very effective.

Technical performance measures should be specified by the tendering and supplier promise for machinery installations. A word of warning on technical installations: it is common for such projects to become so focused on the mechanics of installation that neither the full business benefits nor the full technical effects are met in the first round. These may not become apparent until a second benefits realization activity takes place. If this worried you in the initial round, keep a log of the issues, and keep your steering committee informed. If you are faced with a highly abstract goal, try to quantify it. Perhaps the most abstract will be the vision statement. Say the firm comes up with a statement like "To be the high-quality world leaders in the manufacture and distribution of widgets to third world countries, serving our customers with grace, wit, and enthusiasm." Take the statement and cut it into phrases: "To be the high quality world leaders," "the manufacture and distribution of widgets to third world countries," "serving our customers with grace, wit, and enthusiasm." Now apply a measure to each. Leadership in defect levels, returns, suitability to task; to have the highest market share; to have the highest customer ratings, and so on. Anything can be measured. So, don't forget to measure the performance of the people on the project; they are entitled to know where they stand.

Inform the governing body of any discrepancies and communicate success as soon as possible. If at all possible, structure the project to yield some "quick wins"; that will serve to bolster your supporters and keep your budget and resources intact as pressure inevitably comes on them. Also, consider celebrating failure, particularly if it leads to learning that may lead to success. Where it becomes obvious that there is going to be a failure, ensure it is brought to the surface as soon as possible. Hiding failure very rarely works, because too many people know, and the rumor mill will get you anyway.

Measuring progress is painful and time-consuming. It requires the collection of often hard-to-find information and the maintenance of databases. But it is worth it, because not only can it be a source of personal protection or advertisement of unequivocal success, it provides the focus you need to keep disparate interests in line.

Managing Yourself

The essence of change agent success is self-awareness. You are an integral part of the project, so who you are and how you operate will affect the attitudes of others to the project. High status change leaders provide the project with an aura of respectability in its early days, which is why top management selected them in the first place. You can find yourself drawing on that reserve of good will. If the project is going well this is not a problem, and your reputation is simply augmented. But if the project is failing, it will drain the respect the business has for you, particularly if others try to pin the failure on you. Take great care.

The project will also affect you as a person. A successful project is a terrific high that can make you euphoric. Success can easily make you insufferable to others if it goes to your head rendering you arrogant and self-congratulatory. This is obvious stuff, but it is also very difficult to avoid. As your success increases, so does your feeling that your opinion should carry extra weight. People will start to resent you, especially if you do not share the success. If the project fails you will want to share any blame, so if it succeeds share the glory.

The essence of change leadership is persuasion. If it were to command, you are not really needed except as a messenger. Persuasion is a principal sales task and the best sales people let the customers discover the need themselves and sell themselves on the benefits. In change, this is particularly important. When you return to your regular job, if you have used a hard sell on someone, or tricked him or her, you will suffer a loss of trust in the long haul. Involve people and let them make the sale for you.

Being a change agent is exhilarating, exciting, demanding, terrifying, and simply one of the greatest managerial experiences possible. Part of your success hinges on what the organization and its leaders will allow you to do, but an even larger part is about how you manage yourself. In addition to the above, here are five ideas to help you handle yourself:

- Beware of Your Ego
- Start Where the Patient Is
- Think Risk
- Beware Missionary Zeal
- Listen for Resistance

Beware of Your Ego

Every consultant will tell you the same thing. True success happens when the client implements the solution and feels it was all his or her idea. Change agents are in the same boat. They are catalysts permitting the solution. They are not the solution and this can be very hard to take. Part of the problem comes from the need to get others to own a solution so that they will be committed to it. You have had a terrific idea, or created the circumstances where others could have great thoughts, yet you receive no recognition. As far as they are concerned it is their answer, exactly what you wanted. The first rule of successful change is ego suppression. Promoting yourself by trying to claim a part of this glory will, at best, generate rejection, and at worst will get you accused of manipulation. Once people see you as having a hidden agenda and manipulating them, you are dead in the water. So, how do you survive with your sense of success intact? This is where the role of measurement comes in. You have an area of success that is all yours, meeting the overall targets of the project. People will try to share that glory and perhaps you should let them, but lock in that victory and it takes away the sting of not being recognized for your achievements.

Start Where the Patient Is

Enthusiasm keeps you going when times are hard, but it can also be your enemy in seeking effective execution. We have all had the experience. You have been given a task and you have worked on it diligently for some time. You develop deep insight and a solution, which you now have to take to those who commissioned you. However, your researches have forced you to realize that the original problem has changed and is no longer the best starting point for a solution. Events have changed and you have subtly shifted your ground, but this process has happened so slowly that you don't even know that you have done it.

The day of your presentation arrives. You go in fully prepared and lay out the answer. Instead of the roars of applause you had expected you are greeted by silence. Into that silence, you start to rant on about the wonders of your solution and how it will solve the world's problems. But nothing can avert the disaster and you emerge reeling, wondering what happened.

What happened is simple. In psychotherapy it is called starting where the patient is, that is, starting with the issue that started the patient looking for help. Dave was a successful executive who had had a serious illness about a year ago. However, using a modern miracle drug, his recovery had been very rapid and he escaped the death or debilitation that would normally have accompanied the event completely. Within days he was back at work. Suddenly, in the middle of a meeting, he found himself wanting to cry. Appalled, he left the room and when the problem persisted, sought help. As the therapist worked with him, they found their way from the incident to the illness and the fact that he had never processed this near-death experience. Suddenly, there was a breakthrough and Dave blurted out, "Why me?" The cry of the survivor. Soon they were into issues of unworthiness and all kinds of problems rooted in his childhood. If the therapist had said, based on experience, that a feeling of unworthiness was common in these situations and asked how Dave's parents had treated him compared with his siblings, Dave would have upped and left. He had to find his own way there, or be subtly led there by the probing of the therapy.

In our business example, the audience was not where you were when you made your presentation, and you gave them no bridge to follow you from the original issue that they had mandated you to research. Meanwhile, you had become so convinced that you had become blind to everything except your answer. This combination of blindness and failing to bring people along is common in transformation, no matter what techniques are used. The strategy program, where everyone is not brought to the same place at the beginning, seems to the participants to be driven by a hidden agenda. Meetings held on the same basis end up looking and being merely manipulative. Training does not provide the preconditions which people need to accept before it is rammed down their throats. This behavior occurs again and again and is perhaps the largest single trap a change agent can fall into.

Think Risk

As the bumper stickers say, "Shit Happens," and in transformation, it happens all the time. Transformation in a large organization can take so long and there are so many things that can go wrong that for disaster not to strike would be unusual in the extreme.

Harry and Janet worked with a major profit-challenged clothing manufacturer in the UK and had been developing a whole new approach to the HR aspects of their firm as part of a larger transformation. They had dotted every i and crossed every t, and everyone in top management was in line, but coming into work one Thursday morning the roof fell in. The parent company had replaced the whole top team. Six painful months of work was destroyed in an instant. It could have been a market disaster, an acquisition, or simply someone waking up one day feeling bilious. The random events of the outside world can render all efforts useless. The trick is to be able to walk away from the situation and keep going. Railing against fate will have no effect whatsoever.

In theory, of course, Harry and Janet could have predicted the disaster—it was just one of many risks in the change program. In practice, something like that is rarely assessed—it is just so big you can't deal with it. However, there are many risks that can be assessed. Just as strategists indulge in projecting future scenarios and defining risks, so should the change agent identify all the potential risks: staff losses, money being cut off, loss of a critical supporter, failure of a set of ideas—the list goes on. A risk analysis that lists all the potential risks with their probability should be a normal part of setting up a change project.

Beware Missionary Zeal

Missionary zeal is the passion of the converted combined with a good dose of myopia. "I have understood. I have internalized the new idea. If I see it then so must you. If you don't see it, you are clearly ignorant/blind/stupid/power hungry/old/young/not like me!" The deeper the change, the more profound its implications, and the longer you took to understand yourself, the more likely you are to suffer from the blinding effects of missionary zeal.

Missionary zeal is at once the lifeblood and the downfall of change agents—the lifeblood because it gives them the vision and enthusiasm to carry on; the downfall because it blinds them to other people's unwillingness or inability to change their minds. It also makes it difficult for them to see the very real issues that surround every change. Everything is labeled "resistance" and hands are thrown up in horror. Yet resistance is always logical. If someone won't come along with you it is always for a good and solid reason. At one extreme the proposal has no value in it for them, and at another it is a great threat to them. Then there is always the possibility that they didn't understand a word you said! People have to have a reason to make any change. They have to feel the need to do *it*, whatever *it* is.

Place a person with missionary zeal in a room with a resistant person, and you have a dialog of the deaf that the resister will win, even if the zealot is the boss. Passive resistance, delay, and incomplete implementation are some of ways resisters slow things down. The reality is that getting people to understand something is a process that can force you to go back half a dozen paces in order to carry them forward one pace. It is frustrating and painfully slow, but there is no alternative.

Listen for Resistance

No one comes along and announces to you that they are resisting or at least very rarely, but sometimes they tell you in subtle ways. Successful change agents listen carefully and recognize the symptoms of resistance. Here is a list of some classic ways of degrading an idea.

- Pigeonholing—This is another of Joe's ideas. They never go anywhere.

- Damning with faint praise—A really great idea ... for Joe!

- Backwashing—We've already done this. It is just like the program Joe had back in '99.

- Delaying—We'd love to do it, but we have to get those sales in/products out/end of year accounts finished....

- Not-invented-here—It won't work in this market, this market is different....

- Calling on a higher power—The customer won't like it—The customer was never asked! The boss won't like it—The boss may not like it but is this a problem?

The problem with all of these is that they may carry a germ of truth that is very often difficult to refute. They can put you immediately on the defensive, becoming ever more shrill. So how do you get past them? The solution to resistance lies in understanding it and its sources, and the starting point is to get to know the audiences you are working with. Start by walking in their shoes and understanding why they are saying the things they are. Getting to know your audience involves practicing everything we have just talked about. You have to put your own preconceptions to one side and understand where they are really coming from.

Working with a services firm, it became clear that a large part of the transformation was going to lie in the ability to change the way they did their work. The new methods were not particularly complex or hard to understand and adopting them should not have been such a big deal, but getting people to take them up was very difficult.

Almost all the comments listed above were mentioned at sometime as excuses. A root cause analysis was done on the problem, and what looked like a trivial issue suddenly became very deep.

- This was the third time in 10 years that someone in the firm has mandated a new approach. It was the third time the service staff had rejected it. This really was just another of Joe's (read head office's) ideas.

- It was easy to ridicule the ideas, because at a superficial level they looked remarkably like things a good service provider would do anyway. Chalking this up to the head office catching up with the field was damning with faint praise. The new methods could be safely ignored, because the field was ahead (it wasn't).

- The differences between the new approach and previous ones were small in the eyes of the providers (the new methods were actually much more rigorous). They had been to the previous courses and as soon as the word got out about the similarity, they stopped coming to training.

- There is always a good customer reason why you cannot do something just now.

- The ideas were invented in the international head office, and in this local subsidiary this was an excellent reason for nitpicking.

- The new methods were built on more interaction with the customer, which was a problem for many who were technicians and not comfortable in deep discussion with the customer.

- The boss really didn't like it if the training took time away from billing work.

All these were partly true, but not really true enough. The analysis probed deeper and found a few more realities.

- The new methods demanded more high-level business thinking, and the providers felt inadequately prepared but were not willing to admit their weakness.

- The approaches were different enough that they threatened to show the provider as incompetent. Plus, the way they were being taught drove that message home to the service provider.

- The providers were right that not all customers needed or wanted the new approach. Trying to enforce a single approach was one-size-fits-all thinking.

- The providers were judged by their sales and billings, and if anything disturbed that they would resist it. Having to explain to the customer that the providers' prior ways of doing things were somehow inadequate was not a happy thought.

But this kind of insight was only the starting point. Those trying to put the program across started to look at themselves.

- Were they too highly committed to the program and were overselling it with missionary zeal?
- Were they driven by their own needs to get the program out of the way and off their performance contracts?
- Were they using the right methods?

The result of all this was a total reshaping of the program. They slowed down the delivery schedule and looked for opinion leaders who would try out and endorse the approaches. They changed the training methods from dry lectures to engaging experiential approaches. They set up a local committee to customize the approaches for their market. In short, they started to treat it as a proper change project instead of a training activity. They discovered that your own assumptions and needs can deafen you to the causes of resistance.

* * * * *

There's nothing like being a change agent—it's like playing behavioral chess. To be at the forefront of a significant assignment that calls on your powers of persuasion, leadership, and technical skill is a career high. Successful agents find themselves innovating technically, behaviorally and organizationally, and they find the whole process at once frustrating and exhilarating. Once the game is over you will be changed forever, and going back to a regular job will be a bore. The emotional let-down can be enormous. Suddenly your range of action seems severely restricted, your adrenaline drops, your change team goes their separate ways. Life can be lonely once the roller coaster ride is over. That is why so many good change agents seek the thrill again, climbing onto another horse in the change rodeo.

CHAPTER 6

৪০

Build an
Army of Leaders

In 1999 North American organizations spent an estimated $2 billion on leadership training with third party suppliers, and that was only a fraction of what was spent internally. This commitment is not new; leadership development has been a major industry for over a decade. The reason why is simple. Organizations have been going through profound change and the essence of leadership is change. Managers administer, but leaders change and transform. As we move into the e-world, the pace of continuous transformation is going to pick up yet again, and the quality of e-leadership will become a determining factor in market success, and that will apply not just to top leadership but to every level. As Noel Tichy[1] states, successful organizations will have more leaders at every level than unsuccessful ones. This is so because modern, lean dispersed businesses must react quickly to market changes and require people throughout the organization to take on tasks traditionally reserved to the formal leadership. Success in most of tomorrow's organizations will mean an army of leaders who can inspire teams, divisions, or entire organizations to make the changes that are required to achieve extraordinary results in a timely fashion. So how do you build a leadership army? There are three keys:

---

[1] N.M.Tichy and E. Cohen, *The Leadership Engine: How Winning Companies Build Leaders at Every Level*. New York: HarperBusiness, 1997.

- Commit to Leadership Development
- Send Leaders to Boot Camp
- Lock in Successful Leadership Practice

Commit to Leadership Development

E-leaders know that leadership development is not a quick fix. You can make significant advances in a short time, but to be successful requires a long-term commitment. The reason is simple—leadership is a pattern of behavior; you cannot be inoculated with it; you have to learn, practice, and try to perfect it. This takes time on the leader's part and the creation of an atmosphere conducive to learning, on the organization's. Shell International discovered this when it moved into global leadership development in the middle of the 1990s.

case   In 1996 Shell International was the most profitable business in history. With returns of $8.6 billion that year and a 20 percent annual return since 1992, it made more money than some whole industries. However, for all its good fortune, Shell had a problem. Those dollars did not translate into a satisfactory return on investment and it looked as if the industry was going to turn sour. On this measure of capital efficiency, by 1997, Shell was dead last of the Seven Sisters (the major oil companies) and the $10 billion cash mountain it was sitting on was part of the problem. Some of the issues could be solved by financial engineering, some by divestiture, and other techniques, but the cold reality was that Shell simply had to do its core business better, develop a stronger business orientation, and engage in a dramatic improvement of operations, cost structures, and service levels. In short, it had to become more commercial.

The managing directors came to believe that the critical success factor for achieving the improvement was leadership, and they were not sure that they had the right number or quality of leaders. More specifically, they thought that Shell managers did not have a commercial orientation, so they decided to place significantly more emphasis on leadership development in a multipronged attack. Over the next few years they made changes in the ways they looked for talent, brought talent in from outside, changed the performance management system and compensation, and moved HR from a primary concern with keeping records and managing hiring and firing to a strategic role.

In addition, Shell set up an organization called LEAP (leadership and performance), reporting directly to the top of the business. Its primary role was to kick-start improved, commercial leadership. LEAP's philosophy is based heavily on Noel Tichy's ideas.[2] The author of *The Leadership Engine* had developed a three-part construct working mainly with Jack Welch of GE. First, leaders must take a major role in developing other leaders. Second, hard business results come, in part, from soft behavioral practices. Third, if you are going to use leadership as a tool of transformation, you must move fast and swamp the organization quickly—go for scale and speed.

LEAP realized these ideas through three major programs:

- Focused Results Delivery (FRD) was concerned with leadership skills, but yielded a direct financial return through its use of 90-day projects that not only allow leaders to practice new skills but also make money.

- Business Framework Implementation was concerned with business literacy and financial understanding in a search for a commercial mind-set.

- Shell Leadership Challenge was concerned with team building and connecting to others.

Today, all modules were taken by participants who come from all levels in the organization and were chosen by the business unit depending on the specific needs the unit faced. It was the line management's responsibility to deliver leadership development supported by corporate human resources.

Specifically, in Focused Results Delivery (FRD), Shell put 12,000 people through this program by mid-1999, and as Gary Steel, Shell's Director, Group Leadership & Performance Operation, remarked, "It works and it makes oodles of money!" In the first two years, FRD identified $1.0 billion in directly attributable cost savings. As Steel points out, the financial return on the dollars spent to run the course was over 50:1, a ratio which compares with the best of projects. Moreover, the financial engine was built into the business as the approach led to more and more projects being successfully completed and a concept of continuous improvement.

Hierarchy was not visible in the sessions. Shell's experience was that the most dramatic results of leadership interventions came from people low in the hierarchy, in large measure because these individuals are typically never asked. Steel cites the adage that management is in the position of being "able to purchase a free brain" when they meaningfully involve their people.

FRD has become part of an ongoing effort to shift the culture of leadership in Shell and thereby of Shell itself. The firm's stated

[2] Noel Tichey with Eli Cohen, *The Leadership Engine: How Winning Companies Build Leaders at Every Level.* New York: HarperBusiness, 1997.

preference is to build a new leadership culture organically rather than identifying the culture and then driving home the values. Shell has broad values such as respect for people, which are boundaries to individual behaviors, but it elected initially not to promote specific leadership capabilities, competencies, or indicators. That said, Shell is in the process of identifying and gradually rolling out "people principles" that will serve to integrate the leadership development programs. Based on the FRD program and Tichy's work, the list includes passion (for the business), the ability to take edge decisions (the hard ones), and having a Teachable Point of View—the ability to condense and teach a view on the business and the values needed to drive it. They are also thinking of including innovation, relationships and customer intimacy, and achievement and operational excellence. Shell is currently working on building indicators for leadership development. In Shell's view, the hardest issue in kicking off this new culture is not defining the vision; it is acknowledging the truth about the current reality that the leadership culture and business approaches need to be changed. Peter Senge calls this "dynamic tension,"[3] the need to be grounded in both a desirable vision of the future and the (acknowledged inadequate) current reality.

FRD and its related programs are only one part of Shell's approach to managing its leadership talent. The chair and key reports (committee of managing directors) meet monthly to discuss people in the management development committee. This is the only agenda item. The CEO of the respective subsidiary is included in the meeting. Approximately 200 to 300 people are included in these discussions in the course of the year. When top management started doing talent reviews across the lines of business they believed they had a shortage of management talent, but now the firm feels it is getting to know what is available and that it is considerably better off than was thought. Some people have been added to the list and others dropped. Plus, for the first time in its history, Shell has been successfully hiring off the street at senior levels. This was not easy in the early days, as they sought to bring people with different cultural backgrounds into a deeply established environment, but the buy versus build approach is improving. Indeed, the group HR director was recruited recently from Allied Signal.

Performance assessment makes extensive use of 360 degree feedback. The 360 measures knowledge of products, delivery of service, and alignment to values. Business units choose the specific style (upward, full 360, number of participants). Feedback is attributable (not confidential) and discussed with the supervisor. Considerable

---

[3] Peter M. Senge, *The Fifth Discipline: The Art and Practice of the Learning Organization.* New York: Doubleday, 1990.

training goes into the "gift of feedback and the accountability of the person giving the feedback," says Gary Steel—for example, training in the right time to give feedback. 360s are used both for development and performance management and are an important, single, piece of data. The performance assessment process involves evaluation targets and 360 information. All members of the unit are ranked against a statistical distribution and told where they are ranked, which puts pressure on poorer performers to improve or leave. People with promise are told and this is reaffirmed with share options and other rewards. Pay for performance has three performance thresholds. Measurement in pursuit of performance is rigorously pursued and this is an area Shell is dedicating additional resources to managing.

In the area of compensation, the top 1,500 employees have stock options and the number of employees who can access stock is broadening throughout the organization. Stock awards are also increasingly discretionary rather than an entitlement. With the top 150 in particular, compensation is much more referenced to the market. This group is a key target for headhunters and Shell understands that they must be competitive with the industry. Leadership development and succession planning are not yet tied into the system but soon will be. At the time of writing, Shell had a traditional succession planning system, but it did not have very much profile or credibility. This whole program is in the process of being revamped and buttressed.

As part of this more deliberate route to leadership development, HR is moving to be much more strategic than administrative. The role of the corporate leadership development group is to act as change agents, pushing clients to where they never would have otherwise gone. A measure of the commitment within Shell to the leadership development program came in fiscal year 1998. That was the worst year for financial performance in memory, with $4.5 billion of assets written down and no financial return to speak of. Despite that, the organization still decided to expand leadership development activities.

Shell was driven to overhauling the way it went about leadership development by top management's reaction to results, even though most leaders would have been delighted particularly when they were pretty secure from takeover because of the company's size. However, Shell's feeling was that no one was safe anymore. Every firm faces major challenges in the new millennium from the incredible changes taking place in technology and globalization. E-business technologies provide huge potential to creatively reduce costs, increase revenues, and seize competitive advantages, even for a giant like Shell. Quantum increases in size and fierce competitors accompany globalization. The rapid changes in leadership and direction in many of the most admired corporations are attempts to achieve the growth required to satisfy the seemingly insatiable demands of capital markets. In fact, successful competition in most industries requires grasping the notion that environmental change is not a discrete event that requires a singular corporate reaction. In contrast, the most effective response to the current environmental fluidity is flexibility and adaptability—a continuous journey that demands strong, deep leadership.

Yet most organizations are currently experiencing great difficulty implementing change—partly due to the immense size of our corporations and government agencies that limits their creativity and bureaucratizes the imagination. As Kotter put it: "Over the past decade, I have watched more than 100 companies try to remake themselves into significantly better competitors. A few of these corporate changes have been successful. A few have been utter failures. Most fall somewhere in between, with a distinct tilt toward the lower end of the scale."[4] Most change efforts are faced with a disenfranchised and exhausted workforce that waits for the next "quick fix" program. Shell is one of a large number of major firms that are rethinking their commitment to leadership at a business level as opposed to a traditional skill acquisition level in the expectation that it will help them transform the business.

Shell's problem was a lack of commercial orientation. They had and have some of the finest petroleum engineers in the world. They have been hiring the best and brightest for half a century, and in terms of raw intellectual power, there was no problem. Yet this same organization was a prisoner of its own success and had lost the commercial edge. It was beginning to act like a utility and to share many of the same problems. For instance, privatizing utilities have a severe problem moving in from a monopoly or quasi-monopoly (and even self-regulating) mind-set to a fully competitive and commercial frame of reference. The same problem faces demutualizing insurance companies. Protected for a hundred or more years from commercial pressure, they are fat compared to more exposed organizations. They have poor returns on capital and often weak control systems—all evidence of a lack of commercial vigor. Virtually any business that had been under government control or had had protection of some kind falls into this category—the big railways systems, national airlines, dominant banks, and even some car companies are examples.

---

[4] J.P. Kotter, *Leading Change.* Boston, MA.: Harvard Business School, 1996.

Building a leadership army with a commercial orientation means building a deep understanding of the business, changing existing leadership behavior, and creating new leaders, in high volume and quickly. Sending people individually on leadership courses is too slow, and those traditional courses do not focus on business issues but on behavior and personal skills. While the attendees' personal skill level may improve they will have no more business context, and even worse there is no guarantee that they will practice those new ideas when they arrive home. What is needed is a program that links commercial insight to commercial leadership behavior and locks it in so that a large body of people has the same experience, values, and behavior. For a large organization this points to a major program such as LEAP with the Focused Results Delivery and other programs used in Shell.

Send Leaders to Boot Camp

The solution is a leadership boot camp where everyone has a common experience and is moved from one view of leadership to another. In this kind of experience, the aim is to impart business and leadership skills at the same time, to do it in the context of the business, and to tie work and learning together. Faced with this kind of problem, PricewaterhouseCoopers designed a leadership program for clients based on the Shell experience but carried it much further.

The program was built around four ideas of what it takes to create a commercial leader:

* Build Business Savvy
* Build Successful Leadership Practices
* Teach How to Motivate and Inspire
* Build the Ability to Get Things Done

Each idea was developed as a module, the first three taking two days of classroom time each. The final one was more complex, being a 90-day project that the leaders had to organize and perform. At the end of the project, they would receive feedback on how well they applied their new skills. In practice, the modules were made to fit together as if they were a single program, but by thinking in terms of modules participants could take the training in smaller pieces rather than having to take six days in a single shot. Also, the business savvy module was designed to be taken in natural working groups of people from a single part of the business, as they were required to work on the problems of their operation. The leadership skill parts were intended to be taken in cross-functional groups when people were available and could be released.

Build Business Savvy

The challenge was to build a two-day experience that would leave people much more knowledgeable about a business and able to see their role in a broader strategic context. They also had to live the fundamental reality of a commercial world where no decision stands alone and all risks have to be calculated.

Module Design

The starting point in building business savvy was agreeing on a definition of what was considered commercial. For the sake of this program a commercial orientation was taken to be building shareholder value. Other choices could have been made—such as driving some other financial measure, taking a calculated risk, building market presence—but shareholder value has the advantage of being easy to understand because of its link to share price. The next design issue concerned the material to be taught. Did the participants need lots of tools, lots of business environment background, or did they just need context? The conclusion was that they needed all of these to some degree. So the search was on to find a way of putting a lot of this across without being boring. Third, it was decided that the leaders clearly needed to be focused on where they made a difference—at the operating level—but they also needed an understanding of the firm's grand strategy so they could see their own work in context.

The solution was a two-part module. The first part would focus on the total firm and how its corporate ambitions were to be realized. The second part would bring that down to the operational level and pressed understanding of the detailed operating strategy and how they personally fitted into it. The first part was achieved by the use of a computer-based game, the second by more traditional lectures, workgroups, discussion, and by the use of homework—where participants were expected to take what they had learned and look for value drivers in their own business units.

The Strategy Game

The strategy game focused on the firm's corporate growth strategy. The aim was to communicate the corporate vision such that people understood at a gut level what the business issues were, how the business dynamics worked, and exactly how it was intended to make the words of the vision statement real. The aim, at the end of the game, was to have people able to understand, verbalize, and defend the corporate strategy. Needless to say, success at this level would communicate the firm's vision at a depth never previously achieved.

The actual game was classroom-based and played by three teams of three in head-to-head competition using networked computers. There were real winners and losers. The aim of the game was to maximize shareholder value over a five-year period (20 periods of game play). The computer's role was to keep score and tell each team where it stood. Initially, the game was facilitated with the intention of putting the role of the facilitator into the computer in the form of instructions at a later date. Once this was done independent groups could play the game over the corporate intranet, and in the meantime, every participant walked away with a personal copy of the game in individual play mode. The game was created specifically for this user but was based on the Fastrac game shell, which kept the production cost and coding time down to affordable levels.

The power of a well-constructed game is that it draws the players into its world. For the duration of the game they are the roles they play and as competition hots up they become quite emotionally involved. After the game, win or lose, they will compare strategies and experiences. From a learning point of view, they simply go on learning. In this mode, the following is how a player of the strategy game in the utility industry would describe the experience.

case My colleagues and I had been selected as the new top team of the regional Electricity Distribution Company. This was five years ago when the industry was just re-regulating and we were still owned by the government although there was already talk of an IPO. Our team had been given the job of improving the business, growing it, and, if necessary, taking it public. We were taking a couple of weeks vacation when we got an urgent call from the chairman. While we had been away, the whole face of the industry had changed, with two new players buying into the market. What had seemed like a long-term task to be taken at a measured pace suddenly became urgent. Were we fitted for this tougher environment?

We were lucky in one respect. The utilities our new competitors had bought were as inefficient as we were! So we found ourselves all going through roughly the same stages of change—getting our cost base right, trying to acquire other utilities and trying to build some unregulated businesses. Working our way through these strategies was not easy. Cost cutting meant understanding value drivers and what sequence to attack them in. We discovered that if we mixed hard and soft drivers—say putting in new IT systems with changes to cross-functional cooperation and teamwork—we developed synergies that improved our cost base faster. Get the right combinations and we could even kick ourselves into continuous improvement. However, we knew we could not load the business up with too much change so we were forced into choices that made a huge difference to how fast we improved our operational efficiency and bottom line. Getting this right was critically important, because we needed to get as much of an improvement as possible and enjoy the gains, before the regulator came in and took some of the gain away by driving down our prices. Cost cutting turned out to be a tricky problem.

We were hardly into the cost cutting when the first opportunities to acquire some other utilities appeared. So while we were still trimming the business we had to add acquisition analysis to our problems. Of course, our competitors were also hungry to grow, so picking a price and bidding became very tense. The tension was made worse by the fact that there were only so many really good buys to make. Lose one and we had lost the opportunity forever, and we could never hope to get the economies of scale that the winning bidder would enjoy putting them on a permanently lower cost base than us. The stress was beginning to rise. Decisions we were making on cost cutting that were soaking up investment dollars were affecting how much money we had for acquiring. The outgoings reduced our cash, but the improved operations made our cash position better. What to do? This was where we discovered the discipline of living within our means. In this new world, we no longer had the open checkbook we used to have. Balancing our treasury became an obsession. Then, suddenly we were plunged into the e-business world.

The government had been slow in re-regulating the sale of electricity. Under the previous regime, the actual electrons were simply charged through on the consumer's electricity bill by the monopoly supplier—us. Now the government had decided to create an open market where anyone could buy electricity from the generators and resell it to the consumer. Firms like us in the electricity distribution business would charge separately to carry the electricity to the user in a way very similar to that of the telephone business. We had always assumed (correctly I may add) that there was very little money to be made in this business, the competition would be too great. Then we got a consulting report that showed how we could turn this into an e-business-style opportunity. The key was to sign up as many consumers as possible, then use that base to sell other goods and services. The problem was that the market had not opened up yet, so we had to decide whether to spend money now building an image in the market or whether we should wait. What we knew was that those competitors who got a big lead would scoop the market and we would be locked out of this opportunity. So we now had three sets of decisions to make, to invest in cutting costs, to make acquisitions, or to take an option on an entirely new business. We decided to invest in the e-business, but I am still not sure we did it correctly. I think our competitors were more aggressive, because we could not make headway and eventually sold out, meanwhile it had cost us a whole pot of money!

Then came the IPO. This was a real shock. At the same time as the owners were selling out, we went to market with a secondary offering and had to face the analysts. We had to convince them to buy into our strategy and to support the offering. How much money we got was based on our persuasive powers. It was a hard experience, and I really appreciated in a way I never had before how other CEOs feel. These folks ask tough questions! But it was crucial, because we knew that the moment everyone's shares were on the public market we could raise money to buy other firms. We were conservative. When a big gas utility came up we bid low and let a competitor buy it. Then we used our money to take control of a smaller competitor, so that we are now the biggest electric utility, but who knows for how long. Have we missed our one big opportunity to diversify our business? Will the firm that bought the gas utility now buy us?

What have I learned over the last five years? I have learned a lot about taking calculated risks, about living within my means and the problems of cost cutting, takeovers, and even e-business. We did not create the most shareholder value, but I now appreciate that idea much more than I used to. I have also made some discoveries about working as part of a top management team and the problems of getting agreement when opportunities are balanced on a knife-edge. Oh yes, I have learned that if you are going to face the analysts you have to know your business cold, which I guess is also true if you have to talk to your own employees. Would I do it again—absolutely!

The Strategy Game models most of the decisions that a real-life top management in the utility industry would have to take and players see the connections immediately. In the debriefing that would follow the game, the teams would discuss the ways they formulated their strategies, how they made their decisions, and the leadership implications.

They would also lock in place their understanding of basic concepts like shareholder value, economies of scale, cash management, and so on. A bridge would be made to the real business by discussing its overarching strategy and the cash engine that drives it, showing the real business numbers. By the end of the day, the players would have a dramatically deeper understanding of the firm's overall growth vision, and because of the analyst presentation they would have had to internalize the growth strategy of the actual firm.

Value in Operations

The second part the business savvy module used the game experience to move into a deep discussion of how to drive value from operations. The objective was to take the concepts from the game, supplement them with other insights and help people better understand the dynamics of the business and the present competitive position of the firm. In our regulated electric utility example the practical reality is that such utilities throw off an awful lot of cash, and have some unique dynamics. Dealing with this flow, which can never be fully paid out in dividends, puts pressure on the management to seek higher returns than the regulator will allow them. This restless search drives a lot of strategy.

With this kind of industry-specific background, the design requires the participants to walk through the classic progression of strategy as captured in the game. In the utility example this would mean, a strategy to:

- Drive cost cutting to build the cash flow from regulated operations.

- Seek out opportunities to acquire further regulated income and so get economies of scale in the whole operation.

- Seek out ways to diversify into nonregulated businesses that promise superior returns.

Each of these is discussed in operational terms. Given problems of change overload, which value drivers should you attack first—indeed, what are the value drivers and what is the business case for each? As you improve the business, you do get synergies. What are they and how do they affect the way the business works, its culture, and strategic potential? If you get stuck in cost cutting mode, what are the strategic implications, and what opportunities will you miss? In the real world we know we are going to have to look for value drivers. What would they be in our actual businesses?

When the firm moves into acquisition mode in its main business it is really buying assets. What are the implications for acquisition integration? What will it do to the underlying cost base? What are the implications of sequencing the buys, and how much effect will each of them have—a big one with an established strong culture, versus a little one? Given the practical limits on available acquisitions, how do we decide how much to pay? Is this a rational decision based on calculated returns or is it a strategic decision based on limited opportunity and should this affect the price? What are the effects of bringing in a lot of new people? If we were to make several acquisitions immediately, how would we deal with them in the real world?

The issues of merger integration are taken further with the move to build or acquire other regulated businesses in related energy fields (the gas company in the game). Were these discussed in terms of the implications for such a purchase on operations? Where are the synergies? Is this assumption of convergence real? These are major strategic bets that will have huge implications for the way that the business is run. In getting into unregulated businesses—such as the e-business of the game—would we have the know-how to manage a portfolio of businesses of this kind, where we have little direct experience? What are the operational implications? What are the economics and the competitive drivers? What kinds of people do we need? If we start down this route, what is the strategic logic that ties things together? As we do it, are we really in the product business, or are we becoming a truly customer-oriented operation?

The above gives a flavor of the desired discussion, but it is not all. In the process, the participants are introduced to concepts such as value-based management and some simple tools, such as how to compare different value driver investment opportunities.

Lecturettes, work groups, plenary discussions, and videos were used to promote understanding and to pass on concepts. This session can not compete with the excitement of the game, but interest is maintained by relating back to the game and to the issues in the participants' own operation and setting them up for some analysis of their own business when they leave the classroom. In fact, the timing of the sessions should be lined up with the planning cycle where they would be required to use their new learning in coming up with value building opportunities.

This two-day session is intended to be a highlight in the participants' training experience. The game, with its in-built excitement, lays out the dynamics of a business in a very simple way, leaving participants dramatically more knowledgeable about the firm's vision and its options. The debriefing is designed to pick these issues and drive them home. In transformation terms, the strategy would be communicated, its inevitability based on the fundamental industry and business dynamics of a utility business understood, and people aligned behind it as a result. Various tools would be introduced and real operational learning would take place. Finally, the debriefing concerning decision making would start to set up the rest of the program on leadership.

Build Successful Leadership Practices

If module one, business savvy, was about how to win commercially, module two was about how to win personally. Here, participants would start to understand the nature of leadership and how it acts in a confused and often hostile world. The thesis, born out of research, is that leaders who produce extraordinary results have a very high level of self-awareness and that becoming self-aware is the first step on the leadership journey. Based on this, this module focused on providing leaders with a framework (the 12 practices) and an opportunity to be assessed and to gain insight into how to change themselves.

The time allotted to this module was one day. The challenge was not to provide participants with deep skills in everything—there was not enough time for that—but to provide them with an understanding of where their skill level stood, why the skills were important, how to get started in addressing them, and to develop a plan to acquire the skills they needed help with.

The 12 Practices of Highly Effective Leaders

The inevitable first question is "What skills do you focus on?" The solution to this was research done by Howard Fromkin of PricewaterhouseCoopers. He took the research on leadership for the last 50 years and identified the points at which the analyses overlapped in their expositions of the practices of leaders. These points of agreement were taken as the core skills of effective leaders. The 12 practices include having a future orientation, living clear values, demanding results, teaching continuously, modeling desirable behavior, taking risks and innovating, empowering themselves, mobilizing teams, encouraging participation, selecting and developing winning people, giving recognition, and inspiring trust.

The participants fill in a 60-question questionnaire related to the 12 practices before they came to the course. They complete it for themselves and have five subordinates fill it in also. The questionnaire is filled in electronically through a confidential Web site. The results are collected and compared for each individual, against the distribution for the firm, and with outside databases of highly effective leaders who had also completed the questionnaire. The result is a comprehensive review of each individual leader's skill levels.

As the surveys are completed, a picture of the skill levels in the whole organization appears. These are to be tabulated and used by management as their own benchmark of where the organization stands at that time. The survey, being electronic, is readily repeated in line with performance assessments, thus refreshing the database and indicating the health of the leadership team. The key is that the firm receives the accumulated results, but only the individual gets his or her personal results at this time. Eventually, it is expected that the individual results will also be available to management, but there are issues of trust and a fear that the results could be used as a sorting mechanism for downsizing. If this were the case, it is believed that a significant drop in quality results in compromising the learning opportunity.

In this program the benchmarked result feedback was designed into the first morning of the module. The results for each practice were to be fed back one at a time and the practice and its importance explained. Additionally, for each of the skills, the participants would go through a short experience aimed at helping them diagnose any personal traits or blockages that were preventing them from exhibiting this skill. These short experiences were based on therapeutic techniques and provided deeper insight into individual problems and helped people decide how to improve their skills more efficiently. For example, the module on trust had participants examine how they were perceived in great detail and to plot themselves on a matrix. This created a visual summary of where they stood as well as provoking self-examination. The participant then took the insight and was given help in defining how to improve. This was designed for all the 12 practices.

Skill Development

The benchmarked analysis was designed to provide the basis from which each participant could create a personal development plan. Meanwhile, the organization cover create a curriculum that individuals could work through to improve their skills over the next year or so. They could enter their personal development plan as part of their performance contract. That said, the program was designed to provide some initial skill development and skill reawakening. Many of the participants had been on leadership skill programs before; the problem was that the skills had fallen into disuse, hence the purpose of many of these skill sessions was to remind people of their skills rather than trying to teach them from scratch. Recognizing the limited amount of time, the program focused on coaching, team building, teaching, developing a future orientation, projecting values, modeling behavior, project management, meeting management, and change management. Some of these were covered in this module. Others were covered in the next two modules, either directly or through individual coaching.

The Leadership Model

In the Shell case, the company had decided to introduce people principles aimed at providing a message to leaders on the firm's expectations. The 12 practices of highly effective leaders can serve the same purpose, thereby creating a model of expected leadership behavior. The way this is done involves the whole leadership, so building acceptance. First the vocabulary of the practices is clarified and, where necessary, customized, so that each practice is very easy to understand in the terms of its specific company. Then each practice is exemplified by stories of people who exhibited that behavior or several desired behaviors. These stories are collected and circulated, starting the process of building heroes, a significant part of culture change. Over time, the stories are refreshed with recent examples.

Teach How to Motivate and Inspire

This two-day module was based on the program Noel Tichy developed and used in Shell, GE, and elsewhere. The objective was to get people to reach inside themselves and find a wellspring of personal insight that will give them the emotional energy they can use to inspire others. The approach here was a mixture of personal introspection, discussion, sharing, and video-based examples.

The module starts with a personal journey. Participants are asked to think about their own experience of leadership. Who were the people and what were the events that shaped their perspective on what leadership is. Once they have thought this through, they share it with others, and try to derive the central learning, which almost always settles on a few big issues—that strong leaders provide context, meaning, and passion to the people they lead. Think of the great leaders outside business—Martin Luther King, Mahatma Gandhi, Churchill, Kennedy, Roosevelt, De Gaulle—all were able to provide a story we could buy into, that touched our heartstrings, and inspired us to follow them through their own deeply held passion. All of these displayed what Tichy calls emotional energy, reaching to something inside them in which they passionately believed and using it as a springboard.

The personal leadership journey is only one part of the puzzle. Participants are encouraged to understand the hand they've been dealt, the message being that you have to start from where you are. If you are facing disaster then it is relatively easy to see the issues and assuming you haven't been overwhelmed you should be able to get at the emotional energy you need. However, what do you do if the hand you've been dealt is actually quite good? Jack Welch of GE admits freely that the GE he inherited was a solid organization. Yet he went on to become one of the great transformational CEOs of the late 20th century. How did he do it? He did it through a passion for learning and teaching and a passion for the game of business.

Given an understanding of what leadership means, of emotional energy, and the hand you've been dealt, the last pieces of the puzzle are vision, values, and taking edge decisions. Vision can be personal, but it is also a vision of the business and where it is going, which takes us back to the first module and the deep understanding of the business that was achieved there. Similarly, values can be personal, but in this program participants pick up the values of the firm and decide how those integrate with their personal values. Edge decisions are the really tough ones. This component of the program forces people to confront how they take decisions and the limits that the organization and culture put on them, either real or imaginary.

With a feel for edge decision making, emotional energy, and their vision and values, the participants are ready to put together their Teachable Point of View (TPV). A TPV is a concise statement of their understanding of where the business is going and how it is going to get there, along with the values and behavior that people must display to power the vision forward. Each participant practices delivering his or her TPV, using video to get immediate feedback on his or her performance. They get to keep the video. Once they have developed their TPV, they are expected to put it across to the teams they lead in the next module. The teams will evaluate individual leaders on how well they projected their commitment, and if they are unable to do so they are encouraged to either improve or leave the leadership program. Clearly they cannot raise the passion needed to move the business forward.

Build the Ability to Get Things Done

Leadership demands action. Getting things done is a distinguishing mark of an effective leader, but it is not just getting things done any old way. The aim is to have people make things happen using the values of the business regarding respect for people, dignity, and involvement. Simply forcing compliance through fear is not the idea. Through their TPV, teaching, and the skills they have been given or that have been reawakened in them, the leaders are expected to *lead* and to *develop other leaders*.

This approach demands that every leader undertake a 90-day project that is either something they have already undertaken to do or from a pool of projects that the firm wants doing. The intention is not to create new projects to burden an already heavily worked leadership, but every project is expected to drive value into the business. The project setup takes a day of class time. During that time the project leader pulls together his or her understanding of the project, what the issue is, what its business impact is expected to be, and what the goals, blockers, and help needed are. The others in the class help refine this understanding through constructive criticism. The leader then has an opportunity to share those insights with his or her proposed team and to work through any issues with the project sponsor. Leaders are then expected to go out and achieve.

In real life they go out and do nothing. Time slips by and then suddenly there is a mad panic. There are two schools of thought about this. The first says let them be slow off the start and only put pressure on them at about 30 days. The other says to institute a system of reporting that pressures them to start right away. As there is to be no extension of the time limit, allowing them to blow some time is a learning experience. Keeping tight rein is disempowering in a way. However they act, in the end they are evaluated on the basis of the business results achieved and the way they were achieved. Jack Welch's philosophy on this is famous. Achieve good results the right way and everyone is happy. Get poor results the right way and you get another chance, but get poor results the wrong way and you are probably gone. Get good results the wrong way and you are also gone if you don't change.

At the end of the project the firm has a choice. It can say that this was all a training exercise or it can adopted 90-day cycles as a management philosophy and drive the business that way. This kind of choice faces the business in all dimensions of this program. People absorb the vision, but you need to help them keep refreshing it—teach. Now that they have learned the 12 practices, help them deepen their skills and enforce them. For example, once they have developed a rudimentary skill of inspiring people, help them expand it. Leadership boot camp is the first step in developing a new leadership culture and the primary lever for locking in the new culture is the top leadership. If they do not model the desired behaviors, and live the 12 practices, the whole effort will die.

Lock in Successful Leadership Practice

In the early 1950s Carroll Shartle initiated the Ohio State leadership studies, and since then, studying and developing leadership has burgeoned into a growth industry. Amazon.com listed more than 7,000 recent books on the topic, and beyond that there are articles and the thriving speech market. Debates rage about whether leaders are born or made and about questions of personal style such as charisma. Yet much is known. More than four decades of research has identified a set of competencies and capabilities that fall into one of the following four categories:

- IQ such as verbal and quantitative aptitude.
- Technical skills such as accounting and business planning.
- Cognitive skills such as analytical reasoning, mind-sets, and emotional intelligence.
- Leadership practices such as vision, building relationships, and developing people.

This research has largely settled and little new is being added, but the direction of research has shifted from mass studies to the study of successful leaders. In recent years, a few individuals in leadership positions—Jack Welch of GE, Arthur Martinez of Sears, Andy Grove of Intel, Lee Iacocca of Chrysler, and many others—achieved some extraordinary results. Such observations have shifted the focus from describing and defining leadership as a competence to comparing the behaviors of transformational leaders able to create an environment where everyone is ready, willing, and able to be creative, to take initiative, and to achieve the required results. The emphasis on creating results is crucial. After a careful study of several dozen CEO failures during the last few decades, Charan and Colvin[5] concluded, "In the majority of cases—we estimate 70 percent—the real problem is 'not getting things done,' or execution."

Working with all types of study, Howard Fromkin, of Pricewaterhouse Coopers, synthesized an observable, identifiable, trainable, and measurable set of leadership practices and behaviors that are common to those individuals who transform their organizations into more competitive and viable entities. The implication for leadership development is significant. We can now pinpoint, benchmark, and train people in practices that will make them successful—specifically, more transformational—and measure our success.

Howard Fromkin's research focused upon the observable, measurable, common practices that characterize the behavior of leaders who transformed their organizations to achieve the extraordinary results required to compete successfully in their environment. These common success practices are organized for ease of exposition into five general orientations: the future, communication, mobilization of people, coping with change, and relationships. To yield extraordinary results, you need to exhibit all of these orientations.

The Future

The ability to create, communicate, and enforce a vision of the future is absolutely pivotal to leadership. If you don't know where you are going only the lost will follow you there. This future orientation is not simply to the "what" of the vision, it is also the "how" of values.

Defining a Purpose or Vision

Following a study of what kept some of the world's best from succumbing to the so-called decline of the large corporations, Barlett & Ghoshal concluded: "Although the strategies, structures, and systems

---

[5] R. Charan and G. Colvin, "Why CEOs Fail," *Fortune*, June 21, 1999.

of these companies have little in common, their leaders share a surprisingly consistent philosophy. First, they place less emphasis on following a clear strategic plan than on building a rich, engaging corporate purpose, embedding corporate ambition in something that provides meaning that employees can identify with."[6] In many corporations today, people no longer know—or even care—what their companies stand for or why they exist other than to make money. Goals of return on capital employed, ROI, 20 percent on net assets, or creating shareholder value do not engage frontline managers' affinity or commitment. Most quantitative or financial objectives—a 20 percent increase in sales—yield little more than exhausted stares from overwhelmed staff. They fail to provide meaning or purpose for the average member of the organization. Defining a company's objectives so that they have meaning for employees is exceptionally difficult, and it usually won't be accomplished in a one- or two-day off-site meeting for senior management.

Yet there is absolute consensus among the cognoscenti of leadership that providing a meaningful purpose or vision is the most critical component of successful change leadership. A vision must capture employees' attention and interest by defining the what and how of corporate behavior. Leadership and vision are all about creating an organization with which members can identify, in which they share a common sense of pride, and to which they are willing to commit to exert extraordinary effort. People need an engaging purpose to inspire the extraordinary effort and sustained commitment required to deliver consistently superior performance. The requisite vision or purpose must be a simple mental picture of a future state that is challenging, realistic, and, most importantly, *attractive to the people who have to deliver it.*

Henry Ford's vision imbued the strong enduring emotional attachments required to embed corporate ambition in the personal psyche of each and every member of the organization. He set a goal for the production of the automobile—to eliminate the horse—that his employees could identify with. Change leaders know that they must find a way to soften their strategic focus and to translate their strategic goals into a purpose that has meaning for the average

---

[6] C. A. Bartlett and S. Ghoshal, "Changing the Role of Top Management: Beyond Systems to People," *Harvard Business Review*, May-June 1995, 133-134; also C. A. Bartlett and S. Ghoshal, "Changing the Role of Top Management: Beyond Strategy to Purpose," *Harvard Business Review*, November-December 1994.

employee. AT & T's Robert Allen found himself facing a huge and ancient company that needed to change from thinking and acting like a regulated utility in the context of a highly turbulent industry. The key strategic task was loading more traffic onto the existing telecommunications network and developing new products to meet the needs of an emerging information/communication business. Allen translated these strategic goals into something that could be easily understood and which employees could relate to and take pride in by declaring that the company was determined to be the world leader in bringing people, information, and services together. Wal-Mart promised to give ordinary people the chance to buy a huge range of merchandise, while Mary Kay Cosmetics endeavored to provide unlimited opportunity to its female sales force.

Values

Most established organizations operate from a set of beliefs and a philosophy that is usually implicit and neither forged from emotion or intuition nor compatible with a purpose. Change leaders have learned the truism that a company's culture—the values that it embodies—influences most decisions and choices of its managers and staff. Their values signal the day-to-day decisions required to achieve the organization's vision or purpose. If the purpose is the "what," the values are the "how." They liberate staff from the constraints and limitations of policy and procedures, real or imagined.

Using didactic methods to communicate a company's values will simply call momentary attention to the values and most likely result in organizational cynicism that brushes off these new initiatives as another flavor of the month. It takes more than speeches and wall plaques. Adapting Marshall McLuhan's aphorism regarding the medium, we can say that *management is the message*. That is, implementing the values requires consistent and persistent modeling by senior executives in their daily actions and links to a highly leveraged incentive program. In addition, change leaders devote their time, energy, and creativity to finding ways to convert the new culture and the related values into visible and measurable stretch targets (typically defined in competitive terms), and lead the organization toward that goal through a series of operating challenges.

As discussed earlier, Collins and Porras describe the need for such goals as BHAGs (or Big Hairy Audacious Goals) to support the core vision and core values. For example, Sony's BHAG in the early years was to "become the company most known for changing the world-wide poor quality image of Japanese products."[7] In sum, leaders who assert boldly what they stand for generally attract and retain the kind of employees who identify with their purpose and values and become deeply committed to the person who embodies them. People bear no allegiance to a particular organization but to a set of values that they can believe in and are proud to demonstrate in their daily work lives.

Enforcing Goals and Objectives

If you don't measure results they are rarely achieved, but simply measuring is no guarantee. There have to be real consequences to failure and real rewards for success. Strong leaders arrive at agreed, stretch goals with their people and then insist on their being achieved.

Communication

Getting the vision and values across is one of the most common places for leaders to fail. The vision on the notice board is a classic. Some of this failure can be solved through processes that involve people but some is rooted in the behaviors of leaders who simply cannot communicate at a personal level.

Effective Listening

Achieving extraordinary results requires an understanding about how followers' radar is carefully attuned to the words and behavior that are emitted from the halls of power. In the interest of self-empowerment and personal learning, effective leaders listen nine times as much as they talk and ask questions five times more than they provide answers. They spend the bulk of their time in face-to-face communication with individuals at all levels of the organization. In lieu of ego damaging criticism or second-guessing, they remind people of the compelling future and inquire, "How can I help?" They are keenly aware of the need for consistency and persistence in the "selling" of their vision. Bill Marriott, son of the founder

---

[7] J.C. Collins and J.I. Porras, "Building Your Company's Vision," *Harvard Business Review*, September-October 1996.

of Marriott International Inc., set a task for himself to visit one-third of his hotel and resort properties every year to listen and learn. During these visits, he is heard talking about his vision and values by telling stories that reflect their impact. He proudly talks about unusual staff accomplishments that show the extraordinary level of customer service or outstanding events of recovery that operationalize his ideas about five-star service and his values.

Modeling Behavior

Successful leaders are acutely mindful of maintaining a consistent relationship between their words and deeds to reduce the angst and uncertainty that attends resistance to change. They are aware of the powerful role that their behavior plays in communication. They know that they have to walk the talk more than talk the talk. They frequently scrutinize their daily schedules to search for opportunities to behave in ways that illustrate publicly their vision and values. The CEO of a major food corporation wanted to signal her value about listening to the customer. She unexpectedly arrived at the customer call center, relieved one of the operators, and spent an entire day answering customer calls. By the next morning, the company's informal network had transmitted the message nationally. Occasionally, CEO's communicate with a "big bang" decision such as divesting a profitable business that does not match the organization's vision and values. John Allen, CEO of Stelco Inc., Canada's largest steel producer, was encouraging a change for creativity and innovation at all levels of the organization. As part of this culture change, he commissioned a custom-built 10-day workshop that was designed to bring the required attitudes and skills to the entire company. In spite of pressing competitive demands from a variety of influential and important stakeholders, he personally participated without interruption in the first program.

Mobilization of People

Leaders make things happen through people, so if you have the wrong people, you are condemned to fail. Have the right people and yet be unable to get them to work together or participate, and you will still bring in poor results.

Select and Develop the Right People

Effective leaders delight in recruiting and developing potential leaders at all levels of the organization who are technically competent and share, or can at least live with, their values. They see a large part of their responsibility as mentoring without developing clones. In a careful study of several dozen CEO failures during the last decade, Charan and Colvin concluded that the primary reason for poor execution was "more than any other way, [the] failure to put the right people in the right jobs ... and the related failure to fix people problems in time."[8] Specifically, failed CEOs are often unable to deal with a few key subordinates whose sustained poor performance profoundly harms the company.

Encourage Participation

Achieving sustainable extraordinary results requires leadership not by decree but by consensus building. This form of leadership exhibits a preference for encouraging others to participate and express their views. They favor delegation and stress committee work and task forces, while insisting upon performance, accountability, and results. Although willing and able to take a firm position and override objections, leaders recognize the need to obtain consent from the governed and seek consensus from a sufficiently large critical mass to support continuous movement toward their vision. While it may seem paradoxical, these leaders know how to point the direction and *follow*, to coach people along the way. The CEO of a major Canadian accounting firm led a virtual democracy of independent-minded partners. Intent on the need for innovation, he grasped the suggestion of a new method of compensation and performance management. Expecting resistance from the partnership due to short-term costs in training and utilization, he opted to allow a large group of dissenting partners to spend two days off-site to experience and redesign a pilot program.

Develop Teamwork

Develop cohesive work units committed to achieving stretch goals that are aligned with the organization's vision and values. Their focus upon team building has the fundamental requirement of permeable

---

[8] R. Charan and G. Colvin, "Why CEOs Fail," *Fortune*, June 21, 1999.

boundaries between all work units in the company. Many students of change acknowledge that this is one of the keys to Jack Welch's success at GE. These leaders frequently use "we" rather than "I" and offer people compelling reasons to "get into the boat" with them.

Coping with Change

Leaders change the status quo, mere managers administer it. The ability to deal with change requires the application of a lot of tools and techniques, but those are largely useless if the leader is not mentally and emotionally equipped to handle the risks and the need for self-management that comes with change.

Be Self-Aware and Self-Empowered

Daniel Goleman's studies of leaders of successful high-performing organizations identify emotional intelligence (EQ) as a critical component of extraordinary results.[9] The five components of emotional intelligence are self-awareness, self-regulation, motivation, empathy, and social skill. Persons with strong self-awareness are neither overly critical nor unrealistically hopeful. They are aware of their competencies and their vulnerabilities. People with a high degree of self-awareness are cognizant of how their feelings affect them, other people, and their job performance. With a self-image based upon a realistic sense of one's own accomplishments, visions of the ideal are more likely to be trusted because they are devoid of magical striving for irrational omnipotence and self-aggrandizement. Self-awareness is centrally related to change leadership because it is self-empowering or liberating for self-learning. Change leaders are avaricious learners, always on the lookout for new knowledge and ways of doing things differently.

Accept Risk and Innovation

These leaders devote a substantial amount of time to creating a learning organization, one of the most critical components of creating and sustaining change. A learning culture is inquiry-based and reflective where ideas and information are unfiltered by people who are worried

---

[9] D. Goleman, "What Makes a Leader?" *Harvard Business Review*, November–December 1998; Daniel Goleman, *Emotional Intelligence*. New York: Bantam Books, 1995.

or fearful. It is open to problem finding not just problem solving. Adaptive learning organizations identify and find bothersome problems before they become crises. Further, they encourage the discovery of the ideas and information needed to solve the problems. Learning organizations not only test new ideas to solve problems and provide opportunities to reflect on and evaluate any past actions and decisions, they also encourage calculated risk taking, by being more prone to bring healthy conflict and dissent to the surface and more willing to embrace and learn from error. "If they are not making mistakes they aren't trying hard enough!" They are aware that benefits from improvements in efficiency and effectiveness to gain price, quality, and service advantages rarely occur without some risk to creative solutions. Innovations elude most managers because of their failure to recognize the need for calculated risk taking. In contrast, extraordinary results come from creating an environment that thrives on experimentation, showing great sensitivity to people's feelings and their need to save face, while at the same time insisting that they learn from their mistakes and apply what they learned.

Relationships

Extraordinary results attend a leader who directs time and behavior toward establishing and maintaining supportive relationships with individuals in all constituencies—employees at all levels, customers, unions, vendors, suppliers, brokers, and even regulators. Change leaders have been observed devoting as much as 70 percent of their time to such activities.

Recognize and Reward

Successful leaders devote time to personally reward, publicly and privately, individuals and groups whose performance contributes to the required results. They pay attention to the design and implementation of the organization's compensation and performance management systems to ensure that they are aligned with their vision and values. They understand that the achievement of a vision requires a time frame that often extends beyond people's tolerance for delay of gratification. As a consequence, they make time to celebrate small wins or the achievement of significant milestones on the journey. In addition, they provide a balance of sensitivity and consideration for feelings with a mixture of pressure and praise to motivate and sustain the momentum for change. Rather than seeking personal glory, these leaders' attention to and empathy for individuals results in strong loyalty and bonding and often to the achievement of seemingly impossible goals.

Inspire Trust

The populations of most organizations outlast their leaders. They are accustomed to leaders, like quick fixes, coming and going with a little or a lot of fanfare. In the last few decades the shelf life of senior executives in both the public and private sectors has dropped dramatically. Between 35 percent and 50 percent of all CEOs are replaced within five years.[10] The words and actions of new leaders are scrutinized carefully to see if they can be trusted.

Change leaders engage in practices that generate and sustain trust. They frequently express acceptance, support, and cooperative intentions. They are consistent and persistent in their communications and behavior in relation to their vision and values. They make heavy demands for exacting behavior and results, while at the same time, they shrink from hurting people as individuals or groups. They are constantly on the lookout for opportunities to assist people to cope by sharing their knowledge, skills, experience, and resources. In sum, they treat all people like volunteers who have to be convinced to stay with the business, which, in the case of the best and brightest, is very true. Trust produces stable and effective communication. People will take the risk of expressing their thoughts, feelings, and ideas more openly and operating more cooperatively when the trust level is high. People willingly sign up to serve leaders who respect their dignity, autonomy, and self-esteem. Lastly, when encouraged, people will endure the risks to take initiative and be creative in finding new and different ways of getting things done.

* * * * *

Leadership is the critical difference in effective transformation. Change leaders, who obsessively put into play the above practices, bring to bear an interaction of psychological forces that leads their

---

[10] C.M. Farkas and S. Wetlaufer, "The Ways Chief Executive Officers Lead," *Harvard Business Review*, May-June 1996.

organizations to the required changes that bring about extraordinary results. Leaders are passionate about and inspired by the challenges facing their organization and by the potential opportunity to mobilize their constituents to meet those challenges. Such leaders communicate their vision and values to inspire and tug at the emotional heartstrings of the large number of people they get to deliver it. Persistent and consistent communication in words and deeds builds trusting relationships. Lastly, change leaders develop and facilitate persons at all levels of the organization to engage in the same leadership practices. Change leaders personally own the change challenge and are both inspired and inspiring to convert resisters into willing followers. The difference between compliance and commitment is willing followers.

* * * * *

Fifty years of research into leadership has produced a deep understanding of what the right stuff is and hope for all of us who will find ourselves leading change in this increasingly complex e-world. The central message is that leadership is innate in some people, but the rest of us can learn it by acquiring the skills and business practices of the best players. The actions of hugely successful organizations like Shell make it clear that in the harsh e-world, businesses are going to have to continue to invest heavily in leadership development if they are going to satisfy their shareholders—but with two major differences from previous rounds of leadership training:

1. Leaders must be business literate and thoroughly understand their companies, and
2. Leadership is being pushed farther down in organizations.

The Shell experience and the utility example quoted here are indicators of a new slant on leadership. All leaders must be business literate and able to understand the dynamics and strategies of their specific company. In a way, this is an old problem. Businesses have always needed their leaders to understand the strategic direction and the dynamics of the business. What has changed is the complexity and speed of shifts within businesses. Global players with global strategies are breaking up comfortable assumptions about the ways businesses will operate as they move from local or national to global in reach. A major insurance company recently demutualized and is now faced with operating as a single entity on a global basis. The rules that used to balkanize its capital base, keeping it locked in different countries, fall away as it becomes a joint stock company. Now capital can be moved to the place it is most needed. This one fact alone is sweeping away 100 years of assumptions about the business. The way organizations make money is changing and over the next decade simply explaining the new rules to themselves is going to be a leadership challenge.

Leadership is now being pushed farther down the organization. Increasingly, leaders are being seen less as those with formal leadership title and more as the people who get things done through people. A client with a strong union was looking at upgrading its leadership skills. Traditionally, it would never have looked at the unionized first line supervisors. Today, it realizes that it is at the first line that the business succeeds or fails, and the unionized people were included in their thinking.

The empowered leadership army will have to be smarter about its business and more inclusive, as well as highly skilled at leading.

Conclusion

Barring global warfare or other disasters, the next 10 years will
see one of the greatest bursts of wealth creation in the history
of mankind. For the first time, the bulk of humanity is part of
a single and rapidly integrating market and supply chain. Vigorous
competition will drive out cost and inefficiency and fuel growth. The
Internet will expand dramatically in scope and depth, reshaping
business-to-business transactions, and opening global markets for
everyone. Rising savings from the aging boomers of the rich world
will demand high returns and fund growth. The hyperbole of growth
and the New Economy has been repeated so often, it has become
received wisdom.

Is it true? Probably. The information and communication revolution has released forces that will play out whether we like it or not,
and history shows that revolutions based on technology, communications, and the opening of markets always create huge wealth. The
creation of this wealth is posited on an open, globalizing economy
of freer competition, restless capital, and rapidly evolving technology. Put these together and they spell turbulence. Leaders in this
world will have to create consistent and superior returns for their
shareholders while riding the white water of continuous change. The
challenge is to lead in instability, not to manage or perhaps even
seek a stable system, and such leadership will mean continuous

transformation. The choice of the six imperatives—corresponding to the six chapters—was not accidental.

1. Change on the run points to the fundamental problem of making big changes. Every firm in the world today is faced with absorbing the impact of e-business. Dell, Cisco, and others prove conclusively that Internet-based approaches have lower cost, greater flexibility, and the potential for greater customer loyalty than anything so far seen. The process revolution of the 1980s led to cost drops in the range of 40-plus percent, and there is no reason why e-business cannot do the same. If it does, there is no hiding place for anyone. Mergers, technology assimilation, and profit recovery will be part of everyone's life—more change on the run.

2. Extraordinary financial results are essential. Leaders are measured on their ability to deliver the numbers and the ability to find resilient profits in a turbulent world will be a major challenge. Many things will contribute to this. Excellent strategy, flexible production systems, tight customer linkages, and strong human resource systems, but without cost insight, leaders cannot squeeze the full value out of economic opportunity. The selection of your CFO and the sensitive application of cost insight can turn an indifferent strategy, a poorly performing production system, and an unfocused marketing approach around. Not to decry the other professional skills, but for a leader measured on financial return, cost is king.

3. Uniting people behind your vision is the only way to get it into place quickly, and in an e-speed world this is a requirement. Leaders who have visions and send out a memo are amazingly enough still around, despite the fact that the technique has been proven useless over and over again. The only technique that works is involving people in the creation of their future and keeping them involved.

4. Harnessing people's experience is like being given free money. They already work for you. They are the holders of all the tacit knowledge in the business, and tacit knowledge is what makes a strategic difference. Creating an organization where this happens is a leadership challenge that cannot be delegated. Sure, others can do the mechanics, but you have to model the behavior that says it is safe to fail, that ambiguity is OK and that boundaries are not OK, if they inhibit the transfer of knowledge.

5. Galvanizing change leaders is a continuation of the transformation theme. Top leaders cannot do everything themselves and the availability of high-quality change leaders is a proven difference in the success of the innumerable small or single change initiatives that will be needed.

6. Building an army of leaders is how you energize every corner of the business, and how you project inspiration and vision on a daily basis. Alignment processes will unify people intellectually and emotionally, continuous involvement will get their attention, open environments will encourage them to share, but only local, touchable leadership will hold their interest in place. Leadership has to be ubiquitous in a chaotic and confusing world.

These are the "what" of e-leadership. The "how" as shown in this book is based on the experiences of many leaders, famous or not, over many years. Are their experiences still relevant? Isn't the new world different? In many ways the e-world is different, particularly in its tremendous dependence on knowledge as a competitive weapon, but in two overwhelming ways it is absolutely the same. First, the same basic fears and desires motivate people that have always motivated them, and change is about people. The specific of a resistance may change, but the facts of denial or power hunger do not change and certainly not in 20 years. Second, businesses need to make a profit, and the approaches used by Welch, Martinez, and Gerstner have universal messages even in the e-world.

* * * * *

The idea of e-leadership is the logical extension of thinking that has been evolving for decades. What the six imperatives do is aggregate existing ideas. This is true of all management thought. The issue is not whether it is new, but whether its absorption into the body of strategic wisdom will change the way business is conducted.

Ideas in management follow the same absorption path described earlier. Generally it all starts out with a bright idea often expressed by an academic and based on research into a few bleeding-edge companies. The contribution of the idea initiator is to create and package a simplicity that others can follow. In its early form, the initial packager rarely has tuned the idea, found all its variants, or formed a methodology for putting the idea into practice. That is the contribution of the boutique consultancies that work with the early adopters. Slowly the idea moves into the mainstream and some event pushes it over the top and into the general consciousness. The larger consultancies take it on, bake it into repeatable methods, and help everyone install it. Meanwhile, the universities add it to their curriculum and teach it to the next generation of top leaders. Consultants join their clients and students graduate. Slowly the idea becomes common currency and it is part of the manager's standard kit bag.

It usually takes more than 30 years for an idea to work its way through the business community and mature. Marketing started out in the late 1950s, but it wasn't until the 1980s that it settled into customer focused strategy, and then one-to-one marketing in the 1990s. The first work that led to lean production was done about the same time and arrived at maturity in our thinking in the late 1980s; this became virtual supply chains in the 1990s. Computing started in the 1950s and is now maturing into a concept that we use unconsciously. The Internet as a global communication vehicle is only the latest technology in a communications revolution that has been happening for 40 years. Change as a management concept started out with the burst of management ideas that followed the Second World War and started to mature in the 80s and 90s.

As ideas evolve they change shape, deepening from a tactical idea to something more strategic, often merging with other ideas in the process. Sales and advertising became marketing, which became customer service, then customer focus, customer-oriented strategy, and one-to-one marketing. It is now maturing in the e-business world into owning a customer knowledge flow. Production took a similar route through lean production to mass customization, with Web aggregators using virtual organizations to deliver self-configured and scheduled products. Change evolved from persuasion to transformation and continuous adaptation, and at some point in the 1980s became the defining difference in leadership research marking the boundary between management and leadership.

As an idea matures it produces waves of second-order effects, things that are done because they can be done, not because anyone set out to do them. For instance, the linking of flexible production and customer focus led to the idea of the batch of one in the mid-1980s. That matured into the concept of mass customization[1] and rolled on to Dell and other low-cost customizers changing everyone's

---

[1] Stanley M. Davis, *Future Perfect*. Reading, MA: Addison-Wesley, 1986.

assumptions about products and services—as well as our assumptions about strategy. Once mass customization could be done, suddenly variety became a strategic weapon. A firm that could produce custom product at a low price added variety to the marketplace and destroyed the economics of the inventory-based manufacturer.

This has happened every time; a tactical advantage—lower price or higher quality—becomes a baseline that forces other competitors to scramble. The linking of transformation and leadership may well be at this point. In the 1980s, the ability to change was an advantage as new ideas and fads swept management—essentially reactive. In the 1990s, the ability to move to a completely new structure and reshape industrial age firms in the light of upstart competition held the public transfixed—but big transformation was still essentially reactive. By the end of the millennium enough had been learned about transformational management for a book like this to be written, and we may be moving to a period when the use of e-leadership, high-speed continuous transformational change, may be becoming an overt strategic weapon.

The mass customization world was one of variety, and the strategic option was to increase the variety. The e-world is one of turbulence. What if companies could increase the turbulence? Then their skills in leading rapid transformation would give them an advantage. The strategic intent is to destabilize the industry at all times. This sounds odd, but the reality is that with fast product development and the cannibalizing of business models, this is already happening. In the more frictionless e-business world, where forming a new offering may mean restructuring the membership of an ecology, destabilization may well be the norm. Whatever the final answer, all we know for sure is that a skill that yields competitive advantage will eventually be used aggressively—but that's another book.

Index

Change on the Run

The CEO e-Game

"Intensely engaging and lots of fun."
VP Human Resources
"The use of technology puts traditional games in the shadow."
VP Information Technology

A Fresh Way of Communicating Strategy

Change on the Run: The CEO e-Game is the first of a new breed of business e-games. Designed by experts in business transformation and game technology as a tool for building alignment, it communicates the CEO's vision and strategy to thousands of people in a highly memorable and intensely engaging way.

Change on the Run: The CEO e-Game is a head-to-head competitive experience played in real time. It uses executive quality graphics and easy-to-use interfaces so players focus totally on absorbing the strategic messages. Played on a LAN in a classroom, across an internal Intranet, or across the Internet from the secure Changeontherun server, it can be facilitated or run remotely to reach people throughout the business.

Building Business School Savvy can be Fun

Change on the Run: The CEO e-Game can be readily adapted for business school quality, executive programs focused on building business smarts. Combined with your specific course materials, it provides a fun and highly memorable experience for company or mixed executive groups, as well as a highly effective team-building activity for people of all levels of seniority.

Change on the Run: The CEO e-Game comes with detailed instructions for set up and use and can be run in real time or over several days across the Internet on the Changeontherun secure server. This also allows building the game into remote learning programs.

To find out more about **Change on the Run: The CEO e-Game** look up

www.changeontherun.com

or e-mail changeontherun@changeontherun.com